BACKROADS & BYWAYS OF

OHIO

BACKROADS & BYWAYS OF

OHIO

Drives, Day Trips &
Weekend Excursions

MATT FORSTER

THE COUNTRYMAN PRESS

A division of W. W. Norton & Company

Independent Publishers Since 1923

We welcome your comments and suggestions.
Please contact:
Editor
The Countryman Press
500 Fifth Avenue
New York, NY 10110

or e-mail countrymanpress@wwnorton.com

For information about special discounts for bulk purchases, please contact
W. W. Norton Special Sales at specialsales@wwnorton.com or 800-233-4830

The Countryman Press
www.countrymanpress.com

A division of W. W. Norton & Company, Inc.
500 Fifth Avenue, New York, NY 10110
www.wwnorton.com

978-1-68268-182-4 (pbk.)

10 9 8 7 6 5 4 3 2 1

For the Morrises, whose love and appreciation
of Ohio grows with each passing day!

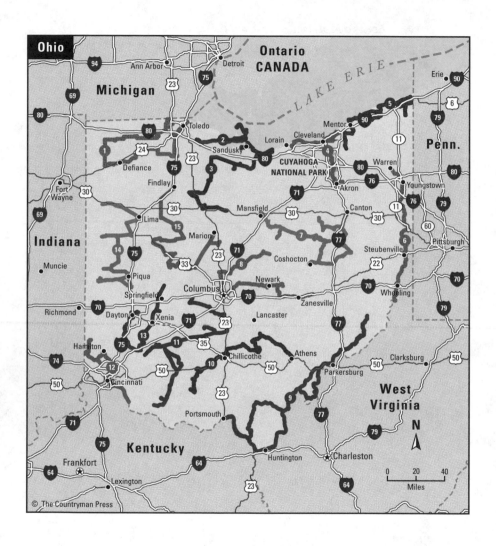

Contents

Introduction

Beautiful Ohio, thy wonders are in view,
Land where my dreams all come true!
—from "Beautiful Ohio"
(Ohio's official state song)

What is it about Ohio that makes so many who are born here look up at the sky early in life and fill with a desire to fly? Before flight was something humans were able to do, the Wright brothers were fiddling around in the bicycle shop and sweating out the mechanics of what would become the foundations of modern flight dynamics. A few generations later, Neil Armstrong soared so high that his feet eventually landed on the moon.

Perhaps it's because there are few frontiers left, and Ohioans are people of the frontier. Ohio has always been a frontier. It was the first frontier, actually—the wild west that preceded the Wild West. The settlers who crossed the Alleghenies were the scrappy ones, the families willing to leave hearth and home for a log cabin in the woods. The folks willing to clear away forests and drain massive swamps to make room for the hard work of farming. The people who followed the rivers, built mills, and started trading. And when the rivers weren't doing the job, they dug canals . . . by hand.

During the era of slavery, Ohioans found themselves on the frontier in another way. The state gave birth to a powerful abolitionist sentiment and became a trunk line for the Underground Railroad, which ferried escaped slaves up from the Ohio River to Lake Erie and freedom in Canada. And when the North and South stopped getting along, and the nation plunged into the Civil War, Ohio was on the frontlines.

Looking at Ohio today, you might be inclined to conclude the state's frontier status has slipped, but Ohio is still leading the way. Every four years around election time, the state simply crawls with candidates. No Republican

THE STATE ROAD COVERED BRIDGE HAS TRELLISED SIDES

has ever won the White House without winning Ohio. With one border touching the Eastern sensibilities of Pennsylvania and another fully absorbing the culture of the South—while firmly placed in the Middle West—Ohio represents America.

My first experience of Ohio was like that of many people: We were on a family road trip, just passing through. From the interstate, Ohio often seems like a particularly dull place to visit. What many travelers don't realize is that just a stone's throw from any exit ramp they can find an unexpected wealth of history, culture, and tradition. A short drive from I-75, for example, offers a chance to see Neil Armstrong's space suit or visit an amazing bicycle museum. All the beauty of the southern shore of Lake Erie lies just beyond the horizon for travelers on I-80. And anyone driving along I-77 south of Cleveland who doesn't know about Cuyahoga River Valley National Park needs to exit immediately and start exploring.

All of these treasures are found on Ohio's back roads and byways. This book presents routes for road trips through twelve different parts of the state, paying special attention to things to see and do off the beaten path. Of course, there are places in this book that a lot of people know about. It would be a shame to not check out the Rock & Roll Hall of Fame in Cleveland; but included with a handful of popular destinations are dozens of out-of-the-way spots that might not be that familiar.

What you won't find in this book is a compendium of everything to do everywhere. Rather than writing a phone book with bullet-point descriptions, I've tried to go deeper, with fuller, more researched descriptions. I've tried to find those tidbits of history that can give a place context and make it all the more interesting. Gallipolis is a pleasant, though rather quiet, community on the Ohio River, but when you learn that it was founded by wealthy French families fleeing the French Revolution, the town suddenly seems different. It's a place where stuff happened. And stuff certainly has happened in Ohio.

This history of this part of the world goes back, at least, to the age of the Hopewell people. They built their great earthworks throughout the Ohio River Valley. Then came the Native Americans we are more familiar with. Battles took place here before the American Revolution, with the British and French hoping to secure trapping trade and transportation routes. These skirmishes were followed by Tecumseh's War and the War of 1812. Canals that connected the entire state to Lake Erie and waterways that flowed south all the way to the Gulf of Mexico bolstered trade. The railroads replaced the canals, and industries grew. Automobile factories, bicycle shops, clay works, glass factories, and factories that supplied the country's cars with rubber tires helped Ohio flourish.

This book will guide you as you stray from the interstate and find the hidden treasures of Ohio. There are plenty of guidebooks for seeing Cincinnati, or Cleveland, or the Erie Isles. Here you will find the most scenic driving itineraries, which will help you explore the state's quieter attractions.

KEY TO PRICING

Lodging

Since inns, B&B, resorts, and hotels and motels can have a great range in the rates for the same room—dependent on the season, day of the week, type of room, length of stay, and even, sometimes, number of occupants—the key below looks at an average low-end rate for a double occupancy room. Since the aim is to give the reader a sense of lodging rates relative to other properties mentioned in the book, these numbers aren't written in stone.

$	Inexpensive (under $75)
$$	Moderate ($75 to $150)
$$$	Expensive ($150 to $250)
$$$$	Very expensive (over $500)

Restaurant

This key considers the average price of a single dinner entrée. Depending on the restaurant, there are often cheaper options—house salads, burgers, and sandwiches—and pricier dishes—lobster tail and filet mignon—and, of course, many people love to pad the tab with appetizers and drinks. But for comparing apples to apples, the price of a midrange plate will have to do. Just recognize that you can, for example, enjoy a $$ meal at most of the $$$ restaurants, and vice versa.

$	Inexpensive (under $10)
$$	Moderate ($10 to $16)
$$$	Expensive ($17 to $24)
$$$$	Very expensive ($25 and over)

AN ORIGINAL LOCK ON THE MIAMI AND ERIE CANAL

1

A GREAT LAKE, AN IMPRESSIVE RIVER, AND A LONG-GONE SWAMP

TOLEDO, MAUMEE, PERRYSBURG, BOWLING GREEN, GRAND RAPIDS, DEFIANCE, BRYAN, ARCHBOLD

ESTIMATED LENGTH: 160 miles

ESTIMATED TIME: 4½ hours

HIGHLIGHTS: This trip begins on Lake Erie's Maumee Bay in Toledo, where you can visit the Toledo Zoo, the Imagination Station, and the National Museum of the Great Lakes. After lunch at Tony Packo's, follow the Maumee River upstream to Maumee and Perrysburg and stop at the Wolcott House Museum Complex and Fort Meigs State Memorial Park. Farther upstream, take a ride on the Bluebird Passenger Train in Waterville before sneaking south to Bowling Green and the Snook's Dream Cars Automobile Museum. Returning to the river, visit the Canal Experience at Providence Metropark in Grand Rapids and AuGlaize Village & Farm Museum in Defiance. Leaving the river and heading north, the route passes through Bryan—where you'll find the lovely Stoney Ridge Winery—before arriving in Archbold and the famous Sauder Village. Returning eastward, stop at Swanton and the Oak Openings Preserve Metropark before one last jaunt north. After visiting the J. H. Fentress Antique Popcorn Museum in Holland, the road trip concludes in Sylvania with a visit to Fossil Park and the Sylvania Historical Village.

GETTING THERE: The trip begins in downtown Toledo. Following the Maumee River upstream, beginning on Anthony Wayne Trail, with stops in Perrysburg and Maumee, the general path continues on US 24 west. After Waterville, there's a detour south for stops in Bowling Green. After which, you return to the river by way of OH 110 to Grand Rapids and US 24. The route continues west to Defiance, and then it follows OH 15 to Bryan. From there, OH 2 returns east through Archbold and Swanton, finishing up in the northwest corner of the metro area in Sylvania.

1. A Great Lake, an Impressive River, and a Long-Gone Swamp

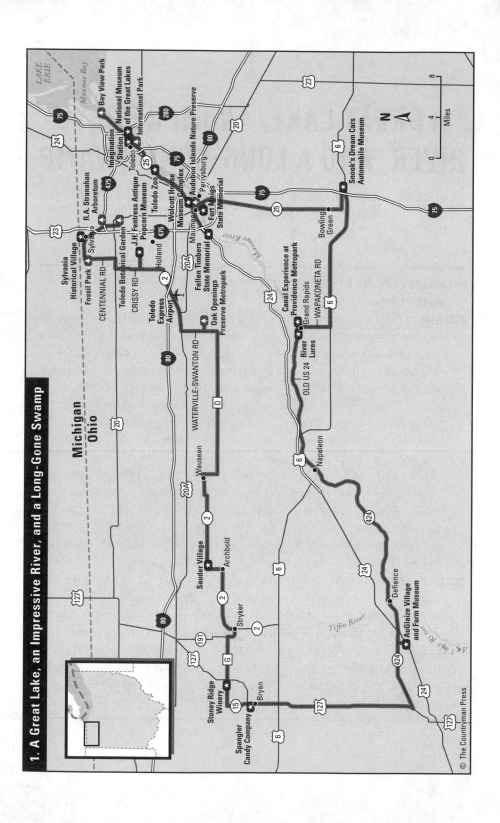

© The Countryman Press

Cities can be like siblings—offspring of the state they call home—and in some ways, their destinies play out as they do in any family. In the case of Ohio, Toledo is the quiet child, while Cincinnati, Cleveland, and Columbus—Ohio's three largest metro areas—get all the attention. But Toledo pushes on, proud in victory and humble in defeat.

The farthest northwest of Ohio's big cities, Toledo inhabits the margins of the state. It sits at the far western shore of Lake Erie on Maumee Bay, near the Michigan border. French trappers and traders were the first Europeans in the region, establishing trading posts along the Maumee River as early as the late 1600s. The river town of Maumee was laid out in 1817, and it seemed destined for a time to be one of the country's premiere centers of commerce. Later, when construction began on a canal system to join Lake Erie with Lake Michigan and the Ohio River, two towns east of Maumee—Port Lawrence and Vistula—joined forces in a bid to become the end of the line for the canals to Lake Erie. When they merged in 1833 to establish the city of Toledo, Maumee faded into the background.

Because wetlands extended 50 miles east to Toledo from Marblehead and to Indiana, the town was, in many ways, cut off from the rest of the state. But Ohioans were passionate about this out-of-the-way burg, and in 1835 they waged war (such as it was) against Michigan to claim an 8-mile strip of land along the shared border that included Toledo—thus the name, The Toledo War. The war didn't amount to much. The only bloodshed in 21 months was the result of a botched attempt by a Michigan sheriff to apprehend Major Benjamin Stickney. The sheriff was stabbed with a penknife by his son Two Stickney.

The canals brought prosperity to Toledo. Canals connected Lake Erie to the Ohio River in both Cincinnati and Indiana to make Toledo a transportation hub. Barges could be towed from Terre Haute, on Lake Michigan in Northwest Indiana, to Toledo, or from Toledo to Cincinnati. Later, railroads would replace the country's complex canal system, but by then Toledo had become an established center of manufacturing, and the trains couldn't stay away if they wanted to.

The region west of Toledo, like much of the rural Midwest, has also had its share of challenges. Threaded by the Maumee River and its tributaries, the area was once known for that immense swamp mentioned previously. The glacially-fed Great Black Swamp put a damper on settlement in northwest Ohio in the early nineteenth century. Roads that cut across the swamp sucked at wagon wheels. Logs laid down to prevent wagons from sinking into the muck turned the roads into teeth-rattling corduroy paths. And, if that wasn't pleasant enough, travelers could always count on summer swarms of malaria-carrying mosquitoes.

In the middle of the 1800s, the state took up the task of draining the swamp. Digging trenches and laying drainage tile by hand was backbreak-

CANADA GEESE FLOAT DOWN THE MAUMEE RIVER

ing work, and the reliance on manual labor meant the job got done slowly. That all changed, however, with the advent of the Buckeye Traction Ditcher. Invented by a local drainage tiler, James B. Hill, the traction ditcher allowed teams of workers to lay drainage tile at a respectably fast rate.

Once drained, the former swampland was settled by farmers looking to sink roots into this extremely fertile corner of the state. The roots took hold, and you will find acre upon acre of farmland stretching west from Toledo to the Indiana border.

The struggles of the American farmer are well documented, and the decline of the country's manufacturing industry over the past several decades has not done Toledo any favors, but the region refuses to surrender. Toledo is a recovering industrial center with a wealth of cultural resources— from the Toledo Museum of Art to the Toledo Zoo—and the small towns that dot the countryside remain bastions of small-town charm and values.

The route begins at Toledo's Bay View Park. Back in 1919, boxing promoter Tex Rickard built the world's largest arena here to showcase the "Fight of the Century," a heavyweight championship bout between Jess Willard and Jack Dempsey. Willard (a.k.a., the Pottawatomie Giant) was the reigning champ, towering over his challenger. Seemingly against all odds, the spunky Dempsey dominated the fight, and by the third round, the Willard team had tossed in the towel. The arena was built to hold 80,000 spectators, but oppressive heat kept the fans away, and almost everyone who had a financial investment in the bloody spectacle—concessionaires especially— ended up taking a beating, too. Controversy still surrounds this, the first of the great Jack Dempsey victories. Dempsey would go on to become a sports legend, but even today folks wonder if he cheated somehow.

The builders of the arena chose the site because the park was flat and full of nothing but dandelions. There are more trees here now, and there are plans to develop the park's peninsula with a restaurant, a lodge, and shops. Right now, however, this is the only place in Toledo where you can really see Maumee Bay. Most of the city is upriver, but here at the mouth of the Maumee River, you get the best view of Lake Erie. Adjacent to the park is the public Detwiler Park Golf Course and the Bay View Yacht Club. The park has an ornamental lighthouse which might draw your interest, but after you've walked out to see the lake, it's time to head upriver to Toledo proper.

Four miles away, on Summit Street, overlooking the river, the Imagination Station attracts kids and families from all over. This sprawling, hands-on science museum is a blast. The museum here used to be known as the Center of Science and Industry (COSI), but that enterprise closed in 2007. After some wrangling, a new millage passed to support the facility, and in 2009 the Imagination Station was born. Some of the more popular exhibitions include the high-wire bike, which is exactly as adrenaline-producing as it sounds, and a Rube Goldberg–inspired contraption that plays music.

Just across the river from the Imagination Station is International Park, which offers a nice view of downtown, seafood, and access to the rail-to-trail pathway along the water. In the same way that Summit Street runs along the northwest side of the Maumee, Front Street runs along the southeast side of the river. Heading east on Front Street will take you to Toledo's newest museum, one that deserves your attention.

In the spring of 2014, the National Museum of the Great Lakes opened on Toledo's waterfront. The museum explores the impact of the Great Lakes on the United States and considers the natural and human history of one of the country's greatest resources. The facility is operated by the Great Lakes Historical Society. Until quite recently, the society operated a museum in

A FEW OF TOLEDO'S BRIDGES ARE QUITE SCENIC

Vermillion called the Inland Seas Maritime Museum. The society closed that museum in order to pursue this larger adventure in Toledo. In addition to the brick-and-mortar museum space you'd expect, it features a 2.5-acre park and a real Great Lakes freighter. The *Col. James M. Schoonmaker* (formerly Toledo's SS *Willis B. Boyer* Museum Ship) was moved to a new home next to the museum and rechristened with its original name.

If you time your trip well, you will finish your exploration of the **National Museum of the Great Lakes** just in time for lunch at the iconic Toledo eatery **Tony Packo's**, found just down Front Street. Known for the Hungarian hot dog—which they serve up with diced onions, mustard, and their special sauce—Tony Packo's has been a Toledo institution since it opened in 1932. Though Toledans always knew they had a good thing, it wasn't until Jamie Farr, the Toledo native who famously played Corporal Max Klinger on TV's M.A.S.H. plugged the eatery on the show that Packo's reputation spread around the globe. In addition to their legendary dogs, the menu includes favorites like chili and chicken paprikás.

If your plans include a night in Toledo, check out **The Casey-Pomeroy House**. Located in Toledo's Vistula Historic District, this historic home is being restored to its original 1870s grandeur. When the restoration is complete, there will be six guest rooms. For now, there are four, each with a private bathroom, hardwood floors, richly detailed rugs, and antique furniture. With an on-site chapel, a large dining room, and a suite large enough to accommodate an entire bridal party for breakfast, hosts of bridal parties often book The Casey-Pomeroy House for at least some portion of the wedding day.

Of course, several days could be spent exploring Toledo. The **Toledo Museum of Art** is a short 2 miles from the Imagination Station and has a famous glass pavilion, and southwest of town, on Anthony Wayne Trail, is the highly regarded Toledo Zoo. The zoo began in 1900, when Carl Hildebrand, a local furniture dealer, donated a woodchuck to the city's Parks Board. It seems an odd donation—how hard would it be to trap a woodchuck if you really wanted one? But the board had plans to start a zoo, and Hildebrand's donation was a start. From these humble beginnings, the **Toledo Zoo** was born. Several decades later, during the Great Depression, workers from the Work

NO VISIT TO TOLEDO IS COMPLETE WITHOUT A STOP AT TONY PACKO'S

THE SCHOONMAKER IS PART OF THE GREAT LAKES MUSEUM PARK

Projects Administration gave the zoo a boost. They built the amphitheater and reptile house, as well as other notable buildings.

Another great summer activity is to catch a baseball game. **The Toledo Mud Hens** is the farm team of the Detroit Tigers. They play at Fifth Third Stadium on Washington Street. Many fans agree that minor league baseball is the best way to enjoy the sport as it once was played. Less inflated egos, fewer celebrities, and cheaper tickets mean fans are once more part of the game. The Triple-A season runs from April through August.

In the early days of settlement, Maumee seemed destined for greatness. The winds shifted, somewhat, and today it is a suburb of Toledo with an interesting past. The next stop on the route is the **Wolcott House Museum Complex**, which is on River Road. To get there, you take Anthony Wayne Trail (OH 25) to Michigan Avenue. River Road is one block south, and the museum is a half-mile upstream, on your right.

Few buildings capture a stretch of history like the Hull-Wolcott House, the only building original to the museum complex. In 1827, James Wolcott built a log cabin on this site. Over the next nine years, the home was remodeled and expanded until it became the fourteen-room Federal-style mansion

The Toledo War

Talk to college-sports fans, and you will learn that Ohio and Michigan have been at war for decades, but for most of that time, the skirmishes have occurred when the Ohio State Buckeyes face the Michigan Wolverines on the gridiron. But the conflict hasn't always been this cordial.

In 1835, when Michigan was seeking statehood, it made a claim on the disputed Toledo Strip, a piece of land created as a result of confusing language in the Northwest Ordinance (passed in 1787) and the Enabling Act of 1802. They were supposed to define Ohio's northern boundary, but they relied on the imprecise location of the southernmost edge of Lake Michigan, 200 miles west of Toledo. Because no one could precisely identify the southernmost edge, the border might have been as far north as Detroit or so far south that it denied Ohio access to Lake Erie.

In order to establish their sovereignty over this 468-square-mile sliver of land, both the state of Ohio and the Michigan Territory passed laws making it illegal for residents of the strip to submit to the other government's authority. And to make their intentions clear, the region's two governors assembled militias and sent them to the Maumee River. With much vehemence, the two sides launched a barrage of insults at each other. There was taunting and even some mocking.

Then, in 1836, Michigan was forced by circumstance to accept a compromise that gave the state three-quarters of what is now Michigan's Upper Peninsula in exchange for Toledo. In the end, more people have been injured in the collegiate rivalry between Ohio State and the University of Michigan than were hurt in the Toledo War.

you see today. Next door is the 1840s Frederick House, and between the two is a stunning flower garden with raised beds and a long arbor.

Other buildings within the complex include the Clover Leaf Depot (1880), the Box Schoolhouse (1850), and the Monclova Country Church (1901). The Maumee Memorabilia Museum sits across the parking lot from the Wolcott House, in a home built in 1901. The museum and the museum complex are open Thursdays through Sundays from April through December.

The Maumee River flows along the other side of River Road from the Wolcott House. Right there in the river are two islands that make up the **Audubon Islands Nature Preserve**. This 170-acre wildlife refuge is accessible only by private watercraft. The river itself is a beautiful stretch of water, and a wealth of birds and other wildlife dwell on sits many islands. One way to explore the river is to sign up for a paddling trip at **River Lures** in Grand Rapids. Though it is a little way upstream, when the water is high enough this outfitter has paddlers traveling as far as Walbridge Park in Toledo. The Orleans trip ends at Orleans Park in Perrysburg, close enough that the enterprising paddler might have an opportunity to explore the Audubon Islands. If tours are unavailable, you can always rent a canoe in Grand Rapids and drive it to Orleans Park. The island has a small, undeveloped boat landing, but it's an interesting enough trip to simply paddle around the island and explore its several inlets.

This stretch of the Maumee River has seen plenty of wars. The Northwest Indian War ended with the Battle of Fallen Timbers here on August 20, 1794, just west of downtown Maumee. The **Fallen Timbers Monument** commemorates the battle and honors those who fought there. General Anthony Wayne led the American forces. Opposing them were 1,500 men from numerous tribes as well as Canadian militia. The Indians hoped that a stand of recently knocked down trees along the river would slow the advancement of Amer-

TO FIND THE WOLCOTT MUSEUM, LOOK FOR THIS HISTORIC HOME

ican troops. It did not. After the victory, there was no major fighting in the territory for 17 years.

Just across the river in Perrysburg is a reconstructed fort that was used in the War of 1812. The **Fort Meigs State Memorial** is located on the site of the original Fort Meigs, which was built in 1813 to exert control over the Maumee River and help supply troops on the Canadian front. The British and their Indian allies attacked the fort twice in 1813, in addition to launching sporadic attacks on parties who left the fort to gather firewood. Fort Meigs, however, remained in American hands. After the war, the property was sold off, and it wasn't until the 1960s that the land was purchased by the Ohio Historical Society and a fort was reconstructed.

The center of Perrysburg is 1.5 miles east of the fort. While you're in the perfectly walkable downtown, there's a really great place to stop for a quick bite to eat. At **Zingo's Mediterranean**, you order at the counter and take your food to eat inside or at one of the café's outdoor tables. Historic Perrysburg provides a pleasant backdrop. With sandwiches, you have the option of traditional pita or Zingo's bread—I lean toward the latter. The menu is stocked with traditional Mediterranean meals. You can order the gyro with the usual lamb or chicken, and you can also order falafel.

Leaving the Maumee River behind for a bit, our route takes us south to Bowling Green. Staying on the back roads, follow Dixie Highway (OH 25) south through Bowling Green, turning left just before the Walmart on East Gypsy Lane Road. After passing over I-75, turn right onto South Dunbridge Road; on the left is the area's most popular attraction (aside from Bowling Green State University, presumably). **Snook's Dream Cars Automobile Museum** is a real find for car lovers. The museum is owned by Bill Snook and his son Jeff. Back in the 1960s, the Snooks took on the challenge of restoring a 1929 Ford Model A. Once he caught the restoration bug, Bill traveled around the country to car shows and swap meets. Along the way, he started to collect odds and ends—vintage oil cans, advertising, etc. He also picked up a few cars.

The automobile museum puts that collection on display. Here you will find the classics—everything from a Morris Mini to a Model A Station Wagon. The two convertibles—a beautiful 1957 red-and-white Chevy Ford Fairlane—will have old cruisers drooling. Adjacent to the museum is a spotless garage, where they repair classic cars, do appraisals, and perform maintenance on the collection. The museum is open weekdays (and if you happen to catch the owner on hand, it's also open on the weekends). Jeff Snook is usually around to answer questions and show visitors around.

Returning to the river, take US 6 west for 13.7 miles, turning right (north) onto Wapakoneta Road. The road ends at Front Street in Grand Rapids. Less than a block to the west is **The Mill House Bed & Breakfast**. The décor is decidedly country, and you will find antiques throughout the inn. There are four rooms for guests; three have exposed brick walls, which give them a historic feel. The innkeepers are gracious and accommodating—and you will find the breakfast to be a special treat. If the weather is pleasant, consider having breakfast on the riverside patio. This is a great place to lay your head when in town for the Grand Rapids Applebutter Festival.

Always held the second Sunday in October, the **Applebutter Festival** celebrates the town's pioneer heritage. The Grand Rapids Village Park features numerous pioneer craft demonstrations—weaving, chair caning, lace making, and, of course, apple butter making. There's a large craft fair with numerous artisans hawking their goods and lots of great food. This event makes Grand Rapids a great autumn excursion for families.

After crossing the Maumee River on the aptly named Bridge Street, turn east onto Anthony Wayne Trail, and follow the signs on your right for the **Canal Experience at Providence Metropark**. There are several places in Ohio where you can learn about the state's historic canals—there's an interesting display on the boats at **Cuyahoga Valley National Park** south of Cleveland, and there's another canal boat ride in Roscoe Village near Coshocton. The canal boat at the Providence Metropark, Volunteer, is a reproduction of a typical cargo-hauling boat of the 1800s. A team of two mules pulls the boat up nearly half a mile of original Miami and Erie Canal Towpath.

The park is what remains of Providence, a canal-era town. The boat passes through Lock #44. Made of limestone and operated by hand, this is one of the nineteenth century's last working locks. As the boat pulls into the lock, costumed reenactors close the lock gates behind and open the wicket gates ahead, allowing water to flow through, raising the boat several feet. After turning around upstream and passing again through the lock, the boat makes a stop so you can tour the Isaac Ludwig Mill and visit the park's General Store.

The mill, built in 1849, is particularly interesting for history-loving types. Because of the original owner's deal with the state, Ohio is obligated to supply water to the mill's turbines. (In exchange, the state was given adjacent land for the Miami and Erie Canal.) Water powers the saw and gristmill. With the dam upriver, there is a consistent supply of water for the mill, but when the river floods, the water levels equalize and the mill loses power. Workers then switch over to the 1890 Erie City Iron Works steam engine, which was installed in the 1970s. Visitors can see how wheat and corn were milled and then head over to the General Store to buy some milled grains to take home.

The next town on the route is Defiance. If time is short, the quickest route is US 24 West. The scenic route, however, follows Old US 24. (To the east it's called Anthony Wayne Trail.) Along the way, the road changes names several times, but for most of the route it simply follows signs for OH 424 into Defiance. It would make more sense to call the road the Maumee River

THERE ARE BEAUTIFUL CARS AND PLENTY OF MEMORIES AT SNOOK'S DREAM CARS

Road since it follows a parallel path north of the river from Toledo to Defiance. In Defiance, several tributaries come together as the Maumee, Tiffin, and AuGlaize Rivers converge and contribute their waters to the now more formidable Maumee. The confluence of the Maumee and the AuGlaize was a critical transportation hub years ago. In 1794, General Anthony Wayne ordered a fort built between the Y of these two rivers on the site of what is today Old Fort Defiance Park.

Close to the center of town, on South Clinton Street, is one of the area's finest B&Bs. The **Elliot Rose Guesthouse** has three rooms and a second-floor suite. Interestingly, the owners don't live on-site, but just down the road. For folks who are uncomfortable with the idea of sleeping in a stranger's home—B&Bs can be rather intimate sometimes—this might be the perfect place to try one out. The inn is tastefully decorated, balancing the home's historic qualities with a contemporary sensibility. Breakfast is served in the dining room, but there's also a three-season porch for an even more relaxed start to the day.

Continuing west of Defiance on OH 424 for about 3 miles, you will turn left (south) onto Krouse Road (OH 146). Less than a mile on, you come to the **AuGlaize Village & Farm Museum**. The site includes several dozen historic buildings gathered from all over. There are one- and two-story log homes, an old telephone exchange building, a blacksmith shop, a cider mill, a cane press, and a schoolhouse, just to name a few buildings. The village is open on the weekends in the summer and during special events, of which they hold quite a few—the Black Swamp Tractor & Engine Show and the Johnny Appleseed Festival are perennial favorites.

The quickest route to Bryan would be to follow OH 18 to OH 15, but there are some tricky turns. A more scenic route continues west on OH 424. When you come to US 127 (about 6.5 miles away), take it north. After driving 15 miles, you reach the town of Bryan. This is the home of the **Spangler Candy Company**—those confectionary geniuses who make Dum Dums and Circus Peanuts. The company began in 1906, when Arthur Spangler bought the Gold Leaf Baking Company, changed the name, and moved it to Bryan. Originally, the Spangler Manufacturing Company produced baking goods like cornstarch and baking powder. Candy was added to the catalog in 1908, and the rest is pretty much obvious. If you visit the Spangler Candy Company on Portland Street, you can get a trolley tour of the factory, visit their museum, and load up for your road trip at the candy store.

If candy is a little too juvenile for your tastes (heaven forbid), the next stop is a bit more grown up. The **Stoney Ridge Winery** is located north of Bryan. Head north on OH 15 to Road G and turn right (east). In exactly 2 miles, you will turn left (north) onto Road 16. The winery will be on your right. The Stoney Ridge Winery has fine wines without a lot of pretention.

COWORKERS STOP TO CHAT ABOUT A CALF AT SAUDER VILLAGE

They happily offer a Pinot Grigio alongside a glass of Country Rhubarb. The winery is situated in a 13-acre vineyard. Open every day but Sunday, a patio overlooks a pond that serves as a backdrop while enjoying wine and cheese.

The next stop is one of the region's most popular attractions, **Sauder Village** in Archbold. The most direct route there is to follow Road G east until it dead-ends at OH 191, which you will follow right (south) and take into downtown Stryker. In the center of town, turn left (north) onto OH 2. You will stay on OH 2 for about 8 miles as it twists and turns and passes through Archbold before arriving at Sauder Village.

Erie Sauder, the founder of Sauder Village, was born in Archbold, Ohio, back in 1904. He was a cabinet maker who began his career at the Archbold Ladder Company. An entrepreneurial spirit led him to strike out on his own in 1934, and he was soon building kitchen cabinets, church pews, and whatever else people needed. Things took off and pretty soon he was specializing in church pews. Using leftover wood from those projects, he designed a cheap, ready-to-assemble table. The story goes that a traveling salesman saw his creation and took it to a furniture show in Chicago. The salesman returned with an order for 25,000 tables. In 1953, Erie received a patent for his knockdown occasional table—the first of its kind—and with that, he launched the ready-to-assemble furniture industry. He soon spun his pew-building operation into the Sauder Manufacturing Company and developed "snap together" furniture for the Sauder Woodworking Company.

Always enamored of the pioneer spirit that led settlers to move to northwest Ohio and conquer the Great Black Swamp, Erie looked for ways to preserve that history after he retired. In 1969, he bought a 17-acre farm on OH 2 north of Archbold, and a few years later, he began moving historic buildings to the property.

The outdoor museum that resulted from his efforts not only captures and preserves the building's implements of an earlier time, but it also honors the skills of those pioneers as well. The village features glassmakers, potters, coopers, blacksmiths, weavers, and other craftspeople. Throughout the village there are regular demonstrations, and the gift shops are full of baskets and bowls and brooms made on site.

Next door you'll find an inn and a campground, and the best place to eat in town, in the adjacent **Barn Restaurant**. Of course, if you are just looking for a snack, there's a bakery and ice cream parlor as well.

Following OH 2 east toward Toledo, turn right (south) onto Shoop Avenue in downtown Wauseon. At Road D (about 1.4 miles from the center of town), turn left (east), and continue 13.5 miles to Waterville-Swanton Road. Turn left (north), then right (east) onto Reed Road. About 1.5 miles on, you come to the main entrance for the **Oak Openings Preserve Metropark.** All told, this park has nearly 4,000 acres for hiking, skiing, and horseback riding. The site features oak savannah, tallgrass prairie, and pin oak flatwoods. There

THIS MODEL T WAS FASHIONED INTO A MOBILE POPCORN CART

are sand barrens and oak woodlands. This is a lot of ecological diversity for a single park. In addition to containing some fairly important habitats, the park features several WPA-era buildings and bridges.

Adjacent to the park is **The Eco Camp**. Situated within the Bluegrass Campground, The Eco Camp features luxury tents with queen size beds. You can enjoy all the amenities of home with all the perks of a campsite by the water. The camp is part of a camping concept, growing in popularity, called *glamping* (glamorous + camping). So, if you have any loved ones who claim not to like camping, this place might provide a great opportunity to change their minds.

The next stop is the **J. H. Fentress Antique Popcorn Museum** in Holland. The museum has no regular hours, but tours are available year-round by appointment. So, if you are a fan of popcorn, popcorn history, or the history of popcorn advertising, you will need to plan ahead. To get there from Oak Openings, head north on Girdham Road to OH 2, which you will follow east to Crissey Road. Take that north to Hill Road, where you will turn east (right). The museum is about 1.5 miles down, on the north side of the street.

The museum features a number of popcorn machines, including an early popcorn wagon and a Model T Butter-Kist popcorn concession. Inside, there is popcorn paraphernalia from all eras, but real aficionados will appreciate that the museum is devoted to Holcomb & Hoke popcorn and peanut machines. The popcorn machines you see in movie theaters and amusement parks are all descendants of the H&H machines.

North of Holland is the Toledo suburb of Sylvania. Returning to Crissey Road, drive 5 miles north to **Fossil Park**. While downtown Sylvania features a bit of local history by way of **Sylvania Historical Village**, Fossil Park goes back a few more years—about 375 million years, to be precise. The 5-acre quarry at Fossil Park is one of only two prime Devonian Era sites on earth. Here you will find trilobites, brachiopods, and various corals. The fossils are not difficult to find, but the use of hand tools (aside from a brush) is prohibited. There are several stations set up to provide some shade, but on sunny days, it's not enough, so bring plenty of water and a hat.

The tour finishes up back in Toledo, whence it began, with two places to appreciate a bit of local nature. From downtown Sylvania (east of Fossil Park), take Main Street south to Sylvania Avenue, heading east. (You will note that Main Street becomes Holland-Sylvania Road.) Less than a mile down on your left will be the **R. A. Stranahan Arboretum**. Managed by the University of Toledo, the Arboretum is open weekdays from 9 until 3. The 47-acre site features an impressive collection of native and foreign

LEFTOVER FINDS AT THE FOSSIL PARK IN SYLVANIA

tree species—from the locally rare flowering Franklin tree to more common American basswood and boxelder trees. The park features old-growth oak forest, prairie, wetlands, and even a ravine.

Returning to Holland-Sylvania Road, continue south another 1.5 miles and turn left onto Elmer Drive. The **Toledo Botanical Garden** is a short distance down on your right. Whereas the arboretum exemplifies a more natural presentation of flora, the botanical gardens focus on cultivation and aesthetics. The gardens are open year-round during daylight hours, and there is no parking or admission fee. Flowers and plants are labeled throughout, so the best way to enjoy your visit is to grab a map from the gift shop and just wander.

IN THE AREA

Accommodations

THE CASEY-POMEROY HOUSE, 802 North Huron Street, Toledo. Call 419-243-1440. Website: casey-pomeroyhouse.com. $$$.

THE ECO CAMP, 5751 Waterville Swanton Road, Swanton. Call 419-482-8406. Website: theecocamp.com. $.

ELLIOT ROSE GUESTHOUSE, 814 South Clinton Street, Defiance. Call 419-956-9981. Website: elliotroseguesthouse.com. $$.

THE INN ON THIRD STREET, 325 West Third Street, Defiance. Call 419-980-0327. Website: secondstorydefiance.com. $$.

THE MILL HOUSE, 24070 Front Street, Grand Rapids. Call 419-832-6455. Website: themillhouse.com. $$.

Attractions and Recreation

APPLEBUTTER FEST, Grand Rapids. Website: applebutterfest.org.

AUDUBON ISLANDS NATURE PRESERVE, located on the Maumee River in Maumee. Website: naturepreserves.ohiodnr.gov/audubonislands.

AUGLAIZE VILLAGE & FARM MUSEUM, 12296 Krouse Road, Defiance. Call 419-782-7255 or 1-866-387-7882. Website: auglaizevillage.com.

THE CANAL EXPERIENCE AT PROVIDENCE METROPARK, Grand Rapids. Call 419-407-9700. Website: metroparkstoledo.com/features-and-rentals/canal-experience.

FALLEN TIMBERS MONUMENT, less than a mile west of the junction of I-475 and Anthony Wayne Trail. The memorial is on a side road, Fallen Timbers Lane. Managed by Toledo Metroparks. Call 419-407-9700. Website: metroparkstoledo.com/explore-your-parks/fallen-timbers-battlefield-ft-miamis.

FORT MEIGS STATE MEMORIAL, 29100 West River Road, Perrysburg. Call 419-874-4121. Website: fortmeigs.org.

FOSSIL PARK, 5675 Centennial Road, Sylvania. Call 419-882-8313. Website: olanderpark.com/olanderpark/fossil-park.

J. H. FENTRESS ANTIQUE POPCORN MUSEUM, 7922 Hill Avenue, Holland. Call 419-308-4812. Website: www.antiquepopcornmuseum.com.

OAK OPENINGS PRESERVE METROPARK, 4139 Girdham Road, Swanton. Call 419-407-9700. Website: metroparkstoledo.com/explore-your-parks/oak-openings.

NATIONAL MUSEUM OF THE GREAT LAKES, 1701 Front Street, Toledo. Call 419-214-5000. Website: inlandseas.org/museum.

R. A. STRANAHAN ARBORETUM, 4131 Tantara Drive, Toledo. Call 419-841-1007. Website: utoledo.edu/nsm/arboretum.

RIVER LURES, 24316 Front Street, Grand Rapids. Call 419-832-0989. Website: riverlures.com.

SAUDER VILLAGE, 22611 OH 2, Archbold. Call 1-800-590-9755. Website: saudervillage.org.

SNOOK'S DREAM CARS AUTOMOBILE MUSEUM, 13920 County Home Road, Bowling Green. Call 419-353-8338. Website: snooksdreamcars.com.

SPANGLER CANDY COMPANY, 400 North Portland Street, Bryan. Call 419-636-4221. Website: spanglercandy.com.

STONEY RIDGE WINERY, 07144 County Road 16, Bryan. Call 419-636-3500 or 1-888-370-8206. Website: www.stoneyridgewinery.com.

SYLVANIA HISTORICAL VILLAGE, 5717 North Main Street, Sylvania. Call 419-517-5533. Website: sylvaniahistoricalvillage.org.

TOLEDO BOTANICAL GARDENS, 5403 Elmer Drive, Toledo. Call 419-936-5566; Website: toledogarden.org.

THE TOLEDO MUD HENS, 406 Washington Street, Toledo. Call 419-725-4367. Website: mudhens.com.

TOLEDO MUSEUM OF ART, 2445 Monroe Street, Toledo. Call 419-225-8000. Website: toledomuseum.org.

TOLEDO ZOO, 2 Hippo Way, Toledo. Call 419-385-5721. Website: www.toledozoo.org.

WOLCOTT HOUSE MUSEUM COMPLEX, 1035 River Road, Maumee. Call 419-893-9602. Website: wolcotthouse.org.

Dining

BARN RESTAURANT, 22611 Ohio 2, Archbold. Call 419-445-2231. Website: saudervillage.org/eat/barn-restaurant. $$.

TONY PACKO'S, 1902 Front Street, Toledo. Call 419-691-6054. Website: tonypackos.com. $.

ZINGO'S MEDITERRANEAN, 106 Louisiana Avenue, Perrysburg. Call 419-872-5800. Website: eatzingos.com. $.

Other Contacts

GREATER TOLEDO METRO CONVENTION AND VISITOR BUREAU, 401 Jefferson Avenue, Toledo. Call 419-321-6404 or 1-800-243-4667. Website: dotoledo.org.

THE MARBLEHEAD LIGHTHOUSE IS ONE OF THE MOST PICTURESQUE LIGHTHOUSES ON THE GREAT LAKES

2

THE JEWEL OF OHIO
THE ERIE ISLES AND THE MARBLEHEAD PENINSULA

GENOA, ELMORE, PORT CLINTON, LAKESIDE, MARBLEHEAD,
KELLEYS ISLAND, PUT-IN-BAY, OAK HARBOR

ESTIMATED LENGTH: 84 miles, plus ferry trips and island travel

ESTIMATED TIME: 6 hours

HIGHLIGHTS: This trip begins in the small town of Genoa, with a visit to Packer
  Creek Pottery. Following OH 163 east and then OH 51 southeast toward
  Elmore, there's a stop at the Schedel Arboretum & Gardens before you
  continue east on OH 105, tagging alongside the Portage River, to Oak Harbor
  and OH 163, which will take you to the Marblehead Peninsula and the Erie
  Isles. The next stop comes in Port Clinton, the home of the Mon Ami Winery
  and Cheese Haven. Eventually you will hop on the ferry in Marblehead, but
  on the way to the dock, you can take in Lake Erie at East Harbor State Park
  on Catawba Island and then visit the historic community of Lakeside. You
  will leave the car behind as the route takes to the water. First stop: Kelleys
  Island, where you can have a bite to eat at the Village Pump before exploring the island by golf cart. Be sure to check out the prehistoric pictographs
  and ride out to the Glacial Grooves State Memorial. After circumnavigating
  the island, jump back on the ferry and sail to Put-in-Bay (a.k.a., South Bass
  Island). Much larger and more touristy than the first stop, you will need to
  time to take it all in. The island's most obvious manmade landmark is the
  Perry's Victory & International Peace Memorial, which has a viewing platform 317 feet above lake level. The downtown area is stocked with bars and
  restaurants and a historic carousel. Inland you will find cave tours, a butterfly museum, wineries, B&Bs, more restaurants, and a fine state park. Heading back to your car in Marblehead by ferry (with a stop at Kelleys Island),
  the trip concludes with a stop at the Marblehead Lighthouse and a few other
  historic sites. If the timing is right, the return trip west will pass through Oak
  Harbor just in time for dinner at the Beekeeper Inn.

GETTING THERE: From I-80, east of Toledo, take exit 71 for I-280. Follow signs for
  OH 420 south. Follow OH 420 for half a mile and turn east onto OH 163 (Genoa
  Road). You will come to the town of Genoa after 5.5 miles. The town of Elmore

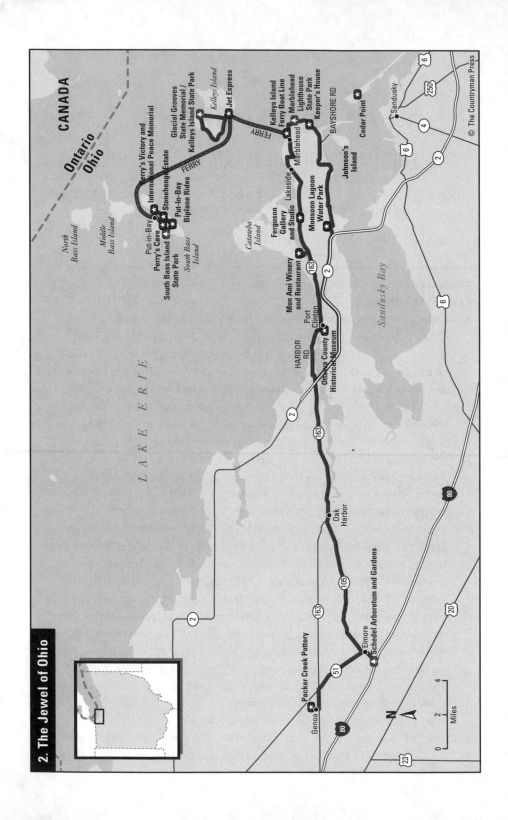

2. The Jewel of Ohio

© The Countryman Press

CANADA

Ontario
Ohio

North Bass Island

Middle Bass Island

South Bass Island

L A K E   E R I E

Kelleys Island

Perry's Victory and International Peace Memorial

Glacial Grooves State Memorial / Kelleys Island State Park

Jet Express

Put-in-Bay

Stonehenge Estate

Put-In-Bay Biplane Rides

Perry's Cave

South Bass Island State Park

Kelleys Island Ferry Boat Line

Marblehead Lighthouse

Keeper's House

BAYSHORE RD

Cedar Point

Sandusky

FERRY

Marblehead

Lakeside

Ferguson Gallery and Studio

Monsoon Lagoon Water Park

Johnson's Island

Catawba Island

Mon Ami Winery and Restaurant

Port Clinton

Sandusky Bay

HARBOR RD

Ottawa County Historical Museum

Oak Harbor

Schedel Arboretum and Gardens

Elmore

Packer Creek Pottery

Genoa

N

Miles
0   2   4

is southeast of Genoa, and from there you will follow OH 105 to Oak Harbor and then OH 163 to Port Clinton. OH 163 continues to the eastern end of the Marblehead peninsula, changing its name to OH 135 as it rounds the point for the return trip westward. The final leg of the journey takes US 2 back to OH 163 west and Oak Harbor.

A chain of islands in western Lake Erie links northern Ohio's Catawba Island (which isn't really an island) with Point Pelee (which is certainly a point) in southern Ontario. The islands provide an easy hop-skip-and-a-jump across Lake Erie for migrating birds and form an important route for their annual journeys north and south. Even more important to our purposes, the islands provide a base for enjoying quite a number of state parks, tourist towns, historical sites, and water sports on Ohio's Great Lake.

For visitors used to driving several hours to spend the day at nearby Cedar Point—passing to the south along I-80/90—the islands' region will come as a bit of a surprise. Midwesterners conditioned to head "up north" for a summer escape little realize that a slice of Great Lakes heaven sits so close to home.

This route begins 12 miles south of Lake Erie in the rural town of Genoa. From Toledo, you can get there by way of OH 51; it's also close to the interstate (take exit 81 for Elmore). Just off Main Street on Eighth Street, you will find **Packer Creek Pottery**. The pottery of Jan Pugh features brightly painted florals and other designs. Jan has had a studio in Genoa since 1979, and her work is featured in many celebrity homes.

WHILE ON KELLEY'S ISLAND, STOP FOR A BIT OF HISTORY AT THE LOCAL MUSEUM

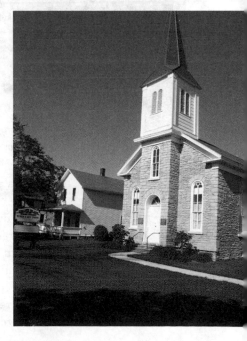

Head east on Fourth Street and then southeast on OH 51 to reach the next stop, which is 5 miles south, in Elmore. Nestled in a bend of the Portage River, the **Schedel Arboretum & Gardens**, with flower-lined brick walks and stone footpaths winding through a master gardener's dream, offers more than 17 acres of meticulous landscaping for public appreciation. The property once belonged to Israel Harrington. After the War of 1812, Harrington set up a tavern in what is now Fremont. He later sold the tavern and purchased land in the Black Swamp along the Portage River. German

THE CENTER OF GENOA IS THE STUNNING TOWNHALL

immigrants moved to the area and helped drain the swamp, establishing the town of Elmore.

By 1969, the Schedel family owned the property. It was the Schedels who saw the potential of this picturesque point. They established the Japanese garden and used their talents in landscape and horticulture to create much of the beauty you see today. Walking tours are available, and twice a week, a tour of the manor and summer cottage can be arranged. Check out the website for seasonal hours. There are also some rules of etiquette to observe; for example, climbing trees is frowned upon.

On the other side of Elmore is the Veterans Memorial Cemetery. Harrington's father—also named Israel Harrington—was a veteran of the American Revolution. Both father and son are buried here alongside the Portage River. According to his tombstone, the elder Harrington fought under Ethan Allen as a member of the Vermont Militia.

Follow the Portage River downstream to Port Clinton by taking OH 105/163 east. Port Clinton is the unofficial gateway to the Erie Isles. This honorific, however, has its drawbacks. The bulk of visitors vacationing on the isles head for South Bass Island, which is more often simply called Put-in-Bay since that's the island's only town. So, even though Port Clinton enjoys more than its share of traffic during the summer vacation season, many folks just see it as a place to park their car while they're enjoying island life. The less-traveled route will take you to the ferry in Marblehead, and since you're relieved of the pressure to catch a ferry, we can breathe easy and enjoy what Port Clinton has to offer.

The first stop is two blocks south of Perry Street on West Third Street. For a summary of county history, there is no better destination than the **Ottawa County Historical Museum**. Ottawa County is in a unique location, surrounded by Lake Erie and intersected by the Portage River. The stories that can be told of Ottawa County include the history of its Native Americans; struggles between settlers and those who were already here; struggles against the French, the British, and the South; the stories of Great Lakes shipping and rock quarrying; and the stories of resort towns and historic towns. The museum is not large, but there's quite a lot here for the history buff.

Heading east on Perry Street for about a mile, Sand Road branches off to the northeast (on your left). If you intend to stay the night in Port Clinton, one of the area's best B&Bs is a few miles up East Sand Road. **The Five Bells Inn** is a grand fieldstone Dutch colonial overlooking Lake Erie. The inn has eight guest rooms and a family cottage for larger parties. Aside from the usual amenities, guests can sit on the front porch or the deck and watch the sunset. All the rooms have a private bath, and two of the suites have a Jacuzzi tub.

If you go to East Harbor Road and continue east about 2.5 miles from the intersection with Sand Road, you will come to Catawba Road. Turn left (north) for the **Mon Ami Winery and Restaurant** (just off Catawba on East Wine Cellar Road). What began as the Catawba Island Wine Company in the late 1800s was acquired by the Mon Ami Champagne Company in the 1930s. Today, Mon Ami is filled with all the traditional charm you'd expect from a winery with this kind of history. The winery also maintains an excellent restaurant. Their wine list pairs well with the menu, which is served in the Dining Room and the Chalet.

On the way to the next stop, be sure to visit the **Ferguson Gallery &**

Studio. In addition to shopping at a great gift shop with plenty of neat ideas for presents you'd like to give to kids, visitors can head to the back and watch glass artisans work. A windowed wall protects you and the gallery from the heat (and likely helps with the air conditioning bill too). After the family gets a chance to see some things made, head back out into the shop to get a one-of-a-kind souvenir of your visit.

The next stop on East Harbor Road is the historic community of **Lakeside**, "The Chautauqua on Lake Erie." What is a Chautauqua? Well you might ask. Back in the late nineteenth century, there was a national adult education movement. Families would leave the city for a time and head out to a Chautauqua (named for the original assembly at Chautauqua Lake in New York), where they could hear fascinating lectures, enjoy soul-enriching music, and socialize with other like-minded families. While many aspects of the movement have faded into the background, the more permanent communities persist.

There are several ways to enjoy Lakeside, a seasonally gated Chautauqua on Lake Erie: You can come for the afternoon, get some lunch, sit by the beach, and catch a concert. Or better yet, you can immerse yourself in the place—stay for a week or more, take advantage of all the community's programming, and become a true believer in self-enrichment. Begun as a summer revival retreat for Methodists in 1873, Lakeside now promotes the four pillars of the Chautauqua movement: religion, education, cultural arts, and recreation.

Religious activities include nightly praise concerts, the appointment of a Chaplain of the Week, and ministries that cater to children and young adults. Summer programming also includes movie nights, an ongoing lecture series, and educational walks. Recreation can be found on the beach and in any of the community's four parks—everything from shuffleboard to competitive capture the flag. Numerous musical acts come through Lakeside each summer. Concerts take place in the beautiful Hoover Auditorium, a structure worth visiting even if there's no event planned. When it was constructed, it had the largest wooden roof in existence. It has since been reinforced with steel, but the curved lines of the exposed wooden beams still inspire visitors and contribute to the building's outstanding acoustics.

The business district is home to a handful of restaurants, cafés, and bars. There's the Fine Print bookstore and a clock shop, as well as places to shop for clothes, antiques, and even kites. The options for lodging at Lakeside are outlined in the lodging section of this chapter and include the historic Hotel Lakeside and numerous inns and B&Bs.

Gate passes are required in the summer (last week of June through August). Passes are cheaper for early and late summer, and not required in the off-season. Weekly and season passes are also available.

For lodging, the **Hotel Lakeside** has been in operation for more than

GUESTS SWIM OFF THE PIER IN LAKESIDE

135 years, earning it recognition as a National Historic Landmark. A long, screened-in porch faces a manicured lawn with a view of Lake Erie. Inside, the hotel boasts a fine restaurant and plenty of public spaces for taking advantage of the hotel's WiFi. This is an important feature for many guests, because the rooms, finely appointed with period antiques, are primarily for sleeping—the rooms don't have televisions or wireless reception. The Victorian feel of the place is evident everywhere, from the décor to the building itself, with its winding wooden staircase and high ceilings.

Another option is the **Idlewyld Bed & Breakfast**, which has a mere 13 rooms. Tucked between cottages on a shady neighborhood street, the bed and breakfast is a short walk from the center of town. There are cozy common areas, where you can enjoy some downtime or get to know other guests. A handful of the bedrooms have private baths, but harkening back to an earlier time, most simply have a bathroom nearby.

For food, there are a number of places to grab a snack and ice cream in Lakeside. For a great pizza, however, check out **Sloopy's Sports Café** on Second Street. The folks at Sloopy's are proud of their pizza and regularly pit their pie against other establishments' offerings in pizza competitions. The result is that their cheesy 'za can honestly claim to be an award winner.

THE LOBBY OF HOTEL LAKESIDE LOOKS MUCH LIKE IT WOULD HAVE A HUNDRED YEARS AGO

If pizza isn't your game, there's no better spot to grab a quick hot dog with delicious heart-clogging sides than **Netty's Chili Dogs,** a short way down from Lakeside on Harbor Road. The chili dog here leans toward the more northern variety, with sauce, mustard, and fresh diced onions, though shredded cheese is available for you southern Ohioans. Fries and popcorn, let's say, round out the meal. And for afters, Nelly's also sells soft-serve ice cream. Nelly's is a chain based in Toledo, but with a mere six locations, it's the kind of chain that has yet to sacrifice a quality product for profits.

Having spent entirely too much of our time on the mainland, the Erie Isles are next. The ferry for Kelleys Island is less than a mile east on Harbor Road (a.k.a., Main Street). The **Kelleys Island Ferry Boat Line** is not as flashy as the competition, Jet Express, but the ferry leaves every hour on the hour (more often during peak summer season) and is the most affordable option around. And since we're talking about transportation, now's the time to mention that most people rent golf carts for getting around the islands. On Kelleys Island, you can pick up a golf cart at the marina when you get off the ferry. If you're not up for exploring, the walk from the ferry dock to downtown is less than a half mile. There you can find places to eat, drink, and be merry. It's a 3-mile round-trip to the north side of the island, however, and to see the whole island you would need to walk a solid 10 miles. So a golf cart comes in handy.

Kelleys Island has had a few names over the years. The first surveyors called it Island No. 6. In 1803, a French settler named Cunningham built a cabin on the island. He lived for a time alongside the Native Americans who had a village there. After he died, the island was called Cunningham Island. In 1833, the Kelley brothers, Datus and Irad, saw potential in selling the island's limestone and lumber. They started buying up parcels of land on the island and soon owned the whole kit and caboodle. Since they could, they changed the name to Kelleys Island.

The history of the island before white settlers came is often hazy. One artifact from that earlier time is the island's Inscription Rock. Along the lakeshore between the ferry dock and downtown, this large slab of limestone is covered in pictographs. Experts believe the etchings date from the mid-seventeenth century. Over time, the weather has worn away much of the art, and a roof has been suspended above the stone to offer some protection from the elements. Thankfully, in 1850, one Seth Eastman thought to record the etchings in detail. From his drawings, a scale model of Inscription Rock was created, giving visitors a sense of what it once was.

Another piece of island history goes back much further. From the center of town, take Division Street north to the north shore of the island. There you will find the **Glacial Grooves State Memorial**. From the small parking lot on the west side of the road, it's a short walk up and around this unique geological feature. Boulders caught in the glaciers were dragged, ever so slowly, across the bedrock, cutting deep, smooth grooves into the stone. A marked path lets you view the grooves from several angles. An unattractive fence keeps you from getting too close.

East of Division Street, **Kelleys Island State Park** takes up the center of the island. Here you can explore a little of the island's mining history. In

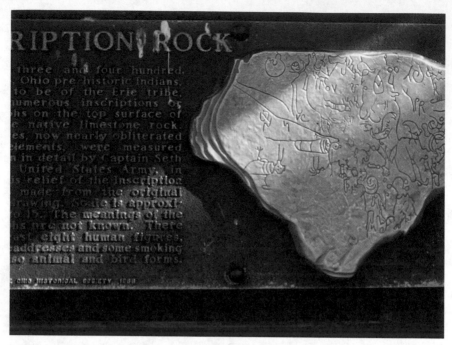

INSCRIPTION ROCK IS OFTEN HARD TO MAKE OUT, BUT THE SIGNAGE HELPS

its heyday, the Kelley Island Lime & Transport Company was the world's largest producer of limestone and lime. The old quarry in the center of the island constitutes much of the state park, though there is a campground on Lake Erie. Plenty of trails will take you out and around the old limestone pit, where you can see how nature is returning to this once barren piece of land.

There is no one road that follows the entire shoreline of Kelleys Island. The most beautiful driving route begins at the glacial grooves and follows Titus Road west to Lakeshore Drive. The road rounds the western edge of the island and returns you to downtown. The **Village Pump**, downtown, was once the island post office. Then it became a bar/gas station (island living, right?). They were pumping gas and pumping beer, so when it came time to name the place, it was a no-brainer. The restaurant is known for its famous Brandy Alexander, but its consistently satisfying menu upholds its reputation. Lake Erie perch is a perennial favorite.

The next stop on the itinerary is South Bass Island, better known as Put-in-Bay. The Kelleys Island Ferry Boat Line won't get you there, but the Jet Express ferry service, which leaves from Port Clinton, will. And there are numerous places to secure a golf cart once you're on the island. Put-in-Bay is the touristy center of the Erie Isles. The island has become popular because of a midway-like downtown, historic monuments, wineries, museums, and family-aimed tourist attractions. Let's begin our visit to the island in town.

The **Chicken Patio** next to the Roundhouse Bar has to be one of my favorite lunch places on the island. Cooked right there on a 21-foot charcoal grill, the smell of BBQ chicken is impossible to resist. Add corn on the cob, a cup of coleslaw, and a puffy white roll to sop up the resulting mess, and you can't go wrong. There are, of course, more upscale options, but the Chicken Patio pairs perfectly with the island's laid-back vibe.

Just beyond the bars and t-shirt shops you will find a historic carousel. My inner ears don't like the spinning, but I love carousels nonetheless. Kimberly's Carousel is special. It's an original Allen Herschell carousel, built in 1917. All the carousel's horses are wooden, hand-carved originals, harkening back to the island's early days as a summer retreat.

Leaving the main strip by way of Catawba Avenue, head southwest out of town for about a half-mile to Perry's Cave. Part of the Perry's Cave Family

THE HISTORIC CAROUSEL IS RIGHT IN THE HEART OF PUT-IN-BAY

Perry's Victory & International Peace Memorial

Americans, by and large, have no collective memory of the War of 1812, but for the people who lived in this part of the country in the early nineteenth century, it was a pivotal moment in the region's history. The first skirmishes of the war were fought here in Ohio when the British encouraged the Native Americans to raid American settlements. Even fewer people realize that a major naval battle was waged on Lake Erie. The 352-foot memorial in Put-in-Bay on South Bass Island commemorates that naval battle.

On September 10, 1813, in the Battle of Lake Erie, the Americans and British fought each other for control of this crucial water route. In what would be the first defeat of a British naval squadron, Commodore Oliver Hazard Perry led his nine American ships against the enemy's six. The battle was hard-fought, but by day's end, Perry would send a message to General William Henry Harrison: "We have met the enemy, and they are ours." As a result of this victory, the British returned Detroit to American hands, and the Indian Confederation, led by Tecumseh, eventually broke apart.

The memorial, which can be seen from a great distance, commemorates that battle and the 200 years of peace—between the United States, Britain, and Canada—that resulted. The memorial was closed for a time, after part of the column fell off, in 2006. By 2012 it was fixed; visitors can now take the elevator to the observation deck once again. From there, they can look across the water to Canada and think back to a time when we weren't the friendliest of neighbors.

Fun Center, the cave almost seems like an afterthought beside the miniature golf, butterfly house, giant maze, gemstone mining, antique car museum, etc. While not breathtaking like Kentucky's Mammoth Cave, Perry's Cave is pretty interesting. Once you're underground, the cave opens up like a very large basement with a low ceiling. A path is marked out to give the wide hall some definition. It's a short tour, so at just about the time the kids start getting anxious, it's time to go.

Also part of the Fun Center is the Skip Duggan Antique Car Museum. Years back, Skip was one of the men who began the island's Sunday Antique Car Parades, which passes through town around 2:15 every Sunday. It's a well-known fact that there are more classic cars per capita on South Bass Island than anywhere else in the good old US of A. This is an informal affair, but every Sunday afternoon, those folks who own classic cars like to tool around the island. It's extra fun if you're not expecting the motorcade, but antique-car enthusiasts will want to plan to catch it.

One thing first-time visitors to the Erie Islands might not expect is that folks have been growing grapes and making wine here for generations. As far back as the mid-1800s, in fact, winemaking has been a treasured tradition on South Bass Island. Right across from Perry's Cave, you can try a bit of this local flavor at **Heineman's Winery.** A German immigrant, Gustav Heineman, started the winery in 1888. In addition to wine, the winery offers tours of the Crystal Cave, which, they boast, puts you inside "the world's largest geode."

Catawba Avenue continues all the way over to the opposite side of the island. Overlooking an inlet on the west shore of South Bass Island, the **South Bass Island State Park** is far enough away from Put-in-Bay to offer some quiet. The park has a campground on Lake Erie and also rents tent-shaped cabins called "cabents" and a rustic cottage. There are glacial grooves here as well, though they are not as celebrated as those on Kelleys Island.

SOUTH BASS ISLAND STATE PARK RENTS KAYAKS AND HAS A GREAT BEACH

Leaving the park and using Meechen Road, you can cut over to Langram Road, which runs parallel to Catawba and makes for a nice loop. When you get to Langram, instead of heading right back into town, turn right (southwest). On sunny summer days, a biplane is parked just on the other side of the fence. **Put-in-Bay Biplane Rides** offers groups of two a chance to ride in one. Imagine a circa WWII biplane, an open cockpit, the Red Baron and all that, and you will get the picture. The pilot gives passengers as much adventure as they ask for, so guests looking to experience some daredevil air antics are in luck (perhaps a few high-air loops?). For groups larger than two (but no more than three), a helicopter ride is a better option. Both the airplane and helicopter will take you on an aerial tour of the islands.

Returning to town by way of Langram Road and Toledo Avenue, turn left at the water and head over to the Doller estate, just west of town. The **Museum of Island Life at the Doller House** tells the story of life on South Bass Island in the nineteenth century. The house itself is a testament to just how upscale that life was for some. Visitors will have a chance to see how folks traveled to and from the island when the lake was frozen over, and how future generations met that challenge in new and better ways. Also on the site is the **Put-in-Bay Winery** and a winery exhibition that takes guests through the process of winemaking, from grape to bottle. And your visit doesn't have to end there, as the educational journey concludes at the tasting room and gift shop. The tasting room includes wines from the island as well as regional favorites.

Being the most visited of the area's islands, there are many options for those looking to spend the night on South Bass Island. The **Vineyard Bed & Breakfast** is one of the nicest. This home was built more than 130 years ago as a farmhouse. Hardwood floors, oriental rugs, and antique furnishings complete the experience of staying somewhere with history. The inn is located on 20 acres, with 700 feet of frontage on the lake. With only three rooms at this B&B, the feeling of quiet solitude is enhanced. Couples might also consider staying at the Arbor Honeymoon Cottage, also located on the property. Finding the place is easy. Just follow OH 357 to the northeast corner of the island. Just before you plunge into the lake, you'll see the signs.

To return to the mainland and your car, you will need to catch the ferry back to Marblehead. This final leg of the loop explores sites in this charming town before you return to Oak Harbor. Marblehead has a few great places to eat. For a sweet morning treat, there's **Jill's Sweet Delite Bakery**. You'll have to get up pretty early if you hope to beat the bakers at Jill's to the worm. (But who wants worms?) Every morning they bake up trays and trays of delicious doughnuts. Nothing too fancy—these doughnuts are straight white bread—but you'd be hard-pressed to find a better doughnut anywhere else. And while you don't have to get there at sunrise, the shop won't have much left by 9 a.m., so don't dally.

A BIPLANE OFFERS A UNIQUE VIEW OF THE ERIE ISLES

On the other side of the main strip is **Schoolhouse Gallery and Gifts**—on the south side of Main Street, just west of the cemeteries. Inside this old, sprawling brick schoolhouse, you will find room after room of gifts, collectibles, and art. The shops are scattered on multiple floors, and travelers can do a lot of gift-buying on just this one stop.

In Marblehead, East Harbor Road becomes Main Street. Leaving town to the east, it rounds the peninsula's horn and becomes East Bayshore Road heading west. At the tip of the peninsula is a very attractive lighthouse, one of the most picturesque in the state. The **Marblehead Lighthouse State Park** was created to preserve the Marblehead Lighthouse and the nearby keeper's house. Inside the keeper's house, the **Marblehead Lighthouse Historical Society** maintains a museum that tells the story of light-keeping on the Great Lakes. The last Fresnel lens used here is on display, and there is a model of some future site development—a Lifesaving Station Education Center. Across Sandusky Bay from the lighthouse, Cedar Point is in clear view. It would be hard to beat a summer afternoon spent sitting on a rock, in the shade, next to the lighthouse in Marblehead, looking out over Lake Erie.

Not to be confused with the keeper's house next to the Marblehead Lighthouse, the **Keeper's House** is south and west, down East Bayshore Road. Much older than its successor, this building housed the lighthouse's first three keepers. It was built on the site of the original keeper's log cabin, which he built in 1809. The stone used to build the home was pulled from a quarry behind the house. The home's interior is furnished in period pieces to give visitors an idea of how it must have been to live here at the time.

Nearby is another interesting bit of history, this one relating to the Civil War, during which the U.S. Army established a Prisoner of War Depot on nearby Johnson's Island. In a little more than three years, 10,000 men passed through its stockade walls. Many never left: Their bodies were interred in a special cemetery, now the **Johnson's Island Confederate Cemetery.** Aside from some earthworks found on private property, this is all that remains on the island to tell these soldiers' story. There is the Johnson's Island Museum, but to visit the Johnson's Island Museum, you must go to Sandusky (see chapter 3). The causeway for Johnson's Island is about 2 miles south of the lighthouse.

Farther along East Bayshore Road, it's hard to miss the **Captain's Lodge**. It's one of the most appealing lodgings in the area. Built to accommodate guests of their charter boat business, this B&B's stately manner makes an impression. The inn has three bedrooms, each with a private bath. Two of the rooms are perfect for couples, while the third—the "bunkhouse"—can handle a family of six.

IN THE AREA

Accommodations

CAPTAIN'S LODGE, 9491 East Bayshore Road, Lakeside Marblehead. Call 419-702-7008. Website: thecaptainslodge.com. $$.

THE FIVE BELLS INN, 2766 East Sand Road, Port Clinton. Call 419-734-1555. Website: fivebellsinn.com. $$$.

HOTEL LAKESIDE, 150 Maple Avenue, Lakeside. Call 1-866-952-5374. Website: lakesideohio.com/accommodations/hotel-lakeside. $$$.

IDLEWYLD BED & BREAKFAST, 350 Walnut Avenue, Lakeside. Call 216-970-4552. Website: idlewyldbb.com. $$.

VINEYARD BED & BREAKFAST, 910 Columbus Avenue, Put-in-Bay. Call 419-285-6181. Website: vineyardohio.homestead.com. $$.

Attractions and Recreation

FERGUSON GALLERY & STUDIO, 5890 East Harbor Road, Marblehead. Call 419-734-0600. Website: fergusongallery.com.

GLACIAL GROOVES STATE MEMORIAL, managed by the Kelleys Island State Park, 920 Division Street, Kelleys Island. Call 419-746-2546 (seasonal number). Website: ohiohistory.org/visit/museum-and-site-locator/glacial -grooves.

HEINEMAN'S WINERY, 978 Catawba Street, Put-in-Bay. Call 419-285-2811. Website: heinemanswinery.com.

JILL'S SWEET DELITE BAKERY, 1002 West Main Street, Marblehead. Call 419-798-0009.

JOHNSON'S ISLAND: CONFEDERATE STOCKADE CEMETERY, Marblehead. Website: nps.gov/nr/travel/national_cemeteries/ohio/Confederate_ Stockade_Cemetery.html.

KEEPER'S HOUSE, 9999 East Bayshore Road, Marblehead. Call 419-798-9339. Website: ottawacountyhistory.org/keeper-s-house.

KELLEYS ISLAND STATE PARK, 920 Division Street, Kelleys Island. Call 419-746-2546 (seasonal number). Website: parks.ohiodnr.gov/kelleysisland.

KIMBERLY'S CAROUSEL, Delaware Avenue, Put-in-Bay. Call 419-285-2212. Website: putinbayattractions.com/kimberlyscarousel.php.

LAKESIDE CHAUTAUQUA, 236 Walnut Avenue, Lakeside. Call 419-798-4461. Website: lakesideohio.com.

MARBLEHEAD LIGHTHOUSE HISTORICAL SOCIETY, 110 Lighthouse Drive, Marblehead. Call 419-798-2094. Website: marbleheadlighthouseohio.org.

MARBLEHEAD LIGHTHOUSE STATE PARK, 110 Lighthouse Drive, Marblehead. Call 419-734-4424 (East Harbor State Park). Website: parks.ohio dnr.gov/marbleheadlighthouse.

MON AMI WINERY AND RESTAURANT, 3845 East Wine Cellar Road, Port Clinton. Call 419-797-4445. Website: www.monamiwinery.com.

MUSEUM OF ISLAND LIFE AT THE DOLLER HOUSE, 392 Bayview Drive, Put-in-Bay. Call 419-285-3343. Website: putinbaywinery.com.

OTTAWA COUNTY HISTORICAL MUSEUM, 126 West Third Street, Port Clinton. Call 419-732-2237. Open Tuesday through Thursday, noon until 3 p.m. Website: ottawacountyhistory.org.

PACKER CREEK POTTERY, 103 East Eighth Street, Genoa. Call 419-855-3858. Website: packercreekpottery.com.

PUT-IN-BAY BIPLANE RIDES, Langram Road, Put-in-Bay. Call 419-285-8042. Website: putinbaybiplanerides.com.

PUT-IN-BAY WINERY, 392 Bayview Drive, Put-in-Bay. Call 419-285-3343. Website: putinbaywinery.com.

SCHEDEL ARBORETUM & GARDENS, 19255 West Portage River South Road, Elmore. Call 419-862-3182. Website: schedel-gardens.org.

SCHOOLHOUSE GALLERIES AND GIFTS, 111 West Main Street, Marblehead. Call 419-798-8332. Website: facebook.com/theschoolhousegallery.

SOUTH BASS ISLAND STATE PARK, 1523 Catawba Avenue, Put-In-Bay. Call 419-285-2112 (seasonal). Website: parks.ohiodnr.gov/southbassisland.

Dining

CHICKEN PATIO, 234 Delaware Avenue, Put-in-Bay. Call 419-285-4595 or 419-285-3581. Website: thechickenpatio.com. $.

MON AMI WINERY AND RESTAURANT, 3845 East Wine Cellar Road, Port Clinton. Call 419-797-4445. Website: monamiwinery.com. $$$.

NETTY'S, 9410 East Harbor Road, Lakeside Marblehead. Call 419-798-5050. The drive-in is open daily in the summer. Website: nettys.com. $.

SLOOPY'S SPORTS CAFÉ, 218 West Second Street, Lakeside. Call 419-798-4457. Website: sloopyspizza.com. $$.

VILLAGE PUMP, 103 West Lakeshore, Kelleys Island. Call 419-746-2281. Website: villagepumpki.homestead.com. $$$.

Transportation

JET EXPRESS, 3 North Monroe Street, Port Clinton. Call 419-732-2800. Website: jet-express.com.

KELLEYS ISLAND FERRY BOAT, 510 West Main Street, Lakeside. Call 419-798-9763. Website: kelleysislandferry.com.

Other Contacts

LAKE ERIE SHORES & ISLANDS—WEST, 770 SE Catawba Road, Port Clinton. Call 1-800-441-1271 or 419-734-4386. Website: shoresandislands.com.

PUT-IN-BAY CHAMBER OF COMMERCE AND VISITOR BUREAU, 148 Delaware Avenue, Put-in-Bay. Call 419-285-2832. Website: visitputinbay.com.

IT WAS NEAR THIS SPOT THAT THE WYANDOT OPERATED A MILL

3

FROM THE SANDUSKY RIVER INTO THE FIRELANDS

BUCYRUS, UPPER SANDUSKY, CAREY, TIFFIN,
FREMONT, BELLEVUE, NORWALK, MILAN, VERMILION,
HURON, SANDUSKY

ESTIMATED LENGTH: 120 miles

ESTIMATED TIME: 3.5 hours

HIGHLIGHTS: Starting in Bucyrus, plan to visit one of the neatest companies around: Bucyrus Copper Kettle Works is the only outfit making hand-hammered copper pots in the country. From Bucyrus, follow the Sandusky River west through the tiny town of Nevada—where you can visit the Wyandot Mission—to Upper Sandusky. The Indian Mill on the river in Upper Sandusky was once the heart of a Wyandot settlement. Leaving the river, the route heads to Indian Trail Caverns in Carey but then returns to the river and a stop at the Overland Inn Museum in McCutchenville on the way to Tiffin, with its history of glassmaking. In Fremont, one of many US presidents from Ohio is remembered at the impressive Rutherford B. Hayes Presidential Center. Heading east, Bellevue offers visitors Seneca Caverns and the Historic Lyme Village. The Firelands Museum in Norwalk puts the region's history front and center. Then, in Milan, you can explore the birthplace of Thomas Edison. Passing through Huron, the trip wraps up in Sandusky. Cedar Point is the big attraction here, but don't let it overshadow all Sandusky has to offer. There are several great museums—the Merry-Go-Round Museum, for one—and a number of fine wineries.

GETTING THERE: This tour begins in Bucyrus, north of Columbus. From I-75, take the exit for OH 15 near Findlay and follow it east to US 30 and into Bucyrus. Or take US 30 north of Lima. Follow that east to Bucyrus. Another option: From I-71 follow US 30 west of Mansfield to Bucyrus. The route essentially follows the Sandusky River, through Upper Sandusky, and Tiffin, into Fremont (by way of OH 53). From Fremont, take US 20 east to Clyde, Bellevue, and Norwalk. From here, take OH 13 to Milan. Vermilion and Huron are next, before the final leg, which follows US 6 along the shore of Lake Erie west to Sandusky.

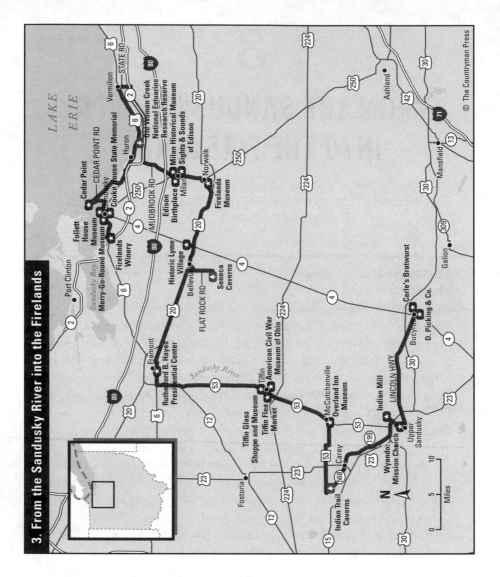

When Europeans landed on the East Coast, they had grand ambitions, establishing colonies and granting themselves lands that extended west from "from sea to sea." Never mind that no one had a good idea of how far west the continent extended—their colonies were bound only by latitude lines and the Pacific Ocean. After the Revolutionary War, many of the colonies gave up their claims on western territories in exchange for wiping out some of their debt to the new American government. Connecticut was one of these, but the state still retained more than a million acres that make up most of what is now northern Ohio. It was called the Connecticut Western Reserve, or more simply, the Western Reserve.

A half-million acres of the western portion of the Western Reserve were set aside for the Connecticut Sufferers—those whose towns had been razed by the British during the war. This region has been known as the Firelands ever since. Interestingly, few of the Sufferers ever settled in the area, choosing instead to sell their land to speculators.

While the Western Reserve included the mouth of Sandusky Bay, the Sandusky River itself flowed outside the reserve, to the west and south. The river begins north of Columbus near the town of Crestline. It flows through Bucyrus, Upper Sandusky, Tiffin, and Fremont before reaching Lake Erie. This part of Ohio is mainly rural in character, but to simply leave it at that would be to ignore the rich heritage and history that give these communities their character.

Every year since 1967, the town of Bucyrus has celebrated the heritage of the region's German immigrants with the **Bucyrus Bratwurst Festival**, held annually on the third full weekend in August. For three days, the town puts on a parade, hosts contests and auctions, and feeds the hungry masses with brats. The festival features an arts and crafts show and a German Heritage Area, where visitors get a chance to rest in the shade, drink beer (in the evening), and enjoy live entertainment.

There used to be more sausage makers in Bucyrus. One of the regular sponsors of the festival, **Carle's Bratwurst**, is the last bratwurst-maker in town. Now, the saying goes that it's best if you don't see how your sausage is made, but don't let that stop you from visiting the source of the best brats around. Harry and Alta Carle founded Carle's Bratwurst in 1929 when they opened a small grocery store in Bucyrus. Today you can stop by to pick up meat for home, or stay and dine in. In addition to bratwurst, they have an incredibly well-stocked meat case, gourmet groceries, domestic wine and beer, and cheeses. You can find Carle's less than a mile east of downtown, on East Mansfield Street.

Another great company still doing things the old-fashioned way is **Bucyrus Copper Kettle Works**. Just a block from the traffic islands in the center of town on Walnut Street, the craftsmen at Bucyrus Copper Kettle Works make hammered copper kettles. The first pots they made, back in 1874, were used to produce apple butter. Eventually the product line was expanded. Today you can purchase kettles for making candy, preserves, and caramel. There are decorative items for around the home, and they even make tympani shells for orchestras. The folks at Bucyrus Copper Kettle Works are happy to show you around, but you will need to call before you visit (419-562-6891).

Heading west out of Bucyrus on West Mansfield Street, the road becomes the Lincoln Highway. Continue west for about 15 miles into Upper Sandusky. You know you're close to your next destination when the street name

MILLSTONES USED BY THE WYANDOT ARE ON DISPLAY NEAR THE RIVER IN UPPER SANDUSKY

changes to East Wyandot Avenue. At North Sandusky Avenue, turn north (right), and drive 0.5 mile to West Church Street. Turn right again, and your next stop, the Wyandot Mission Church, will be on the left.

Upper Sandusky was founded on the site of a Wyandot village of the same name. The Wyandot people came from the north, driven into Ohio by the Iroquois. They settled all over northern and central Ohio. Like many Native American tribes, they fought alternately on the side of both the French and the British, as both nations sought to secure the continent for themselves. When Mad Anthony Wayne—a general in the new American Army—defeated the British and their native allies at the Battle of Fallen Timbers in 1794, the Native Americans were forced to sign the Treaty of Greenville, which gave the United States much of Ohio and other strategic sites on the Great Lakes.

In 1816, a missionary named John Stewart came to Ohio to share the Christian faith with the Indians. Stewart was originally from Virginia, born to free black parents, and his ancestry included a mix of races. Settling in Upper Sandusky among the Wyandot, Stewart established the first successful Methodist Episcopal Native American mission. In 1824, the Wyandot Mission Church was built. The Wyandot continued to worship at the mission until political pressure led them to relocate to Kansas in 1843. The church is open to visitors in the summer months on Friday, Saturday, and Sunday afternoons. The cemetery is always open; visitors can view the graves of John Stewart and a number of Wyandot converts.

For a number of years, the Wyandot people lived side by side with settlers who had moved from the east. They adapted well to the changing environment. During the War of 1812, the Wyandot fought against the British, and to thank them for their efforts, the United States built a mill for the tribe on the Sandusky River. To see the site of the mill, return to North Sandusky Avenue and head north. After 0.5 mile, turn right onto Indian Mill Drive. The mill is 2 miles north, on the right.

Indian Mill sits on the banks of the Sandusky River. The original mill was located about 300 feet from the current mill's location. The newer mill was built in 1861 after the Wyandot were relocated. Today it describes itself as an "educational museum of milling." Given the importance of mills to the development of the country—nearly every settlement with a river had at least one—the museum tells an important story. In the autumn, the red mill sits on the water against a backdrop of fall colors. From Indian Mill Park, which sits across the river, the result is a ridiculously picturesque scene, perfect for color-tour photographers.

From Indian Mill, return to US 23, and drive 2 miles to OH 199. Indian Trail Caverns, in Carey, is 12 miles to the north and west. In Carey, OH 199 joins US 23 and heads due north, but you will want to continue straight on OH 568 (West Findlay Street).

The **Indian Trail Caverns** and the associated Sheriden Cave are treasure troves for archaeologists and prehistory buffs. The Sheriden Cave is a karst sinkhole, and over the millennia it has gathered the remains of now-extinct animals from the Late Pleistocene Age as well as tools from Paleo-Indians. Archeologists have discovered thousands of specimens and artifacts, such as the remains of stag moose, short-faced bear, and giant beavers. Visitors can tour the caves on weekends in the summer.

Heading back to the Sandusky River, you can pick up County Road 58 just north of the caverns. Follow the county road east until it dead-ends at Wenner Road. Turn left and go north a block to County Road 59 and turn right (east) toward OH 53 and the town of McCutchenville. The Sandusky River meanders along its lazy path east of the small town, but on the main road (OH 53; a.k.a., Clay Street) is the **Overland Inn Museum**. The inn was built in 1829 by Joseph McCutchen along the route between Columbus and Lake Erie. The Harrison Trail, as it was known, was a busy stagecoach route, and over the years the structure served travelers making their way north and south. Owned and operated by the Wyandot County Historical Society, the inn is now a museum and offers a passel of classes and programs focusing on traditional crafts, from making hairpin lace to spinning wool.

Heading north on OH 53, the next big town is Tiffin. Straddling the Sandusky River, five bridges connect the two halves of the town. The seat of government for Seneca County, Tiffin dates back to the War of 1812. After natural gas was discovered nearby, the town became a minor industrial hub. It is the home of the National Machinery company, Webster Industries, and others. Until a recent move, the American Standard Company had its headquarters in Tiffin. And one of the town's proudest industries was the Tiffin Glassworks, which kept residents working for nearly a hundred years.

The legacy of the glassworks can be seen at the **Tiffin Glass Museum**. There are several glass studios and shops in town, but the Tiffin Glass Museum is something different. The museum seeks to preserve the unique history of Tiffin Glass. Exhibitions display glass pieces chronologically, so visitors can walk through nearly a hundred years of the evolution of glassmaking in Tiffin. The museum is located on South Washington Street, near the river.

Another museum that is also a working shop is **The Enchanted Moment Doll Shoppe, Museum, and Gallery**, a few blocks south of the Tiffin Glass Museum and one block to the east, on Jefferson Street. The non-profit museum has over 3,000 vintage dolls on display. The shop carries everything from new accessories to antique dolls. And there is even a doll hospital, where experts in doll restoration can return your favorite friend to good health.

Finally, not to be missed is the **American Civil War Museum of Ohio**. Located at the corner of Washington and Main Streets, the museum is housed in what was once the Tiffin post office. Just look for the neoclassical stone façade. Ohio is full of Civil War history. While only two battles, relatively minor ones, were fought in the state, Ohioans participated in nearly every campaign in the war. Being in the geographical center of the country helped make Ohio an important player in the conflict. The museum in Tiffin follows the Civil War, with an eye to both the larger picture—the causes of the war and changes in the history of warfare—and the intimate portrait, examining the lives of the soldiers who fought during our most divisive period.

In between visits to the museums, if your trip falls on one of the special weekends in the summer when it is open, you will want to shop at the **Tiffin Flea Market**. You will find it on the west side of town, a block south of Market Street on Hopewell Avenue. A good flea market is hard to find these days. Many have too much junk—knock-off designer purses, fake Rolex watches, no-name electronics—and not enough of the good stuff. The Tiffin Flea Market is something special. This is the largest flea market in the region, and sellers offer all sorts of antiques, old books, records, collector's items, etc. Check the flea market website (tiffinfleamarket.com) to find out on which weekends it will be held.

Afterwards, be sure to stop at **Jolly's Drive-In**, just a half mile farther east on Market Street. As rare as a good flea market, these classic drive-ins are few and far between these days. Built as an A&W back in 1947, this independent drive-in is still in the family—three generations on. In addition to classic chili dogs (the kind spread with creamy cheese), Jolly's serves sloppy joes, delicious chicken and roast beef sandwiches, and their own root beer (the same recipe that was used when the drive-in first opened). You won't find fries or onion rings, but popcorn and chips can be added as sides.

Returning to OH 53, head north, with the Sandusky River on your right. The next stop is Fremont and the **Rutherford B. Hayes Presidential Center**. To get there, drive 16 miles to US 6 (Hayes Avenue) and turn right. The center is 2 miles east of OH 53. Rutherford B. Hayes was the nineteenth president of the United States, as well as the twenty-ninth and thirty-second governor of Ohio. He was born in 1822 in the town of Delaware, Ohio, a short distance north of Columbus. After finishing law school, he moved to Fremont (then called Lower Sandusky) and opened a practice. He was eventually elected to office as city solicitor in 1859, but two years later he had to leave Fremont to fight in the Civil War.

After the war, Hayes's political career took off when voters sent him to Congress and later to the Ohio governor's office. In 1877, after a highly con-

THE MUSEUM AND LIBRARY ARE A CENTERPIECE OF THE HAYES HISTORIC SITE

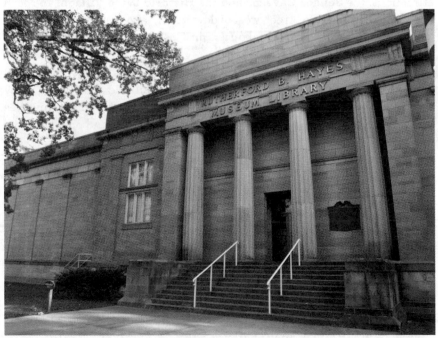

tested election, the Republican went to the White House. Hayes lost the popular vote, but as a result of the Compromise of 1877, the Democrats ceded the election on the condition that Hayes would pull federal troops out of the South. Most historians cite this as the end of Reconstruction.

The **Rutherford B. Hayes Presidential Center** is located on the Hayes estate. The centerpiece of the property is a sprawling thirty-one-room mansion. The mansion was originally built by the president's uncle and guardian during the Civil War; Hayes continually expanded and remodeled the house up until his death in 1893. After he passed away, the property was donated to the state, and a museum was added. The museum features more than 19,000 items that once belonged to the president and his family.

While you tour the property, be sure to take note of the trees. Hayes was fond of having honored guests touch various trees on the property. These trees were then marked with a plaque. For example, you might see a hickory once touched by Grover Cleveland, the twenty-second and twenty-fourth president of the United States. There's also a marker that indicates the spot where, in 1790, Peggy Fleming was rescued by the Wyandot Indian chief, Tarhee, from being burned alive by the Cherokees. The Wyandot then returned her to her family in Pittsburgh.

After following the Sandusky River for nearly its entire run, our path now turns east, into the Firelands. The first stop is Bellevue, 15 miles east of Fremont, on US 20. A hard-working Midwest town, Bellevue has two main attractions: the **Seneca Caverns** and the **Historic Lyme Village**. To reach the caverns, from Main Street, west of downtown, take Flat Rock Road south 3.5 miles to County Road 178 and turn right. The caverns will be on your left, less than a mile down the road.

Driving through Ohio south of downtown Bellevue, the last geological feature you would expect to find would be caves. Nothing about these many square miles of level farmland suggests that something interesting lies just beneath the surface. But it does. Discovered in 1872 and opened to the public for tours in 1933, Seneca Caverns can be explored on seven levels, going down 110 feet. (Below that, water fills the caves, though in dry seasons spelunkers have gone down to 220 feet.) Tours take about an hour. Visitors will go down to where the Ole Mist'ry River flows through the caverns. It's always about 54 degrees in the caves, so bring a jacket or coat.

Returning to downtown Bellevue, if you plan to spend the night, you might consider The **Victorian Tudor Inn** on Main Street. Bellevue is not the likeliest place for a bed and breakfast, though the town does have plenty of charm. The inn itself is one of the most attractive of the neighborhood's historic homes. There are five rooms, and guests can make themselves at home in any one of the inn's public areas—including the Hot Tub Room. In the summer, you can sit out on the porch or enjoy the spacious gardens.

East of downtown Bellevue—north of US 20 on OH 4—our tour continues

JUST NORTH OF BELLEVIEW IS THE HISTORIC LYME VILLAGE

with a visit to the **Historic Lyme Village**. Recreated to represent a village in the 1800s, a two-hour tour of the Historic Lyme Village gives visitors an up-close look at life in the Bellevue area during the early nineteenth century. The village is a collection of historic buildings from all over the area. They provide an appropriate backdrop for the staff of volunteers who reenact life during this period for guests.

Head east on US 20 for 15 minutes to get to Norwalk. Approximately 8 miles from Bellevue, the town can be reached by the exit for Main Street, which will take you to the center of town and our next stop, the **Firelands Museum**.

During the Revolutionary War, the British raided and seriously damaged nine towns in Connecticut. The Connecticut legislature compensated the residents of these towns with land to the west: a half million acres in northern Ohio, the aforementioned Firelands. The museum in Norwalk (named for Norwalk, Connecticut), tells visitors about this unique bit of American history and how the war and the events that followed had an impact on this part of the state. Bits and pieces from everyday life are on display, from aprons to pistols. From this, you get a decent sense of how colonial life translated to the rapidly populating frontier.

THE FIRELANDS MUSEUM IS LOCATED IN THE HISTORIC PRESTON-WICKHAM HOUSE

The finest B&B around is the gorgeous **Georgian Manor Inn** in Norwalk. Its 9,000 square feet, twenty-seven rooms, and immaculate grounds draw guests to Norwalk from all over Ohio. The home was built in 1906 in the Georgian Revival style. Fully restored, the inn features hardwood floors and period antiques. There are numerous public areas where guests can relax, including two porches. The gardens are especially nice. The inn has four guest rooms.

The next town on the tour is less than 10 minutes away. US 250 approaches Milan from the south and then skirts the western edge of town. Continue on the highway until you come to Church Street, where you will turn right. This will take you to the center of town.

Bounded by Front and Church Streets to the north and south, and Main and Park Streets to the west and east, Milan's town square is an idyllic slice of America, a throwback to less cynical times when the promise of the country was expressed through small yet vibrant communities. That feeling lives on. At the north end of the square is a gazebo. At the other end lies a statue of a young Thomas Edison. In the center is a monument to those from Milan who served in the Civil War. On Labor Day Weekend, the town square is the site of the annual **Milan Melon Festival**. A car show, carnival rides, musical acts, and a parade are just parts of what draw 50,000 festivalgoers every year. The event has been held in Milan for more than 50 years.

When Thomas Alva Edison was born in Milan on February 11, 1847, his hometown was a bustling canal port. Work on the Milan Canal began in 1833, and it finally reached Lake Erie in 1839. Canals were a boon for many small towns, and Milan exemplified that like few others. Located just a little more than 7 miles to the south of Lake Erie, Milan became one of the busiest ports on the Great Lakes.

By the 1850s, the heyday of inland water transportation had passed, and

THIS HUMBLE BRICK HOME WAS THE BIRTHPLACE OF THOMAS EDISON

THE SIGHTS AND SOUNDS OF EDISON HAS AN INCREDIBLE COLLECTION OF RESTORED PHONOGRAPHS FOR SALE

the railroads began to dominate. (Coincidently, the year of Edison's birth was the busiest year on the canal for Milan.) But such is the legacy of Thomas Edison that, though he lived here just seven years, his memory survives in a dozen ways, while the memory of the canal lingers only faintly.

The **Edison Birthplace** on North Edison Drive in Milan is where the legend began. Aside from Ben Franklin, no other American inventor has left a cultural legacy as significant as Thomas Edison's. The incandescent light bulb would have been plenty, but he also gave us the phonograph and the motion picture camera. The birthplace, however, harkens back to a simpler time in the inventor's life. A tour of the home takes you from the birth room to the kitchen. Many of the items in the home belonged to family members.

Afterwards, walk a block southeast to the **Milan Historical Museum**. Anticipate spending an hour or so here. The museum has six buildings of exhibitions, covering everything from the visual arts to the life in old Milan. When you're done, there's always time for Milan's second claim to fame: antiquing.

Before heading back to downtown to browse the shops on the square, be sure to visit **Sights & Sounds of Edison** on South Main Street. Specializing in the history of recorded sound, this antiques shop has counters full of restored cylinder Edison phonographs, gramophones, and record players. With their decorative horns and buffed wooden cases, the phonographs are as much works of art as they are pieces of history.

Finally, for overnight accommodations, reserve a room at the **Angel Welcome Bed & Breakfast**. There's no better place to rest your head in Milan. Built in 1828, the inn was one of the first six homes to be built in town. The original owner built the house across the street from the general store. Today, there are three well-appointed guest rooms. The B&B is walking distance from downtown, and the Edison birthplace is just around the corner. Best yet, you will find your hosts at Angel Welcome to be extremely hospitable and gracious.

After leaving Milan, it's time to spend some time on Lake Erie. Head north by taking US 250 and veering right onto Old Mudbrook Road. Follow Old Mudbrook north to OH 2 and head east. Continue until you reach the exit for State Road, which you will follow 2 miles north to downtown Vermilion.

There are few people who remember the days when the economy of entire communities was supported by fishing the Great Lakes. Everyone—from the men on the boats to the boat makers, wholesalers, and the folks who made the shipping crates—was part of the industry that made the fortune of many towns like Vermilion. Named for the river that empties into Lake Erie, Vermilion never had a harbor big enough for commercial shipping, but smaller boats did well. From the early years onward, there were fish shanties on the river.

Charter fishing outfits still sail out of Vermilion, but where shanties used to be, there are now parks and cottages. Developers dredged the marsh at the mouth of the river carving out the Vermillion Lagoons—a community of homes close to the lake, each with its own boat dock. A handful of marinas a little farther upriver also help house the fleet of boats used by recreational boaters out of Vermilion.

Even if you don't get out on the water, however, Vermilion is a great little town for walking. There are shops and restaurants along Liberty Avenue and Main Street, and at the north end of Main Street, there's a public beach. One of the town's mainstays is the **Old Prague Restaurant**. Specializing in Czech cuisine, they have a number of imported Czech beers on tap and dishes like chicken paprikash, served with dumplings or spaetzle. The restaurant has seasonal hours—open daily in summer, much less often in winter.

For fine dining on the water, there is really only one option. **Chez François** on Main Street sits on the Vermilion River, with views of the river and the Vermilion Lagoons. The restaurant offers a decidedly upscale French menu, a stunning wine list, and a calendar of culinary events that make Chez François a destination in itself.

Both of these restaurants are within walking distance of the **Gilchrist**

Guest House Bed & Breakfast on Huron Street. The inn's property fronts Lake Erie and is next door to the now-closed Inland Seas Maritime Museum. (The museum moved to Toledo and is now the National Museum of the Great Lakes.) This charming bed-and-breakfast features four guest rooms, each with antique wooden beds and furniture. The home was built in 1885 for J. C. Gilchrist—at the time a big name in lumber and Great Lakes shipping. This is the perfect home base for exploring Vermilion: Guests can stroll the property, walk down to the local beach, or hike the easy two blocks to downtown.

As you drive west along the coast of Lake Erie to Sandusky—following US 6 (Cleveland Road) toward Huron—you will pass the entrance to the **Old Woman Creek National Estuarine Research Reserve**. This 572-acre preserve is popular with bird watchers, nature lovers, and folks who enjoy a nice walk in the woods. The centerpiece of the park is the Old Woman Creek estuary. Two miles of trails wind in and out of oak-hickory forest and take visitors to an observation deck on the water. In addition to native waterfowl and migrating species, you may see a bald eagle or two on the lookout for dinner.

Leaving the preserve and continuing west for about 2 miles, you will come to the town of Huron and a restaurant with a proud local reputation. **Berardi's Restaurant**, just east of the river, is owned by the Berardi family. They own several eateries in the area. Back in 1942, Al Berardi opened a french fry stand at Cedar Point amusement park. By the time the stand closed at Cedar Point in 1978, the outfit was selling 2 million pounds of potatoes a year. The concession was a favorite with regular visitors to the amusement park, and even now, 30 years later, it's hard to find decent fries at the park. But the tradition of serving decent food and great fries continues at the family's restaurants. The Italian dishes are excellent, and there's a full menu of burgers and sandwiches, but whatever you order, make sure it comes with a plate of hand-cut fries, just like Al used to make.

Outside of northern Ohio, Sandusky is synonymous with **Cedar Point**. The roads that lead you through town to the amusement park are the best-maintained in the area, lined with signs that keep drivers pushing ahead to the park. Cedar Point has a long and fascinating history—beginning as a launch for Sandusky fisherman, serving as a line of defense when Confederate soldiers were imprisoned on nearby Johnson's Island, and providing Americans with an entertaining way to escape the summer heat—though it is admittedly hard to see much of that history now.

That is not to say the park is without its attractions. More than three million people visit every year. And even those who would rather avoid roller coasters find a lot to keep themselves entertained. These visitors are treated to many easy-going rides, plenty of concessions, and family-friendly live entertainment. Adjacent to the amusement park is the Challenge Park, with

FLOWERS BORDER THE STREETS OF DOWNTOWN VERMILION

a couple of adrenaline-pumping rides and high-speed go-karts as well as the Soak City waterpark.

Sandusky itself, however, is often overlooked, as families make a beeline for the Cedar Point parking lot. Those willing to put in an extra day will find a lot to see here, like a handful of beautiful historic homes. The **Cooke House State Memorial** is less than a mile southeast of downtown, right on Columbus Avenue (the street that splits Washington Park). The Cooke House is unique in that, even though it was built in the 1840s (and moved to its present location in 1874), it has been restored to look as it did in the 1950s. There are a few pieces of furniture from the nineteenth century, but that would have been expected in the 1950s. In this respect, I believe the home is truly unique. While other museums capture a period with very era-appropriate furnishings, the Cooke House captures the period and also shows how it would have been influenced by the periods that came before. It's a fabulous house to tour—the three-story mansion has a surprisingly large kitchen, and the landscaping is stunning.

Another house worth visiting is the historic **Follett House Museum** on Wayne Street. Essentially a branch of the Sandusky library system, the Follett House is a fine example of Greek Revival architecture. In fact, it's on the list of National Historic Landmarks. Not at all a "moment in time"–type attraction (like the Cooke House), inside you will find a more traditional

THE MERRY-GO-ROUND MUSEUM IS A FUN DIVERSION

museum that preserves local history. Four floors tell the role Sanduskians played in events ranging from the War of 1812 to World War II.

At the corner of Washington and Jackson Streets, you will find another museum that captures a piece of local history: the **Merry-Go-Round Museum**. Considering that people have been coming to Sandusky to be amused for well over a hundred years, few places are as appropriate a home for a merry-go-round museum as this town. The highlight of the museum is the 1939 Allan Herschell Carousel. As it spins, the air constantly fills with the sound of the band organ. In addition to displaying antique carousel figures, the museum also restores old pieces. If they're lucky, visitors might have a chance to watch professionals work on bringing some of these wooden animals back to life.

After checking out the Merry-Go-Round Museum, head across Washington Park to the **Red Popcorn Wagon**. This snack cart has been in Washington Square since 1910. It has become such a fixture that it was added to the National Register of Historic Places. Over the years, ownership of the popcorn wagon passed through many hands. Today, it's owned by the city and operated by the United Way.

If your tour of Sandusky has you wandering downtown around mealtime, there's a great little restaurant not to be missed: the **Zinc Brasserie**, found a block north of Washington Park, on Columbus Avenue. In France, bar tops are often covered in zinc, and the neighborhood bar is often called Le Petit

Zinc. But in the lingo of French restaurants, a brasserie is a step up from a local bar. The Zinc Brasserie captures this contradiction wonderfully. While it is certainly a step up from most dining in Sandusky, its feel of a neighborhood hang-out is not lost. It's wonderfully comfortable, with a classic French menu—a place that does justice to steak frites is not to be missed.

Heading west from town on US 6, the tour winds down with a visit to the **Firelands Winery**. You will pass the Toft's Ice Cream Parlor at the **Toft Dairy** along the way, so you will have to decide if wine pairs well with a delicious sundae. Serving better ice cream than any soft-serve stand and most hard ice cream places, the folks at Toft's cook their vanilla, giving their ice cream an uncommon richness. The dairy is the oldest in Ohio, and some of its history is on display at the parlor.

Continuing along US 6, just past the light where US 6 turns to follow Fremont Avenue, you will turn left (south) onto Bardshar Road. The Fire-

STOP AT TOFT'S FOR A PERFECT SUMMER TREAT

lands Winery is 0.5 mile down. The winery was built in 1880 and originally called the Mantey Winery. Different signs have hung over the door through the years, but in 2002, the winery became known as the Firelands Winery, becoming the flagship property of the company that also owns Mon Ami in Port Clinton. The largest producer of wine in Ohio, Firelands prides itself on using grapes from local vineyards for its presses.

IN THE AREA

Accommodations

ANGEL WELCOME BED & BREAKFAST, 2 Front Street, Milan. Call 419-499-0094. Website: angelwelcome.com. $$.

GEORGIAN MANOR INN, 123 West Main Street, Norwalk. Call 419-663-8132 or 1-800-668-1644. Website: georgianmanorinn.com. $$$.

GILCHRIST GUEST HOUSE BED & BREAKFAST, 5662 Huron Street, Vermilion. Call 440-967-1237. Website: gilchristguesthouse.com. $$.

THE VICTORIAN TUDOR INN, 408 West Main Street, Bellevue. Call 419-483-1949. Website: victoriantudor.com. $$.

WAGNER'S 1844 INN, 230 East Washington Street, Sandusky. Call 419-626-1726. Website: lrbcg.com/wagnersinn. $$.

Attractions and Recreation

AMERICAN CIVIL WAR MUSEUM OF OHIO, 217 South Washington Street, Tiffin. Call 419-455-9551 or 419-509-0324. Website: acwmo.org.

BUCYRUS BRATWURST FESTIVAL, Bucyrus. Website: bucyrusbratwurst festival.com. Held annually on the third full weekend in August.

BUCYRUS COPPER KETTLE WORKS, 119 South Walnut Street, Bucyrus. Call 419-562-6891. You'll need to call ahead if you would like to visit the shop. Website: bucyruscopperkettle.com.

CARLE'S BRATWURST, 1210 East Mansfield Street, Bucyrus. Call 419-562-7741. Closed on Sundays. Website: carlesbrats.com.

CEDAR POINT, 1 Cedar Point Drive, Sandusky. Call 419-627-2350. Website: cedarpoint.com.

COOKE HOUSE STATE MEMORIAL, 1415 Columbus Avenue, Sandusky. Call 419-627-0640 or 1-877-734-1386 Website: ohiohistory.org/cooke.

CROSBY'S ANTIQUES, 4 North Main Street, Milan. Call 419-499-4001. Website: facebook.com/pages/Crosbys-Antiques/160183097335467.

EDISON BIRTHPLACE, 9 North Edison Drive, Milan. Call 419-499-2135. Website: tomedison.org.

THE ENCHANTED MOMENT DOLL SHOPPE, MUSEUM, AND GALLERY, 174 Jefferson Street, Tiffin. Call 419-443-0038. Website: theenchanted momentdolls.com. Open Wednesday through Saturday.

FIRELANDS MUSEUM, 4 Case Avenue, Norwalk. Call 419-668-6038. Website: firelandsmuseum.com.

FIRELANDS WINERY, 917 Bardshar Road, Sandusky. Call 419-625-5474 or 1-800-548-9463. Website: firelandswinery.com.

FOLLETT HOUSE MUSEUM, 404 Wayne Street, Sandusky. Call 419-627-9608. Website: sandusky.lib.oh.us/follett_house.

HISTORIC LYME VILLAGE, 5001 OH 4. Bellevue. Call 419-483-4949. Website: lymevillage.com.

INDIAN TRAIL CAVERNS, 722 OH 568, Carey. Call 419-387-7773. Website: indiantrailcaverns.com. The caverns are open on Saturday and Sunday afternoons in the summer. There is a fee to tour the caves, and they accept only cash.

INDIAN MILL, 7417 County Highway 47, Upper Sandusky. Call 419-294-4022. Website: visitwyandotcounty.com/indian-mill.

MARITIME MUSEUM OF SANDUSKY, 125 Meigs Street, Sandusky. Call 419-624-0274. Website: sanduskymaritime.org.

MERRY-GO-ROUND MUSEUM, 301 Jackson Street, Sandusky. Call 419-626-6111. Website: merrygoroundmuseum.org.

MILAN HISTORICAL MUSEUM, 10 North Edison Drive, Milan. Call 419-499-2968. Website: milanhistory.org.

MILAN INN-TIQUES, 29 East Church Street, Milan. Call 419-499-4939. Website: shoresandislands.com/things-to-do/milan-inn-tiques?id=12361.

MILAN MELON FESTIVAL, Village Square, Milan. Call 419-504-8664. Website: shoresandislands.com/local/events/milan-melon-festival?id=10338.

OHIO VETERANS HOME MUSEUM, 3416 Columbus Avenue, Sandusky. Call 419-625-2454, ext. 1447. Website: dvs.ohio.gov/main/ovh-sandusky -military-museum.html.

OLD WOMAN CREEK NATIONAL ESTUARINE RESEARCH RESERVE, 2514 Cleveland Road East, Huron. Call 419-433-4601. Website: wildlife .ohiodnr.gov/oldwomancreek.

OVERLAND INN MUSEUM, 283 OH 53 North, McCutchenville. Call 419-294-3857. Website: wyandothistory.org.

RED POPCORN WAGON, Washington Park, Sandusky. Call 419-627-5833. Website: facebook.com/RedPopcornWagon.

RUTHERFORD B. HAYES PRESIDENTIAL CENTER, Spiegel Grove, Fremont. Call 419-332-2081. Website: rbhayes.org.

SENECA CAVERNS, 15248 Township Road 178, Bellevue. Call 419-483-6711. Website: senecacavernsohio.com.

SIGHTS AND SOUNDS OF EDISON, 21 South Main Street, Milan. Call 419-499-3039. Website: edisonman.com.

TIFFIN FLEA MARKET, 100 Hopewell Avenue, Tiffin. Call 419-447-9613 or 1-888-736-3221. Website: tiffinfleamarket.com.

TIFFIN GLASS MUSEUM, 25 South Washington Street, Tiffin. Call 419-448-0200. Website: tiffinglass.org.

TOFT DAIRY, 3717 Venice Road, Sandusky. Call 419-625-4376 or 1-800-521-4606. Website: toftdairy.com.

THE VICTORIAN TUDOR INN, 408 West Main Street, Bellevue. Call 419-483-1949. Website: victoriantudor.com.

Dining

BERARDI'S RESTAURANT HURON, 218 Cleveland Road East, Huron. Call 419-433-4123. Website: berardisrestauranthuron.com. $$.

BRICK OVEN BISTRO, 1012 Cleveland Road, Sandusky. Call 419-624-1400. Website: brickovenohio.com. $$.

CHEZ FRANÇOIS, 555 Main Street, Vermilion. Call 440-967-0630. Website: chezfrancois.com. $$$$.

JOLLY'S DRIVE-IN, 66 East Market Street, Tiffin. Call 419-447-4998. Website: jollysdrivein.com. $.

OLD PRAGUE RESTAURANT, 5586 Liberty Avenue, Vermilion. Call 440-967-7182. Website: oldprague.com. $$.

ZINC BRASSERIE, 215 East Water Street, Sandusky. Call 419-502-9462. Website: zincbrasserie.net. $$$$.

Other Contacts

DESTINATION SENECA COUNTY, 19 West Market Street, Suite C, Tiffin. Call 567-220-6387. Website: destinationsenecacounty.org.

HURON COUNTY VISITOR BUREAU, 10 West Main Street, Norwalk. Call 419-668-4155 or 1-877-668-4155. Website: visithuroncounty.com.

LAKE ERIE SHORES & ISLANDS—EAST, 4424 Milan Road, Suite A, Sandusky. Call 1-800-255-3743 or 419-625-2984. Website: shoresandislands.com.

WYANDOT COUNTY VISITOR BUREAU, 108 East Wyandot Avenue, Upper Sandusky. Call 419-294-3556 or toll free at 1-877-992-6368. Website: www.visitwyandotcounty.com.

4

CLEVELAND TO AKRON
THE SHORES OF LAKE ERIE AND THE CUYAHOGA RIVER VALLEY

BAY VILLAGE, ROCKY RIVER, CLEVELAND, EUCLID,
CUYAHOGA VALLEY NATIONAL PARK, AKRON

ESTIMATED LENGTH: 100 miles

ESTIMATED TIME: 3 hours

HIGHLIGHTS: Your journey starts with the Burrell Homestead at the French Creek Reservation. This short, historic stop is followed by a visit to the impressive Lake Erie Nature and Science Center in Bay Village. Then we head north to US 6, which runs along the Lake Erie shoreline. Heading east, touches of suburbia give way to the feeling that Cleveland is near. You'll want to stop for lunch at Melt Bar & Grilled as you make your way into the city. Right downtown on the waterfront are the crowning jewels of Cleveland's cultural center—the Rock & Roll Hall of Fame and Museum and the Great Lakes Science Center. Then it's off to explore Cleveland's neighborhoods: Tour the museums and botanical gardens on the campus of Case Western Reserve University, visit Little Italy, stop for a Polish Boy at Seti's, and do some shopping in Coventry Village. Diving further into Cleveland's proud immigrant culture, your next stop is a short jaunt north to Euclid to visit the National Polka Hall of Fame. Then it's time to leave metropolitan Cleveland. The route follows the Cuyahoga Valley—which you can explore by car or train—with stops at a handful of waterfalls and a visit to the Hale Farm and Village. The final leg of the trip passes through Tallmadge and finishes at the Stan Hywet Hall and Gardens in Akron.

GETTING THERE: This route begins at the French Creek Reservation in Sheffield Lake. It's on the Black River, which is west of Cleveland and southeast of Lorain. To get there, take I-90 for Detroit Road (exit 148). As you head west, the first intersection is Gulf Road/East River Road. Turn right, and you will find the entrance to the Burrell Homestead, about 2.5 miles north of the intersection.

LEFT: A GREAT WAY TO EXPLORE THE CUYAHOGA VALLEY IS A RIDE ON THE SCENIC RAILROAD

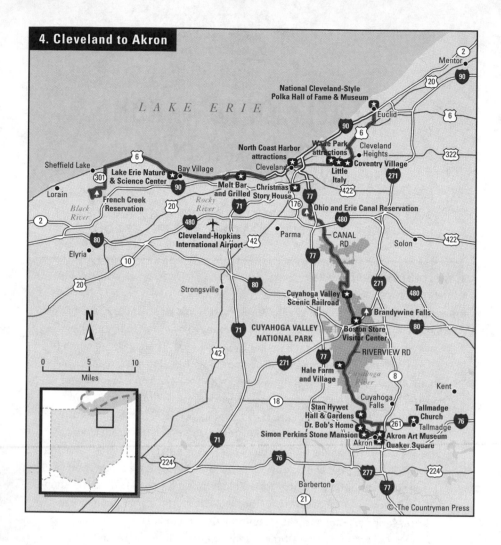

4. Cleveland to Akron

The heart of this itinerary is Cleveland, and—contrary to what you might have heard about the health of cities in the industrial Midwest—it's still beating. The city bears the name of one General Moses Cleaveland, who led the team of surveyors who first divvied up the territory into townships back in 1796. Moses never planned to stay in Ohio once the job was complete and soon left. The first settler, a fellow by the name of Lorenzo Carter, built a cabin in the area not soon after, but it was nearly two decades before the Village of Cleaveland became a legitimate entity.

Cleveland's location at the mouth of Cuyahoga River, on the shores of Lake Erie, made growth inevitable, but with the advent of the canal system, Cleveland's location became even more of an asset. The city was connected to the Gulf of Mexico by way of the Ohio and Mississippi Rivers. The Erie Canal connected Cleveland to the East Coast. And while the railroad put many a canal town out of business, it only strengthened the value of Cleveland's ports. Soon Cleveland was a Midwest transportation hub and industrial powerhouse. Ore and coal made its way here by boat, and local companies made all sorts of things, including steam and electric automobiles. As manufacturing flourished, the business community found Cleveland a great town for making money.

All this success attracted attention. Germans, Irish, Polish, and Italian immigrants came to northern Ohio to find work, and they found it. Seeking a place that felt like home, they gathered in neighborhoods, started businesses, and raised families. Eastern Europeans were a big part of the mix: At one point, the only place with more Hungarians per square mile was Budapest. These communities brought with them great food, rich musical traditions, and an old-world ethic that embraced hard work and kept family close.

The latter half of the twentieth century was tough on every city that had come to rely on manufacturing. Many jobs have left by now, and the economy is still, in many ways, transitioning to a post-industrial economy, but the boom years established a wealth of cultural institutions and resources that continue to make this a great town to live in and visit.

THE ROCK & ROLL HALL OF FAME HAS BECOME A BIG DRAW FOR DOWNTOWN CLEVELAND

West of Cleveland, two significant waterways empty into Lake Erie. The closest is the Rocky River, which is the namesake of the town at its mouth. Further west is the Black River, which feeds into Lake Erie in Lorain. Metroparks and nature preserves line both rivers. Adjacent to the Black River in Sheffield Lake, on Colorado Avenue, is the **French Creek Reservation**, a natural oasis that also preserves some of the region's early history.

Begin your visit with a stop at the park's **Burrell Homestead**. In 1816, Jabez Burrell moved with his family from Massachusetts to Ohio and built a log cabin at the confluence of the Black River and French Creek. The War of 1812 was a recent memory, and Ohio saw an influx of settlers, now that hostility on the frontier had cooled. A few years later, Burrell began working on the homestead you see today. The brick for the Federal-style home was fired right there on the farm.

The next generation of Burrells made the property a stop on the Underground Railroad. Runaway slaves were hidden in the grain house. When the coast was clear, a sympathetic boat captain would spirit the slaves down the Black River and across Lake Erie to freedom in Canada.

In addition to the homestead, the French Creek Reservation features 450 acres of forest, rolling woodlands, cliffs, and creeks. At less than 2 miles long, the Big Woods Trail is a great way to explore the preserve. The hike begins at the Picnic Tree Picnic Area. For a shorter hike with more personality, you might try the Nature Center Trail. The trailhead is found just outside the Nature Center doors, and there are a couple of scenic overlooks along the way. This trail also connects to the park's other trails, so you can extend your hike to fill your available time.

The next stop is the **Lake Erie Nature & Science Center** in Bay Village. Travelers who like to meander can head north to US 6 and follow the shoreline to Porter Creek Drive. The center is at the corner of Porter Creek Drive and Wolf Road. For those who want to make like a bee, you can follow I-90 east to Crocker Road (exit 156). About 1.5 miles north, you will turn east onto Wolf Road. The center is 0.7 mile down, on the north side of the road.

The Lake Erie Nature & Science Center is quite a place, especially if you have children. The center leases the property from the Cleveland Metroparks, and it adjoins the park system's **Huntington Reservation**. Inside, you will find a small planetarium as well as wildlife exhibitions. Local citizens bring injured animals here for treatment and rehabilitation. If you're not content to look at simple specimens of taxidermy, much of the wildlife here is alive and kicking. One of the hallways features a beehive. Connected to the outside and enclosed in Plexiglas and screening, visitors can hear the buzz of a thousand bees working hard at making honey. There's a small zoo out back that contains turkey vultures and deer. There is also a small pond stocked with frogs, fish, and turtles.

A trail across the street from the nature center connects this section of the Huntington Reservation with the park's Huntington Beach on Lake Erie. A very popular place for sunbathing and swimming in the summer, the beach stretches nearly 0.5 mile. When the weather's warm, be sure to stop at **Mitchell's Ice Cream**. There are several locations in the area; the closest here is in Westlake. The Mitchell brothers have perfected the recipe for great ice cream. It's all about the ingredients: "We don't use ingredients that your grandmother wouldn't have used in her own cooking." This translates into locally sourced dairy products from family farms that feed their cows a diet of grass, fruits from local orchards and farms, and nuts and chocolate from Cleveland-based companies. If you visit the area in the off-season, you will need to go to one of their year-round locations. There are eight locations around metropolitan Cleveland.

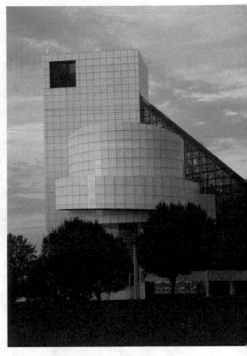

RIGHT ON THE WATERFRONT, THE GREAT LAKES SCIENCE MUSEUM PROMISES A LOT OF FUN FOR KIDS AND ADULTS ALIKE

Since we're on the subject of food, as you head east on US 6 toward Cleveland, you will find yourself near one of the area's most popular eateries. Just before the highway crosses the Rocky River, take Lake Road south to Detroit Road east. This is also called Alt-US-6. **Melt Bar & Grilled** is less than 2 miles east of the river on Detroit Road. Melt is known for one thing—grilled cheese sandwiches—but don't let the simplicity of this idea trick you into thinking this place must have a boring menu. Au contraire! Melt has more takes on the grilled cheese sandwich than you can imagine. There's the Parmageddon, stacked with pierogi, vodka kraut, and sharp cheddar cheese. The Godfather is essentially cheesy lasagna between two slices of bread. There's even a chicken curry sandwich.

Melt has expanded in recent years—there are now five locations—so maybe the pressure has eased, but you need to plan ahead if you intend to eat there. In the past, reservations have been a must. If you stop by on the weekend for lunch without calling ahead, you might wait an hour or two to be seated.

Continuing east on Detroit Avenue, you will jump on OH 2 and follow it into the heart of Cleveland. The next stop is the North Coast Harbor. During the summers of 1936 and 1937, this was the site of the Great Lakes Exposition, which attracted 11 million visitors to the city's waterfront. The visitors

"A Christmas Story": On Location

A Christmas Story did not do well when it arrived in movie theaters a week before Thanksgiving in 1983. Critics were rather positive—Siskel and Ebert gave it "two thumbs up"—but moviegoers seemed to miss it altogether. By Christmas, most theaters had dropped it from the lineup. Thankfully for people who didn't catch it on the big screen, that wasn't the end of the story.

Over the years the film gained a huge audience. Television networks played it around Christmas time, folks bought and rented the movie to watch at home, and pretty soon the movie earned a spot on the proverbial list of much-loved Christmas classics. Today the movie is so popular that a cable network can justify broadcasting a 24-hour *A Christmas Story* marathon on Christmas Eve and Christmas Day.

The movie, based on Jean Shepherd's book *In God We Trust, All Others Pay Cash*, takes place in a fictional city in Indiana, centering on Ralphie Parker and his family. Fans will recognize the *A Christmas Story* **House** in Cleveland right away. All the exterior shots of the home were filmed here. Since the interior wasn't used in the movie, the homeowners have made some efforts to re-create the look and feel of the movie's sets—but the layout is different and it feels dramatically less lived-in than you might imagine.

Across the street is a little museum, and locals who participated in the film shoot are often on hand to share stories of the experience. There's a great gift shop that sells leg lamps, as well as Red Ryder BB guns, pink bunny pajamas, and Randy's blue scarf.

The *A Christmas Story* House is south of downtown Cleveland, in a quiet neighborhood southeast of the I-71/I-90 junction.

---

are still coming, but now they come to tour the Rock & Roll Hall of Fame, the Great Lakes Science Center, the USS *Cod*, and the Steamship *William G. Mather* Maritime Museum. Another big draw is FirstEnergy Stadium, where the Cleveland Browns play.

Most of the people who make it to the **Rock & Roll Hall of Fame and Museum** come from out of town. Since 1995, when it opened, 9 million visitors have made the trip. Cleveland has a proud rock heritage. Alan Freed, a Cleveland disk jockey, was the first to use the term "rock and roll" to describe this black R & B that all the white kids were listening to in the 1950s. In the 1980s, Huey Lewis told us that "the heart of rock and roll was still beating, in Cleveland." In the 1990s, the Drew Carey Show kicked off with a weekly reminder from Mott the Hoople singer Ian Hunter: "Cleveland rocks!"

This reputation has been enhanced by the Rock & Roll Hall of Fame (though there's something a bit off about a corporate-sponsored institution that commemorates the anti-establishment anthems of street-scrapping kids and garage bands). The impressively large facility is packed with artifacts celebrating rock-and-roll culture. Not only will you find instruments, costumes, and other memorabilia belonging to these counter-cultural icons (some are on loan to the Rock Hall), but you will also get a thoughtful look into the roots of the music.

New acts are added annually to the Rock Hall's roster. This yearly induction process brings some controversy to Cleveland—there are more worthy bands than there are spots available, and fans are a passionate bunch—but it also brings some great music. Numerous concerts, lectures, and symposiums put the music into context, exploring the bands and musicians who led the way and the cultural climate that gave birth to the music.

Next door to the Rock Hall is another great Cleveland institution, the **Great Lakes Science Center**. Once they pay admission, guests can feel free to leave a lot of museum etiquette at the door. Museums all convey information differently—there's often a lot of reading, and sometimes there are short videos—but the Great Lakes Science Center skips some of that and invites guests to learn by doing something. Start a miniature tornado, or watch your neighbor's hair stand on end. This is a hands-on museum, and as such, it's really popular with kids.

THE OMNIMAX THEATER AT THE GREAT LAKES SCIENCE MUSEUM PUTS THE AUDIENCE INTO THE MOVIE

In addition to the science exhibitions that deal with natural phenomena, biology, and space, there's a room especially for kids under 7, an OMNIMAX theater, and an actual Great Lakes steamship to explore. The theater typically has a fascinating schedule of shows, and sometimes experts will give a short talk beforehand.

In the summer, there is one more stop in the North Coast Harbor that you may want to make time for. The **USS *Cod*** is a World War II–era submarine that you can tour. The *Cod* had more than its fair share of adventures during the Second Great War, and that history really comes alive when you have a chance to experience the space these men had to inhabit. The submarine was active in the Pacific during the war and then moved around quite a bit before landing in Cleveland

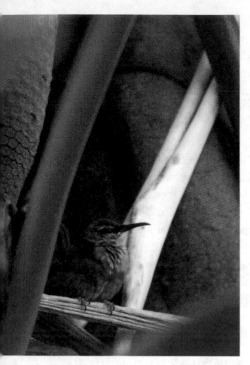

THE CLEVELAND BOTANICAL GARDENS IS HOME
TO DOZENS OF BIRDS

as a training vessel for the Navy. When the Navy was done with the ship, it was passed on to a group of locals intent on preserving the submarine as a memorial. If you are uncomfortable in tight spaces, you may want to prep yourself for the tour. The ship has been restored, but no accommodations have been made to make it easy for visitors to get around. You will use the same ladders and hatchways its sailors used in the 1940s.

Continuing east on OH 2, drive for roughly 4.5 miles, and exit the highway at Martin Luther King Jr. Drive. This scenic street winds through a greenway that straddles Doan Brook all the way into University Circle. The Circle is an amazing neighborhood full of enriching cultural activities. It includes the campus of Case Western Reserve University, several theaters, botanical gardens, historic churches, a history museum, art museums, and a museum of natural science. There are plenty of restaurants and coffee shops, and the neighborhood is adjacent to Cleveland's Little Italy.

A number of great institutions are clustered around Wade Park. Families can plan on a whole day of touring the Cleveland Botanical Garden, the Cleveland Museum of Natural History, and the Cleveland Museum of Art. There's also the History Center in University Circle—care of the Western Reserve Historical Society.

The **Cleveland Botanical Garden** is a particularly pleasant diversion when the weather is chilly. In a few short steps, you can go from the cutting cold of a Midwest winter to the Garden's Glasshouse, which features two different climates: a desert of Madagascar and a Costa Rican rainforest—both warm enough to raise your core temperature back to normal in minutes. In addition to hundreds of different plants, the Garden plays host to a diverse collection of birds and butterflies. One nice surprise is the Garden Store, which carries gardening books, landscaping tools, bird-watching gear, and a nice variety of gifts. If there's a gardener on your Christmas shopping list, be sure to take a moment to browse.

The **Cleveland Museum of Natural History** is just across the street from Wade Park. Despite its small size, it is packed with dinosaur fossils, Ohio archaeology, astronomy, and even live animals. It's just the right size for a well-rounded few hours before you head over to the **Cleveland Museum of Art** next door (not to be confused with the Museum of Contemporary Art Cleveland down the street).

The Museum of Art goes back to 1913. This large space, which comprises the original 1916 building plus an impressive addition, has an incredibly diverse collection that spans many periods and many cultures. There are, of course, the usual galleries dedicated to traditional European paintings and sculpture from ancient Greece, the Renaissance, and early America. There are also works from ancient Egypt and Native American, Islamic, and African cultures. On level one, you can have lunch at the Provenance Café or Restaurant and make a day of it. And, like most good art museums, they have an excellent Museum Store.

Just east of University Circle is Cleveland's **Little Italy**. The neighborhood centers on the crossroads of Mayfield Road and Murray Hill Road (east of Euclid Avenue). There are more than two dozen places to grab a bite along

THE CLEVELAND NATURAL HISTORY MUSEUM HAS AN IMPRESSIVE COLLECTION OF FOSSILS

a stretch of road that's less than a mile long. Of course, you will find excellent Italian—from Michelangelo's Restaurant to Valentino's—but a few standouts offer alternative cuisine, such as Chutney Rolls (Indian fusion) and the Washington Place Bistro (high-end American fare).

The bistro is adjacent to the **Washington Place Inn**. This intimate boutique hotel has only seven rooms and a great location that makes it an excellent option for those wanting to make the most of Cleveland. Each room is a classy retreat from the ordinary cookie-cutter hotel décor. Weekend guests can enjoy a really nice Sunday brunch. Best of all, the city is just five minutes away, and the University Circle museums are less than a mile from the inn.

Continuing east on Mayfield Road, the next neighborhood stop is Coventry Village for a bite to eat at **Tommy's**. Back in the day, Rolling Stone magazine made the bold claim that Tommy's Coventry Road served the best milkshake east of the Mississippi. A few decades have passed, and Tommy's is still a contender, but this place is worth a visit for so much more than a milkshake. The classic eatery has been serving diners in the Coventry Village business district since the 1970s with a menu as eclectic as you can imagine. Not only do they serve burgers and amazing house-cut fries but also tofu, falafel, hummus and babaganoush, meat pies, and incredible soups. The vegetarian dishes are a big draw: at Tommy's, herbivores and carnivores dine in harmony.

Right next door are two great shops. The first is **Mac's Backs-Books**, a used bookstore with books stacked three stories high. (That's two floors plus the basement.) Book lovers will have no trouble losing an hour browsing here. The shop is connected to Tommy's, so you don't even need to put your coat back on to visit.

Next door to that is another Coventry Village legend, the **Big Fun Toy Store**. It would be easy to simply call this place a toy store, but it's not where you'll find the newest Fisher-Price doohickey or this Christmas's "must have" thing-a-ma-bob for under the tree. To say it's a novelty shop would add some needed color, but wouldn't acknowledge the vintage merchandise. (Lots of folks stop by to visit their collection of retro toys—old Disneyania, Star Wars figures, and lunchboxes from the 1970s and 1980s). The name of the store pretty much covers it. The shelves are stocked to the ceiling with goodies from your childhood. This is where you shop for big fun.

Before the path turns to the south, one more stop offers a piece of local culture. By taking US 20 northeast to East 222nd Street north, you will come to the **National Cleveland-Style Polka Hall of Fame and Museum** in Euclid. Rock and roll may be paying the bills these days, but the heart of Cleveland is pure polka. Adjacent to the Euclid City Hall, this small museum captures the glory days of a very particular piece of the polka experience. Even folks whose experience of polka is limited to a tune or two heard in passing on the Lawrence Welk Show might recognize the name of the legendary Frank

The Polish Boy

Chicagoans have the pizza, Philadelphians have the cheesesteak, and Clevelanders have the Polish Boy. This fine specimen of regional cuisine is essentially a kielbasa on a hot dog bun, piled high with coleslaw, French fries, and barbeque sauce. Some variants swap in hot sauce for the barbeque, but either way, this is one of the messiest meals you can find in town. A number of places have the Polish Boy on the menu, but one of them stands out as a local favorite. **Seti's Polish Boys**, at the corner of Woodland Avenue and East 34th Street, is a food truck, which is totally in keeping with the down-to-earth street food they serve. You could order the Polish Boy with additional chili and cheese if you brought an extra shirt to change into after eating, or you could try their other variations on the sausage and hot dog theme. (If you're traveling by interstate, you'll find Seti's just east of exit 162A off of I-77.)

Yankovic, America's Polka King. Yankovic was born in South Euclid and is a real favorite son at the museum. Others are honored as well, though, and the museum does a great job of highlighting the style of polka particular to Cleveland.

The Cuyahoga River Valley begins south of Akron and follows the river all the way to Lake Erie. A large swath of the valley is a national park, but closer to Cleveland is the **Ohio & Erie Canal Reservation**, which comprises 4.4 miles of the old canal and sections of the Cuyahoga River. To get there, take I-90 west to I-77 south. Take exit 159A for Harvard Avenue, turn west (right) at the first intersection, and then head south on East 49th Street, which you take 0.8 mile to the park.

The Ohio & Erie Canal plays a big part in the region's history—interesting fact: President James Garfield once worked as a mule boy on the canal—but the reservation is more about the ecology of the park than its history. For a look at the history, you will need to stop at the Boston Store Visitor Center at **Cuyahoga Valley National Park**. The best way through the park is by driving along the Ohio & Erie Canalway Byway. To get there from the reservation, continue south on East 49th Street to Canal Road. A little over a mile after the road turns into Valley View Road, turn south (right) onto Chaffee Road, making a jog west on Chippewa Road to Riverview Road. This eventually turns into Merriman Road as it enters Akron.

There are a number of ways to explore Cuyahoga Valley National Park. The **Cuyahoga Valley Scenic Railroad** follows the river and offers a host of options. Visitors take scenic train rides through the park; cyclists can also pedal the Tow Path Trail and take the train back to their cars for a nominal fee. Diesel locomotives, of which the park has a few, pull vintage coach, observation, and concession cars. From time to time, visitors can take special tours of a steam locomotive that makes an occasional appearance.

Another way to experience the park is to chase down a few of the area waterfalls. The most popular, and easiest to get to, is Brandywine Falls. Cascading 60 feet down a sheer cliff of Berea sandstone and layers of shale, the falls create a bridal veil effect. It's a short hike to the falls from the parking area. The river gorge is rather steep, so much of the path consists of wooden walkways. There are a number of stairs, but it's not a difficult walk by any means.

Just across the gorge from the observation deck is **The Inn at Brandywine Falls**. The inn was once the home of James Wallace. George Wallace, James's father, built a mill at the head of the falls in 1814, which led to the founding of the Village of Brandywine. The town is gone—as is the mill—but guests will appreciate that history when they visit the inn.

THE BRANDYWINE FALLS ARE THE MOST ACCESSIBLE WATERFALLS IN THE NATIONAL PARK

At the south end of the park, west of Riverview Road is the Hale Farm & Village. Owned and operated by the Western Reserve Historical Society, the Hale Farm is described as a "living museum." Your visit begins at the Gatehouse/Visitor Center, where you can purchase tickets, maybe pick up lunch at the Village Café, and browse the Museum Store. The Gatehouse is your gateway to the farm, and beyond its doors, you will find the original Hale homestead. The primary buildings here are the Jonathan Hale House, a three-story brick home built in 1825; the Pioneer House log cabin; and the various barns and work buildings. Jonathon Hale moved to the Western Reserve in 1810, purchased 500 acres, and began to carve a living out of this wild frontier land. This side of the Hale Farm focuses on that legacy. The farm itself remained in the family for three generations. Today it gives visitors a chance to experience the life of a nineteenth-century homesteader.

Across the road from the farm is Wheatfield, a fictional village composed of historic buildings, most of which were brought here from somewhere else. There is a law office, a meetinghouse, a log schoolhouse, and numerous gardens, sheep pens, and chicken coops. The Jonathan E. Herrick House was brought here from Twinsburg, Ohio. The home, originally built in 1845 in the Greek Revival style, has a stone façade that gives it a solid feeling—like living in Fort Knox. Here at Wheatfield, the building is the home of the fictional Meredith family. These details help the costumed interpreters tell the stories of life in the Cuyahoga Valley two hundred years ago.

Those who appreciate artisan craftsmanship will want to stroll down the village's Industrial Row. Here you can see folks making bricks and throwing pottery. Just beyond is a barn dedicated to glassblowing. In fact, throughout the entire village, you can often find people making candles, spinning wool, and weaving baskets.

Leaving the national park, follow Riverview Road, which becomes Merriman Road along the way, south for 6 miles to Memorial Parkway. Heading east on Memorial Parkway, follow it into the center of Tallmadge. This road changes its name as well, becoming East Tallmadge Avenue and then West Avenue before it reaches Tallmadge Circle.

From above, the city of Tallmadge resembles a compass rose, with appropriately named roads mapping the four cardinal directions (North, West, East, and South Roads) and the four intermediate directions (Northwest, Northeast, Southwest, and Southeast Roads). At the center is the town square—alternatively called Tallmadge Town Square Historic District or Tallmadge Circle Park—which is circumnavigated by a busy traffic circle. The 4.5-acre park is not only the geographical center of town but also its historic center.

At the north end of the park stands the historic **Tallmadge Church**. The role New Englanders played in the establishment of this town is clear when you look at this white clapboard house of worship and its soaring steeple.

SHEEP GRAZE NEAR WHEATFIELD, THE VILLAGE ACROSS FROM HALE FARM

The building was dedicated in 1825 and served as the First Congregational Church for 144 years. Today, the church is owned by the Ohio Historical Society and managed by the city. You will often see parties gathering here for a wedding on weekends. Opposite the church is the Old Town Hall (1859), which the Tallmadge Historical Society uses as its headquarters. The park has a lot of potential for photographers, but with no official museum, the opportunities for exploration are quickly exhausted.

From Tallmadge Circle, take West Avenue to Akron's North Main Street. Turn south and follow that into the heart of Akron. The town was strategically settled at the high elevation point of the Ohio & Erie Canal. Its name comes from the Greek *akron*, meaning "summit." An industrial center, Akron was known for most of the twentieth century as the place that made tires. Goodyear, Goodrich, and Firestone all had headquarters here. Goodrich still remains. Today, Goodyear Airdock—owned by Lockheed Martin—manufactures blimps.

Heading into the city, at East Market Street you will see the first stop in Akron, the Akron Art Museum. The museum's stunning modern architecture is hard to miss. Irregular angles are accentuated by the glass-and-steel façade. In a reversal of a hen protecting her chicks, the newer section of the museum extends a long wing over the older brick-and-limestone library that was the museum's first home.

When visiting the museum, it helps to have some knowledge of the layout. The newer building has several distinct sections. The space called the Crystal is the naturally lit entrance area, illuminated by sun shining through soaring walls of glass. The Roof Cloud diffuses some of the sun's light, providing shade where the museum needs it. The Gallery Box, by contrast, has no natural light at all. This is where you find the art. Here, the museum's collection is displayed in a controlled environment protected from the damaging effects of the sun.

The Akron Art Museum displays the works of native Ohioans and artists from around the world. By and large, the collection features work from the nineteenth, twentieth, and twenty-first centuries. You will find the works from some familiar artists, including portraits by Chuck Close, prints by Andy Warhol, and photographs by Ansel Adams.

Returning to East Market Street, head northwest to North Maple Street and follow it west to the **Simon Perkins Stone Mansion**. Construction of this unique Greek Revival estate was completed in 1837. It was the home of Colonel Simon Perkins, the son of General Simon Perkins, who founded Akron. Appropriately, the mansion is now a museum that tells the story of the Perkins family, the city of Akron, and the surrounding Summit County. The property also houses the offices of the Summit County Historical Society.

Return to East Market Street again, this time via Rhodes Avenue, a block east of the Perkins mansion, and head a block northwest to North Portage Path. This road approximates the route of a trail that predated settlers coming to Akron. The Portage Path linked the Cuyahoga and Tuscarawas Rivers and was a main transportation artery for American Indians. It connected the Great Lakes with the Ohio and Mississippi Rivers and the Gulf of Mexico. After 1.3 miles on North Portage Path, you will come to the **Stan Hywet Hall & Gardens**.

Located at the northwest corner of the intersection of North Portage Path and Garman Road, the gated entrance to the property is at the same time hard to miss and easy to recognize. The stone gate seems too narrow for such a grand estate, but if you see a Tudor-style home off to one side, you know you're at the right place. The grand mansion overlooking the 70-acre estate was completed in 1915 for F. A. Seiberling, the founder of the Goodyear Tire and Rubber Company. Of course, it took some time to put this 65-room home together—construction actually began in 1912. Don't waste too much time trying to figure who Stan Hywet was and how he could afford what was once considered the 12th largest home in the country. There was no Stan Hyet. Rather, the name comes from Seiberling, who christened his home with the Old English term for "stone quarry."

Several tour options give visitors a chance to enjoy a docent-led presentation of the estate, or they can simply roam at their own pace with a guidebook in hand. In addition to the architecture and historical trappings, there are also a number of gardens to explore.

Returning toward West Market Street, you might be interested in spending the night at **The O'Neil House Bed & Breakfast**, which is located on West Exchange Street, one street down from West Market Street, west of the Portage Path intersection. The inn was the home of another Akron tire magnate: William O'Neil, the founder of the General Tire Company. Built in 1923 in the Tudor style, the inn has four guest rooms, each with a private bath.

There's an interesting museum close to the B&B that many will find inspiring. It is **Dr. Bob's Home**, the birthplace of Alcoholics Anonymous. This is where Dr. Robert Holbrook Smith and Bill Wilson established the method and organization that would go on to help an untold number of people in their struggle with alcohol. Best of friends, both struggled with alcoholism. It was Wilson who first followed a spiritual path to recovery. He then led his friend down that path. They would go on to help thousands and publish a book about the method's principles.

Before you leave Akron, you won't want to miss grabbing a bite to eat at the local **Swensons Drive In**. It is a special-to-Akron sort of place. There are a handful of these drive-ins around, but the original Swensons is on South Hawkins Avenue. Burger-lovers will need to order the Galley Boy, a double-decker cheeseburg (that's how they say it: hamburg and cheeseburg) with two special sauces. The olive on top is a nice touch. With the exception of the veggie burger, there's not much to surprise regular drive-in diners. There are chicken strips and onion rings, sloppy joes and hot dogs. The real surprise is the price. You can do really well here on a budget.

IN THE AREA

Accommodations

HOMESTEAD HOUSE BED & BREAKFAST, 38111 West Spaulding, Willoughby. Call 440-946-1902. Website: homesteadhousebb.com. $$.

THE INN AT BRANDYWINE FALLS, 8230 Brandywine Road, Sagamore Hills. Call 330-467-1812 or 1-888-306-3381. Website: innatbrandywinefalls.com. $$$.

THE O'NEIL HOUSE BED & BREAKFAST, 1290 West Exchange Street, Akron. Call 330-867-2650. Website: oneilhouse.com. $$–$$$.

WASHINGTON PLACE INN, 2203 Cornell Road, Cleveland. Call 216-791-6500. Website: washingtonplacelittleitaly.com. $$$.

Attractions and Recreation

BIG FUN TOY STORE, 1814 Coventry Road, Cleveland Heights. Call 216-371-4386. Website: bigfunbigfun.com.

BURRELL HOMESTEAD MUSEUM, French Creek Reservation, 4530 Colorado Avenue, Sheffield Village. Call 440-949-5200. Website: metroparks.cc/french_creek.php.

CHRISTMAS STORY HOUSE, 3159 West 11th Street, Cleveland. Call 216-298-4919. Website: achristmasstoryhouse.com.

CLEVELAND BOTANICAL GARDEN, 11030 East Boulevard, Cleveland. Call 216-721-1600. Website: cbgarden.org.

CLEVELAND MUSEUM OF ART, 11150 East Boulevard, Cleveland. Call 216-421-7350. Website: clevelandart.org.

CLEVELAND MUSEUM OF NATURAL HISTORY, 1 Wade Oval Drive, University Circle, Cleveland. Call 216-231-4600 or 1-800-317-9155. Website: cmnh.org.

CUYAHOGA VALLEY NATIONAL PARK, 15610 Vaughn Road, Brecksville. Call 330-657-2752. Website: nps.gov/cuva.

CUYAHOGA VALLEY SCENIC RAILROAD, Rockside Station in Independence, 7900 Old Rockside Road, Independence. Call 1-800-460-4070 ext. 1. Website: cvsr.com.

DR. BOB'S HOME, 855 Ardmore Avenue, Akron. Call 330-864-1935. Website: drbobshome.com. The home is open every day, except Christmas, from noon–3 p.m.

FRENCH CREEK RESERVATION, 4530 Colorado Avenue, Sheffield Village. Call 440-949-5200. Website: www.metroparks.cc/french_creek.php.

GREAT LAKES SCIENCE CENTER, 601 Erieside Avenue, Cleveland. Call 216-694-2000. Website: greatscience.com.

HALE FARM & VILLAGE, 2686 Oak Hill Road, Bath. Call 330-666-3711. Website: wrhs.org/plan-your-visit/hale-farm/.

HOWER HOUSE, 60 Fir Hill, Akron. Call 330-972-6909. Website: hower house.org.

HUNTINGTON RESERVATION, 28728 Wolf Picnic Area Drive, Bay Village. Call 216-351-6300. Website: clevelandmetroparks.com/parks/visit/parks/huntington-reservation.

LAKE ERIE NATURE AND SCIENCE CENTER, 28728 Wolf Road, Cleveland. Call 440-871-2900. Website: lensc.org.

LITTLE ITALY, Cleveland. Website: www.clevelandlittleitaly.com.

MAC'S BACKS – BOOKS ON COVENTRY, 1820 Coventry Road, Cleveland Heights. Call 216-321-2665. Website: macsbacks.com.

MITCHELL'S ICE CREAM, 26161 Detroit Road, Westlake. Call 440-250-0952. Website: mitchellshomemade.com.

NATIONAL CLEVELAND-STYLE POLKA HALL OF FAME AND MUSEUM, 605 East 222nd Street, Euclid. Call 216-261-3263. Website: clevelandstyle .com.

THE OHIO & ERIE CANAL RESERVATION, 4524 East 49th Street, Cleveland. Call 216-206-1000. Website: clevelandmetroparks.com/parks/visit/parks/ohio-erie-canal-reservation.

SIMON PERKINS STONE MANSION, 550 Copley Road, Akron. Call 330-535-1120. Website: summithistory.org/Community/museum_perkinsmansion.html.

ROCK & ROLL HALL OF FAME, 1100 East 9th Street, Cleveland. Call 216-781-7625 (that's 781-ROCK). Website: rockhall.com.

STAN HYWET HALL AND GARDENS, 714 North Portage Path, Akron. Call 330-836-5533. Website: stanhywet.org.

TALLMADGE CHURCH STATE MEMORIAL, 115 Tallmadge Circle, Tallmadge. Call 330-633-0855. Website: ohiohistory.org/visit/museum-and -site-locator/tallmadge-church.

USS *COD* SUBMARINE MEMORIAL, 1201 North Marginal Road, Cleveland. Call 216-566-8770. Website: usscod.org.

Dining

MELT BAR & GRILLED, 14718 Detroit Avenue, Lakewood. Call 216-226-3699. Website: meltbarandgrilled.com. $$.

SETI'S POLISH BOYS, 4699 Lorain Avenue, Cleveland. Call 216-240-0745. Website: setispolishboys.biz. $.

SWENSONS DRIVE IN, 40 South Hawkins Avenue, Akron. Call 330-864-8416. Website: swensonsdriveins.com. $.

TOMMY'S RESTAURANT, 1824 Coventry Road, Cleveland Heights. Call 216-321-7757. Website: tommyscoventrycleveland.com. $$.

Other Contacts

AKRON/SUMMIT CONVENTION AND VISITOR BUREAU, John S. Knight Center, 77 East Mill Street, Akron. Call 330-374-7560 or 1-800-245-4254. Website: visitakron-summit.org.

CLEVELAND VISITOR CENTER, 334 Euclid Avenue, Cleveland. Call 216-875-6680 or 1-800-321-1001. Website: thisiscleveland.com.

LORAIN COUNTY VISITOR BUREAU, 8025 Leavitt Road, Amherst. Call 440-984-5282 or 1-800-334-1673. Website: visitloraincounty.com.

5

A LAND OF COVERED BRIDGES, A VALLEY OF VINEYARDS

ASHTABULA COUNTY, CONNEAUT, ASHTABULA,
GENEVA-ON-THE-LAKE, GENEVA, MENTOR-ON-THE-LAKE,
WILLOUGHBY, CHAGRIN FALLS

ESTIMATED LENGTH: 120 miles

ESTIMATED TIME: 4 hours

HIGHLIGHTS: This trip begins with a short tour of eight of Ashtabula's covered bridges, broken up by stops at two local wineries—Tarsitano and Markko Vineyards—and Brant's Apple Orchard. When you reach Conneaut, you can visit the Conneaut Historical Railroad Museum before heading west to North Kingsville and the Covered Bridge Pizza Parlor. Continuing west to Ashtabula, the Ashtabula Harbour Commercial Historic District has some excellent shops, some great places to eat, and a fine coffee shop. On the hill overlooking the harbor is the Ashtabula Maritime and Surface Transportation Museum. Also worth a visit is the Hubbard House Underground Railroad Museum. Next, follow the shoreline of Lake Erie to the unique tourist town of Geneva-on-the-Lake. The next stop is to a series of wineries and vineyards along the Grand River valley. Then you return to the lake, head west, and make a stop in Mentor. Finally, go back south, following the Chagrin River Valley to Chagrin Falls, with a short detour to the Holden Arboretum.

GETTING THERE: From I-90, take exit 241 for Center Road (OH 7) south. This is south of Conneaut. After 10.5 miles you will come to Caine Road. Head west to the Caine Road Bridge, the first stop on the itinerary. The route then follows Stanhope-Kellogsville Road (TR 33) north before returning east to OH 7, which you will take north to Conneaut. (The tour of covered bridges explained later is omitted here for brevity's sake.) From Conneaut, the route follows US 20 west to North Kingsville, then goes north on Main Street (OH 193) to Lake Road (OH 531). Following the shoreline west, there are stops in Ashtabula's historic harbor district, then the more-touristy Geneva-on-the-Lake. Traveling on Broadway south through Geneva, there are a series of stops in the Grand River Valley wine region, mostly along North River Road (OH 307).

LEFT: THE CREEK ROAD COVERED BRIDGE IS A LITTLE WAYS OFF THE BEATEN PATH

However, you can bypass these and head straight over to Mentor-on-the-Lake by way of US 20 and OH 2. Then after a short side trip to Willoughby, you catch up with River Road and follow it all the way south to Chagrin Falls.

This route begins south of Conneaut, in the land of covered bridges and wineries. Depending on how you're counting and who you ask, Ashtabula County has the most covered bridges of any county in Ohio. Fairfield County, in the center of the state, is a close second. Then again, maybe Fairfield has the most. It all depends on what "covered bridge" means. That said, Ashtabula County has 17 covered bridges that allow car traffic and another handful that have been decommissioned for vehicular use but are still open to walkers.

The start of this tour is a whirlwind round-up of eight covered bridges. Now, there is absolutely no need whatsoever to go driving around Ashtabula County at breakneck speeds, stopping only for a quick look at a covered bridge before jumping back in the car. In fact, that approach sort of defeats the whole ethos of touring the countryside. So, while you could see all these bridges in 75 minutes or so, I recommend taking more time to visit this sampling of the county's river crossings. In fact, I recommend taking a

THIS HALF OF A COVERED BRIDGE IS HOME TO COVERED BRIDGE PIZZA IN NORTH KINGSVILLE

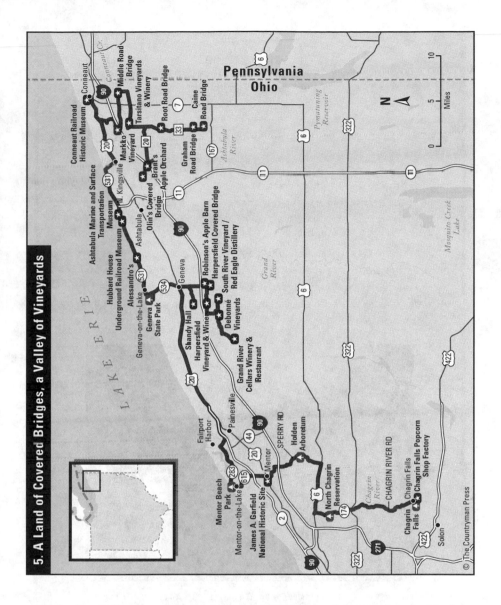

whole day. Add some wineries into the mix. Enjoy a leisurely lunch. Maybe even book a room at a local B&B. That said, this guide will get you through eight bridges in a little more than an hour if you're so inclined.

The tour starts at the west branch of the Ashtabula River. The first three bridges are just off Stanhope-Kelloggsville Road (TR 33). Beginning at the southernmost point, the Caine Road Bridge is just east of TR 33 on Caine Road. This bridge was constructed in 1986 to commemorate Ashtabula County's 175th anniversary. Moving north to Graham Road, the Graham Road Bridge is decommissioned and no longer supports traffic. It was moved to a site near the river on the south side of the street. It dates from 1903, built

Covered Bridges

These days, covered bridges are most often built to protect people from the elements—as in pedestrian walkways between buildings. So why were so many covered bridges built in the nineteenth century? They seem rather grandiose for a rural setting, and they must have taken much longer to build than an uncovered bridge.

The answer is pretty simple. The enclosure protects the structural elements of the bridge from the weather. Without a roof, rain and snow would sit on the bridge platform, seep into the beams and joints, and dramatically shorten the bridge's lifespan. The roof prolonged the life of the bridge and in turn protected the investment made to build it.

That said, other reasons are often given to explain the building of covered bridges. One of the more interesting ideas is that covered bridges look a lot like barns. Farmers who needed to move livestock across a river had an easier time convincing a herd of cows to pass through a barn-like building than they would an open bridge.

THE RIVER NEAR THE BENETKA ROAD COVERED BRIDGE LOOKS TO BE A PERFECT SPOT TO SIT IN THE SHADE AND CAST A LINE

Because of their roofs and walls, covered bridges often look similar, but underneath the shingles and siding, some interesting features often go unnoticed. The next time you stop to look at a covered bridge, take a closer look. Go inside and look for supports. Look up to see how the roof was framed. Get underneath the bridge to see what's holding it up. Because these bridges attract visitors, many have a placard that summarizes some technical details, such as the support type and the year it was built.

from an earlier bridge that was damaged during a flood. The final bridge on this stretch is the Root Road Bridge, which spans the Ashtabula River proper. It was built in 1868 and renovated in 1983. The renovation lifted the 114-foot structure 18 inches and added a concrete pier for extra support.

Continuing down the Ashtabula, the tour heads west on Plymouth Ridge Road (via Monroe Center Road). Just before you cross over I-90, turn south onto Benetka Road to reach the Benetka Road Bridge. This is one of the most picturesque bridges on the short tour. You can park near the bridge and head down to the water for a look upstream. Inside the bridge, you will see the two large laminate arches that were added in 1985 for extra support.

On the other side of I-90, turn north onto Dibble Road and stop for a moment at **Brant's Apple Orchard**. This family-run outfit offers 21 varieties of apples in season. There's an exceptional bakery on site, and visitors can watch the process of turning fruit into cider at the cider mill. The orchard is open from August through November. In the off-season, you will just have to imagine how wonderful the cider doughnuts might have been.

Just past the orchard, turn left onto Dewey Road. Where the road crosses the Ashtabula River, you will see Olin's Covered Bridge. The Olin family has owned the property adjacent to Olin's Covered Bridge since it was built in 1873. Surprisingly, it's the only covered bridge in the county named for a family.

The tour's final three bridges all span Conneaut Creek. Return to Stanhope-Kellogsville Road and head north. The road actually changes its name to State Road north of Monroe Center Road. Just past Hatches Corners Road, you will see the State Road Covered Bridge, built in 1983. A different covered bridge here spanned Conneaut Creek from 1831 until 1898.

As you return to Hatches Corners Road and drive a little way west, the **Tarsitano Winery & Café** is the perfect spot to take a break from bridge-viewing and sample some of the region's wines. Ken and Kelly Tarsitano opened their winery in 2001 on a farm that had been in Ken's family for generations. In addition to wine, the winery serves simple antipasto dishes that pair nicely with wine tastings—artisanal cheese plates, warm breads, and cured meats.

Continue east on Hatches Corner Road, cross Center Road (OH 7), and turn left (north) onto Middle Road. The Middle Road Bridge, which also crosses Conneaut Creek, was built in 1868 and reconstructed in 1984.

The final bridge on this tour is the Creek Road Bridge. To get there, cross the Middle Road Bridge, and head west on South Ridge Road. After dipping under I-90, the road comes to a T. Directly across from the intersection is one of the most respected wineries in the area. The **Markko Vineyard** is open every day but Sundays, but you need to call ahead for tastings. Turn right at the intersection and follow Under Ridge Road east to Keefus Road, and then turn north. The first road you come to on your left is Creek Road. Turn onto it, and in less than a quarter-mile you will reach the Creek Road Bridge. Built in the 1800s (the exact date is not known), this 112-foot is perched 25 feet above Conneaut Creek. It was renovated in 1994.

Returning north on Keefus Road, head east on US 20 into downtown Conneaut. This small community thrived on the railroad for generations. Several lines passed through town. The Water-Level Route, as it was known, connected New York with points west, including Conneaut, along a route with very little change in elevation. Other routes connected the ports of Lake Erie with Pennsylvania. In the early spring of 1953, a three-train collision east of Conneaut killed 20 people. The remoteness of the location exacerbated the accident. Rescuers had to hike in a quarter-mile and carry victims to ambulances waiting on a narrow dirt access road.

The **Conneaut Historical Railroad Museum**, located in the old railroad passenger depot on the aptly named Depot Street, tells the story of the 1953 wreck as well as other stories related to the role of the railroad in Conneaut's history. There are restored and preserved train cars, steam engines, model railroads, and plenty of photos. The museum also has a nice collection of tools and accessories necessary for running a railroad. Take note: The museum is open only in the summer.

After touring the museum, head west on US 20 to North Kingsville. In 1972, an enterprising pizza shop owner bought the old Foreman Road Cov-

ASHTABULA COUNTY'S AGRICULTURAL CHARACTER IS EVIDENT EVERYWHERE

Remembering a Tragedy

Historical markers usually have more positive stories to tell than the one you will see on Lake Avenue, near where the railroad bridge crosses the Ashtabula River. The plaque commemorates one of the worst train wrecks in the country's history. On December 29, 1876, the iron-truss bridge that spanned the nearby gorge collapsed, and a train carrying 159 passengers plunged 90 feet to the bottom. A blizzard made rescue efforts difficult, and passengers who might have survived perished when the heating stoves that were warming the cars caused fires that spread through the wreck. All told, 92 people died. One of the dead was Philip Bliss, a hymn writer who is best known for his song "It Is Well with My Soul."

As a result of the disaster, the railroad's engineer, Charles Collins, committed suicide, according to investigators. The police believed, however, that he might have been murdered, though a recent reappraisal of the evidence (which included a look at Collins's remains) suggests that he did indeed commit suicide. Two other things resulted from the wreck. First, the federal government took an active role in investigating railroad accidents. And, second, the town of Ashtabula built a hospital.

ered Bridge. He chopped the bridge in half and made the halves into two pizza parlors. One is in Andover, and the other is on Main Street in North Kingsville, spitting distance from US 20. As you drive through town, look for the horse-drawn buggy in front of the **Covered Bridge Pizza Parlor**. The pizza is pretty good, and you won't find a more unique setting.

From the pizza parlor, take Main Street north toward Lake Road (OH 531), and then follow the shore of Lake Erie west. The next town is Ashtabula. One of the unique features of these towns along Lake Erie is that many of them have a sister city closer to US 20. There are Geneva and Geneva-on-the-Lake and Mentor and Mentor-on-the-Lake. Ashtabula's sister city is the Ashtabula Harbour Commercial Historic District. It is much closer and exists as part of Ashtabula as a registered historic district. Ashtabula Harbour was once one of the busiest ports on the lake. Ore was off-loaded here and sent by train to the steel mills of western Pennsylvania. To meet the needs of industry, immigrants by the score flocked to the Ashtabula, causing this small downtown to boom. It is said that the port town was one of the seediest in the world, sharing the same reputation for lawlessness as Calcutta and Shanghai.

The days of bar fights and foul-mouthed stevedores have passed, and with their passing, the Harbour District has gained a new reputation. Department stores and groceries have been replaced by boutique shops selling home décor and women's clothing. Bars and taverns have been transformed into coffee shops and fancy restaurants. There are a couple museums off the main drag, and recreational boaters dock south of the bridge.

The **Bascule Bridge Grille & Wine Bar** is a fine example of the kind of dining you can expect to find in the Harbour District. While the sign out front that stresses the dress code ("sideways or backwards caps, bandanas, skullcaps, beanies, knit hats, and gym wear will not be permitted") and restricts diners to guests who are eight years old and older may be off-putting—even to hatless 40-year-olds—the restaurant receives rave reviews for its upscale, seasonal menu. This is the kind of place where the food, the ambience, and the wine list are as important as the service and how the entrees are presented.

Right across the street is **DeFina's: The Harbor Store**. This classy gift shop is an extension of DeFina Auctions. (Though they used to hold auctions, the firm now acts as consultants.) The Harbor Store is filled with unique gifts—handmade purses, books for kids, and items for the house.

West of this row of businesses on Bridge Street, the bricked-paved Hulbert Avenue leads up the hill to the **Ashtabula Maritime and Surface Transportation Museum**. From this high vantage point, you can see the mouth of the Ashtabula River and the entire port area. The museum will soon be expanding, but for now, it's located in a two-story house with a nice addition off the back. Facing the water is a real pilot house from a retired freighter that visitors can climb into for a look around.

Two blocks west on Walnut Boulevard at Lake Avenue is the harbor area's other museum, the Hubbard House Underground Railroad Museum. This home was a terminus on the Underground Railroad, and it is the only ending point on the trail that is open to the public today. The view from the Hubbard House, overlooking the expanse of Lake Erie, would have swelled the heart of many an escaped slave who had a chance to look upon it in the daytime. Although the Canadian shore cannot be seen from this distance, it was less than 50 miles from here to freedom.

The museum does a great job of telling the story of the Railroad. Locals played a big part in the abolitionist movement, and many even joined John Brown's raid on the arsenal at Harper's Ferry. Other bits of local history are also on display, including information about the bridge disaster of 1876. The home itself is an exhibition, furnished with antiques from the mid-1800s.

From Ashtabula, follow OH 531 west to Geneva-on-the-Lake. On the way, you will pass a place that serves the best Italian food in northeast Ohio. Guests at **Alessandro's** used to be plagued by long waits. Popular restaurants can be like that. Though the restaurant is no less popular now, this problem has been relieved somewhat by the addition of dining room space and an update to the entire property. The menu is prepared by Alessandro Pilumeli, who was born in Sicily and came to the states by way of Florence,

THE GENEVA AREA HAS A NUMBER OF PICTURESQUE WINERIES

Italy. Of course, the restaurant offers pizza and calzones, but regulars know to order an entrée or a meal from the pasta menu. The Trota alla Rustica, for example, is pure gold: trout sautéed with garlic olive oil, tomatoes, and capers. Or try one of the classics. A simple plate of spaghetti with Alessandro's meat sauce can't be beat.

After driving a little more than 3.5 miles west on OH 531, you come to Geneva-on-the-Lake. One of the most highly recommended places to eat in town, **Eddie's Grill** will give you an idea of the local culture. This walk-up eatery serves burgers, foot-long hot dogs, and fries. There are stools along the counter and a covered open-air patio for getting out of the sun or rain. There's also a great doughnut shop just down the road. For more than 75 years, **Madsen Donuts** has been a local favorite. On a summer morning, there's a line out the door, so be sure to go early. They make what they can, and when the food is gone, the doors close.

For entertainment, the most obvious attractions are the arcades. Geneva-on-the-Lake has a few, and they are touted on bright signs up and down the strip. For a more-relaxing activity, the beach on Lake Erie at **Geneva State Park**—just west of town (take North Broadway south to Lake Road west, and

GENEVA-ON-THE-LAKE IS PAINTED UP LIKE A MINIATURE CONEY ISLAND

follow the signs north on Padanarum Road)—is excellent. The park is a bit out of the way, so you'll encounter little traffic—just people like yourself hoping to spend some time on the water. The result is a relatively quiet spot to catch some rays and enjoy the lake. There are restrooms and changing rooms, and Ohio state parks are always free. So all you need is a swimming suit and a towel.

Backtracking just a little way, take North Broadway (OH 534) south to Geneva. You've visited a few wineries on this trip already, but Geneva is the gateway to northeast Ohio's Wine Country. The Grand River flows south of town, and its broad valley defines the Grand River Valley Appellation. The west–east running valley, its proximity to Lake Erie, and other natural features give local grape growers a unique microclimate conducive to the cultivation of excellent wine grapes. Many vintners have set up shop in the valley to take advantage of these conditions.

On your way to Fairport Harbor, you will pass four wineries and a distillery. There is also a historical site, an outstanding produce stand, and one of the longest covered bridges in the state.

Beginning closer to town, the first stop in Geneva is **Shandy Hall**. Originally built as a four-room home in 1815—which was early in the settlement in the Western Reserve—the building eventually grew to seventeen rooms. The house has been maintained as it would have been maintained in the 1830s. There are murals in the dining room, but the most interesting room to visit is the basement kitchen.

Shandy Hall is open by appointment only. So, if a tour of the house is on your list, be sure to call early on in your planning to see what kind of access you can arrange (216-721-5722). The Hall is on South Ridge Road West. Just head west on South Ridge Road from Broadway.

Just west from Shandy Hall is the **Warner-Concord Farms Bed & Breakfast**. You wouldn't know it to look at it, but this 8,000-square-foot home was once a barn. After 150 years of service, the barn was dramatically remodeled in the early 1990s to create the perfect space for a night in wine country. The B&B overlooks the Warner-Concord Farms vineyards. Each of the small inn's guest rooms has its own private bath. Throughout the home, you will see architectural features of the original barn peeking through. Hand-hewn posts and beams abound, giving the feeling that the building is still very much connected to the land and its agricultural heritage.

Returning to Broadway, drive south to North River Road. On the southeast corner of that intersection is **Robinson's Apple Barn**. In the fall, the folks at Robinson's sell apples, fresh-pressed apple cider, and apple fritters. But their inventory is not limited to the orchard. They sell all sorts of fruits and vegetables, jars of jelly and jams, pickled cucumbers, and their own maple syrup.

South of the Apple Barn, as the road crosses the Grand River, you can look west to see the Harpersfield Covered Bridge. This is the third-longest covered bridge in Ohio, and when the lighting is right, and you have the right lens, it makes for a great scenic photograph. To get a closer look, head west on North River Road and take the first left onto Harpersfield Road. The bridge is a double-span truss bridge, with an adjoining pedestrian walkway. At the north end of the Harpersfield Covered Bridge is an Ashtabula County MetroPark. In the summer, many anglers fish from the dam here.

From Geneva take US 20 west to OH 2 west. Near Fairport Harbor, take the exit for OH 283, which will lead you on a winding path toward Mentor-on-the-Lake. The **Mentor Beach Park**, on Lakeshore Boulevard at Andrews Road, is not a great place for swimming. The shoreline is rocky, and there is no beach to speak of. If you love lakes, however, it's a fine place to stop and watch the water for a while. When the wind picks up, the waves can hit the shore with some violence—the water smacks against the large stones, sending the spray skyward. The park is a surprisingly large 13 acres and has a small playground, restrooms, and a picnic area.

The Grand River Valley Winery Tour

There are too many wineries in the Grand River Valley to give them all decent coverage here. This little tour, which can be incorporated into the route outlined in this chapter, will take you from Broadway and North River Road, south of Geneva, to Chardon-Madison Road, south of Madison.

Driving west along North River Road, the first Grand River winery you find is the **Ferrante Winery & Ristorante**. The Ferrante family has been making wine for three generations, so they know what it's about. This is a winery with all the bells and whistles—there is, of course, a wine-tasting room, and tours of the facility are available in the summer months, but there's also an excellent restaurant that serves lunch and dinner. The menu is pure Italian, and there are Ferrante wines to pair with every meal.

A mile and a half west is the **Harpersfield Vineyard**. This property could perhaps be described as cozier than the Ferrante Winery. In addition to the tasting room, there is a kitchen that serves sandwiches and flatbread pizza. On the weekends, there is live music.

South of the Grand River on South River Road—you can cut across on County Line Road—is the "old church winery, otherwise known as **South River Vineyard**. This picturesque winery is housed in a nineteenth-century church that was moved from Shalersville, Ohio. The back of the church has been expanded to offer guests a stunning porch overlooking the vineyards.

Next door is something a little different. **The Red Eagle Distillery** is hard to miss. It is a bright red barn surrounded by vineyards. The folks at the distillery make whiskey, in particular, bourbon. They craft their small batches from locally sourced grains, intentionally avoiding genetically modified corn.

Continuing west on South River Road, you will come to **Chalet Debonné Vineyards**. Like the Ferrante Winery, the folks at Debonné have a restaurant. All summer the Grill at Debonné serves sandwiches and appetizers in a sprawling outdoor dining area. There's also a food menu in the tasting room. Their Riesling is very popular.

When South River Road crossed the county line, it became Doty Road. Follow Doty Road west until it comes to a T at Emerson Road. Head south (left) to Ross Road, and turn west (right) onto it. At Chardon-Madison Road turn south (left). Just a little way down is the final stop on the winery tour, the **Grand River Cellars Winery & Restaurant**.

Opened in the late 1970s, the winery was originally called the Grand River Wine Company. After more than 20 years, the original owners decided to sell the business, and the property was bought by a partnership of experienced wine folks, who have turned it into the Grand River Cellars Winery & Restaurant. The same hand that crafts the wine at Debonné Vineyards works its magic here. Check their website (debone.com) for hours—in the winter they are closed on Mondays and Tuesdays.

Heading south on Andrews Road (still OH 283), when the road comes to a T, turn east (left) and follow OH 615 south to US 20. Turn to the west, and the **James A. Garfield National Historic Site** will be on your right.

The large farmhouse was purchased by James A. Garfield in 1876. At the time, he was a U.S. Congressman with a large family. Four years later, he was running for president from the porch of the house. The reporters who flocked to Mentor to interview Garfield nicknamed his estate Lawnfield. The name stuck. After her husband's assassination, Lucretia Garfield added a memorial library to hold his papers.

Today, the property is managed by the National Parks Service and the Western Reserve Historical Society. The interpretive center's exhibitions commemorate the significant events of Garfield's life. This includes his early career, his work as a congressman, his important elections, and his unfortunate death.

Describing how to get to the next stop on the tour, the Holden Arboretum

LAKE ERIE CAN MAKE PLENTY OF WAVES WHEN THE WIND PICKS UP

THE HOLDEN ARBORETUM HAS PAVED AND UNPAVED PATHS FOR VISITORS

in Kirtland will take some explaining. Essentially, the Arboretum is 5 miles to the southeast. To get there, return to OH 615 (Center Road) and head south. At the first major intersection, at Johnnycake Ridge Road, turn east. At the intersection with Hart Road, turn south. At Baldwin Road there's a jog to the east, then a quick turn again south onto Booth Road. Turn left onto the first road you come to, Sperry Road. Less than 2 miles down, on your right, will be the entrance road for the park.

The 3,600-acre **Holden Arboretum** is a nature-lover's paradise. Over 20 miles of trails wind through the arboretum's woods. They circumnavigate several ponds, a lake, and a bog. Birdwatchers come from all over to see various local species as well as the flocks passing through on their annual migrations.

There are trails of differing lengths. You can enjoy a short hike and remain close to the visitor center. Or you can really stretch your legs and put in a rugged 3 or 4 miles. Sign up for a guided hike to see parts of the preserve that are generally inaccessible. One such hike is the tour of Stebbins Gulch. This part of the Arboretum is a National Nature Landmark, and therefore

DOWNTOWN CHAGRIN FALLS EVOKES A FEELING OF NEW ENGLAND

THE POPCORN SHOP IS A POPULAR STOP WITH VISITORS

access is limited. The tour covers only 1.8 miles, but the hike introduces visitors to a wealth of natural beauty. Rock outcroppings provide a nearly complete overview of the region's geological history. There are waterfalls and cascades, and a guided tour will give you a glimpse of what a naturalist might see when walking through these woods.

Hiking is not for everyone, and many folks end up simply meandering through the arboretum's gardens. The gardens closest to the visitor center have been planted to attract butterflies. Further out you will find wildflowers, swaths of rhododendron and viburnum, and lilac gardens.

From the arboretum, continue south on Sperry Road, and then head west on US 6. After 5.5 miles, turn south onto River Road (OH 174). This is the scenic route. The road follows the Chagrin River upstream to Chagrin Falls. Throughout the drive, the terrain is varied, which is the result of water draining north to Lake Erie for thousands of years. Along the way you pass through the **North Chagrin Reservation**. Closer to Chagrin Falls, you can access the Forest Ridge Preserve. These two parks bookend the Chagrin River Valley, offering hiking trails and other outdoor recreation.

As you drive into Chagrin Falls, there's a stop sign at an intersection with the aptly named Summit Street. From there, it's a short descent into town. If you weren't looking for the river, you just might miss it. The bridge is lined with cars that are parallel-parked and is nearly indistinguishable from the rest of town. A gap between storefronts is your biggest clue that something is different. On the far side is the red-white-and-blue awning of the **Chagrin Falls Popcorn Shop Factory**.

The Popcorn Shop sells more than just popcorn. There's ice cream, coffee, and custard too. The building was once the home of the Pride of the Falls Flour Mill, but back in the 1940s, the Popcorn Factory took its place. It's the perfect spot to grab a cone before you wander around back for a view of the falls.

There are, in fact, two sets of falls on the river. Across from the Popcorn Shop are manmade falls created by a wide dam. A small park has a view of it. To the left of the Popcorn Shop is a wooden walkway that leads down from the shops on Main Street to a view of the impressive natural falls. Dropping about 20 feet, the falls are surrounded by buildings, creating an impressive effect. Across the way, you can see the dining room of **Jekyll's Kitchen**, an amazing restaurant with an equally amazing view. (The restaurant burned down in late 2013, but the owners plan to rebuild. Look for it in 2015.)

IN THE AREA

Accommodations

WARNER-CONCORD FARMS BED & BREAKFAST, 6585 South Ridge Road West, Geneva. Call 440-428-4485. Website: warner-concordfarms.com. $$$.

Attractions and Recreation

ASHTABULA MARITIME AND SURFACE TRANSPORTATION MUSEUM, 1071 Walnut Boulevard, Ashtabula. Call 440-964-6847. Website: facebook.com/AshtabulaMSTMuseum.

BRANT'S APPLE ORCHARD, 4749 Dibble Rd, Ashtabula. Call 440-224-0639. Website: brantsappleorchard.com.

CHAGRIN FALLS POPCORN SHOP FACTORY, 53 North Main Street, Chagrin Falls. Call 440-247-6577. Website: www.chagrinfallspopcorn.com.

CHALET DEBONNÉ VINEYARDS, 7840 Doty Road, Madison. Call 440-466-3485. Website: debonne.com.

CONNEAUT HISTORICAL RAILROAD MUSEUM, 363 Depot Street, Conneaut. Call 440-599-7878. Website: facebook.com/chrrm.

DEFINA'S: THE HARBOR STORE, 1009 Bridge Street, Ashtabula. Call 440-964-0054. Website: facebook.com/DefinasTheHarborStore.

FERRANTE WINERY & RISTORANTE, 5585 North River Road West, Geneva. Call 440-466-8466. Website: ferrantewinery.com.

GENEVA STATE PARK, 6069 Padanarum Road West, Geneva. Call 440-466-9004. Website: parks.ohiodnr.gov/Geneva.

GRAND RIVER CELLARS WINERY & RESTAURANT, 5750 South Madison Road (OH 528), Madison. Call 440-298-9838. Website: grandrivercellars.com.

HARPERSFIELD VINEYARD, 6387 North River Road West, Geneva. Call 440-466-4739. Website: harpersfield.com.

HOLDEN ARBORETUM, 9500 Sperry Road, Kirtland. Call 440-946-4400. Website: holdenarb.org.

JAMES A. GARFIELD NATIONAL HISTORIC SITE, 8095 Mentor Avenue, Mentor. Call 440-255-8722. Website: nps.gov/jaga.

MADSEN DONUTS, 5426 Lake Road East, Geneva-on-the-Lake. Call 440-466-5884. Website: madsendonuts.com.

MARKKO VINEYARD, 4500 South Ridge Road West, Conneaut. Call 440-593-3197. Website: markko.com.

MENTOR BEACH PARK, 7779 Lake Shore Boulevard, Mentor-on-the-Lake. Call 440-974-5720. Website: cityofmentor.com/departments/parks-recreation/facilities/mentor-beach-park.

NORTH CHAGRIN RESERVATION, 401 Buttermilk Falls Parkway, Willoughby. Call 440-473-3370. Website: clevelandmetroparks.com/parks/visit/parks/north-chagrin-reservation.

RED EAGLE DISTILLERY, 6202 South River Road West, Geneva. Call 440-466-6604. Website: redeaglespirits.com.

ROBINSON'S APPLE BARN, 5202 OH 307, Geneva. Call 440-466-6780. Website: robinsonsapplebarn.com.

SHANDY HALL, 6333 South Ridge Road West, Geneva. Call 216-721-5722. Website: wrhs.org/plan-your-visit/historic-properties-2/shandy-hall-in-geneva.

SOUTH RIVER VINEYARD, 6062 South River Road West, Geneva. Call 440-466-6676. Website: southrivervineyard.com.

TARSITANO WINERY & CAFÉ, 4871 Hatches Corners Road, Conneaut. Call 440-224-2444. Wine tasting by reservation only. Website: tarsitanowinery.com.

Dining

ALESSANDRO'S, 6540 Lake Road West, Ashtabula. Call 440-964-5766. Website: alessandrosrestaurant.com. $$.

BASCULE BRIDGE GRILLE & WINE BAR, 1006 Bridge Street, Ashtabula. Call 440-964-0301. Website: basculebridgegrille.com. $$$$.

COVERED BRIDGE PIZZA PARLOR, 6541 South Main Street, North Kingsville. Call 440-224-2252. Website: coveredbridgepizzaparlor.com. $$.

EDDIE'S GRILL, 5377 Lake Road East, Geneva-on-the-Lake. Call 440-466-8720. Website: eddiesgrill.com. (Cash only.) $.

JEKYLL'S KITCHEN, 17 River Street, Chagrin Falls. Call 440-893-0797. Website: jekyllskitchen.com. $$$–$$$$.

Other Contacts

ASHTABULA COUNTY CONVENTION & VISITOR BUREAU, Ashtabula County. Call 1-800-337-6746. Website: visitashtabulacounty.com.

TRUMBULL COUNTY TOURISM BUREAU, 321 Mahoning Avenue Northwest, Warren. Call 1-866-360-1552. Website: exploretrumbullcounty.com.

LANTERMAN'S MILL IS ITSELF REASON ENOUGH TO VISIT MILL CREEK PARK

6

A PARADE OF MUSEUMS

WARREN, NILES, YOUNGSTOWN, COLUMBIANA, EAST
LIVERPOOL, WELLSVILLE, STEUBENVILLE, MARTINS FERRY,
BELLAIRE (MOUNDSVILLE)

ESTIMATED LENGTH: 116 miles

ESTIMATED TIME: 3 hours

HIGHLIGHTS: This route is all about museums. In Warren, there are art museums and history museums, an automobile museum (National Packard Museum) and a nearby museum dedicated to a former president (McKinley Birthplace Home in Niles). Mill Creek Park in Youngstown offers a combination of interesting historical sites such as Lanterman's Mill and outdoor recreation. Along the Ohio River, the museums get a bit smaller and even more specialized. In Columbiana, East Liverpool, and Wellsville, you will visit the Log House Museum, the Museum of Ceramics, and the Wellsville River Museum. Further south in Steubenville, there is a recreation of old Fort Steubenville, and in Martins Ferry, there is the Sedgwick House Museum. For those who really appreciate the art of Lego building blocks, the Toy and Plastic Brick Museum in Bellaire is a definite must. And those interested in the region's glassmaking history will want to stop at the National Imperial Glass Museum. The final stop is the Grave Creek Mound and associated museum in West Virginia. The ancient burial mound is just over the bridge from Shadyside in the town of Moundsville.

GETTING THERE: This trip begins in Warren and the northern suburb of Niles, 15 miles from the border with Pennsylvania. Following US 422, the route continues south to Youngstown and then Columbiana. From there, you will travel south again to East Liverpool, on the Ohio River. From here the route follows the river closely. OH 7 passes through Wellsville, Steubenville, Martins Ferry, and Bellaire. Those interested in ancient North American history will extend the trip to Shadyside and cross the river into Moundsville, West Virginia.

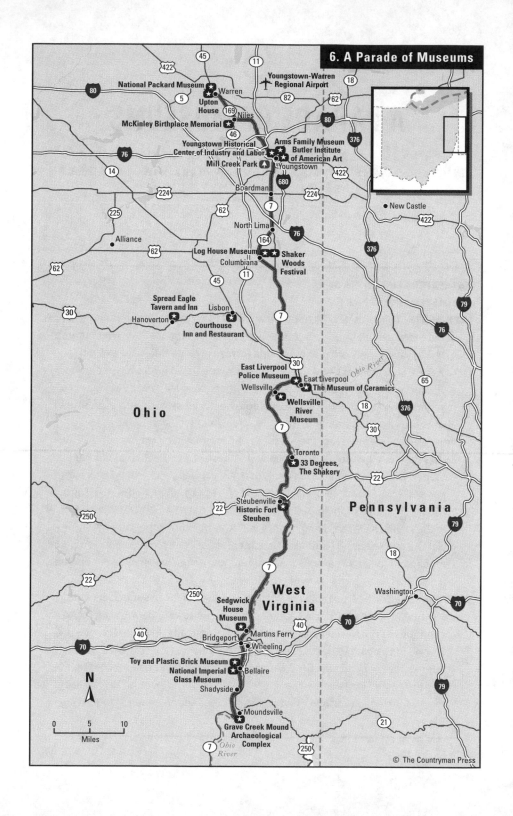

6. A Parade of Museums

422
45
11
80
National Packard Museum
Warren
Youngstown-Warren Regional Airport
18
5
82
62
Upton House
169
Niles
McKinley Birthplace Memorial
46
376
Youngstown Historical Center of Industry and Labor
76
Arms Family Museum
Butler Institute of American Art
Mill Creek Park
14
Youngstown
Boardman
680
224
224
New Castle
76
62
North Lima
225
164
76
Alliance
376
62
Log House Museum
Shaker Woods Festival
65
62
Columbiana
45
11
79
Spread Eagle Tavern and Inn
Lisbon
30
Hanoverton
Courthouse Inn and Restaurant
76
Ohio River
East Liverpool Police Museum
30
East Liverpool
The Museum of Ceramics
Wellsville
65

Ohio

18
Wellsville River Museum
376
7
30
Toronto
33 Degrees, The Shakery
22
250
Steubenville
Historic Fort Steuben
22

Pennsylvania

79
22
7
18
West Virginia
250
Washington
70
70
Sedgwick House Museum
40
40
Bridgeport
Martins Ferry
70
40
70
Wheeling
Toy and Plastic Brick Museum
National Imperial Glass Museum
Bellaire
Shadyside
79
N
0   5   10
Miles
Moundsville
21
7
Ohio River
Grave Creek Mound Archaeological Complex
250
© The Countryman Press

Drop a twig in the Mahoning River, which flows through Warren, and you could watch that twig float through the center of Warren, then Niles, and then Youngstown before crossing the border into Pennsylvania. There it would pass into the Ohio River before passing us in East Liverpool, Wellsville, Steubenville, Martins Ferry, and Bellaire. Aside from paddlers and waterfront campers and those with an interest in healthy ecosystems, rivers don't get a lot of attention. They're taken for granted, except when they flood or catch on fire. This route takes us from one museum to the next—institutions that have memorialized history, art, and industry—but I try to remember that the Mahoning River, Meander Creek, Mill Creek, and the Ohio River form an important backdrop to this route through eastern Ohio.

Our adventure in eastern Ohio begins in Warren. The city sits on the banks of the Mahoning River and is centered on the picturesque **Courthouse Square**. Most of the attractions here in town are located off of Mahoning Avenue, which begins at the northwest corner of the square and follows the river for a time before heading north and becoming OH 45 (which makes a beeline north all the way to Ashtabula). In the neighborhood of Perkins Park, you will find the Trumbull County Tourism Board, Warren's Riverwalk Path, the Sutliff Museum, and the historic Upton House and John Stark Edwards House. All of these are within easy walking distance. The National Packard Museum is about a mile north.

The Packard Electric Company was founded in 1890 in Warren, Ohio. The region was part of the Connecticut Western Reserve when it was established in 1798. It was the frontier then, but by 1890 Warren could boast a population of nearly 6,000 residents. Railroads connected Warren's bustling factories and businesses to the rest of Ohio. The Packard Electric Company began as a manufacturer of incandescent light bulbs—and made Warren the first town in the country to light its streets with electric lamps. Within ten years, Packard began producing cars, as well.

The electric and automobile sides of the business eventually parted ways. General Motors picked up the electric business and developed wiring harnesses used in millions of vehicles. It eventually became part of Delphi Automotive Systems.

The Packard Motor Car Company produced its first cars in Warren before the operation moved to Detroit. A Packard was not your run-of-the-mill automobile. While Ford was pushing down the price of Model Ts to expand his market, the price of a Packard made sense for the high-end consumer it attracted. These vehicles—cars still valued by collectors—competed with the most luxurious models coming out of Europe, like the Mercedes and Rolls-Royce.

The Packard nameplate died in 1962, but the legacy is still remembered at the **National Packard Museum**. The museum has a 1900 Model B, the earliest known production car, and a 1903 Model F, the last known Packard built in Warren. The collection includes cars from the company's entire run, up to a 1956 Packard Caribbean, including examples with the company's famous twin-six engine. There are also exhibitions that explore the role the automotive industry still plays in eastern Ohio. (The nearby GM Lordstown Complex builds the Chevy Cruze.) Open year-round, and closed only on Mondays and holidays, there's no excuse to miss this one.

Heading toward the center of town on Mahoning Avenue, Perkins Park will be on the right, as is the Tourism Bureau. The park is a hub of activity, especially in the summer. The Riverwalk path follows the Mahoning. At the south end, tucked in between three parks, behind the Tourist Bureau office, is the Warren Community Amphitheatre. **River Rock at the Amp** brings a host of tribute bands and rising stars to the amphitheater for a series of summer concerts.

Across the street, the **Sutliff Museum** is located on the second floor of the

THE UPTON HOUSE STANDS OUT AMONG AN IMPRESSIVE STRETCH OF HISTORIC HOMES

Warren–Trumbull County Public Library. This small museum preserves the legacy of the Sutliff family. Influential in Warren, the family first came to Ohio as pioneers in 1804. In addition to preserving family documents and sharing the family's participation with the Underground Railroad, the museum has a collection of objects from the Victorian period.

THE FRIES AT THE HOT DOG SHOPPE IN WARREN ARE EVERY BIT AS GOOD AS THEY LOOK

The Upton House sits across Monroe Street from the library. The home is the third oldest in Warren, which in itself is pretty neat. It was also the home of Harriet Taylor Upton. As a political activist, Upton was a leader in the national suffrage movement, and for a short time, the house here on Mahoning Avenue was the headquarters for the National American Woman Suffrage Association.

It's a short walk, two houses north, on Monroe to the **Trumbull County Museum**, located in the John Stark Edwards House. While the neighboring museums have a narrower focus, the Trumbull County Museum takes a look at a larger patch of history—from the prehistory of eastern Ohio to the present.

Before leaving downtown Warren, you can grab a bite to eat at the original **Hot Dog Shoppe**. It's just south of the river on Market Street. There are few of these places in the area, but this is the first one. This excellent eatery was founded in 1946 just after Paul Trevelline and Ralph Middendorf returned home from World War II. The specialty of the house is the chili-cheese hot dog (best topped with onions in my humble opinion), but don't ignore the fries, which you can also get with chili and/or cheese.

For diners who would prefer something more upscale than a hot dog joint, there's **The Mocha House Café and Eatery** on High Street. This place opened as a coffee shop in the early nineties. Today, they offer a full menu of basic American fare—from burgers and fries to spaghetti with meatballs. (In this case, the latter qualifies as American cuisine.)

Niles is perhaps best known as the birthplace of the twenty-fifth President of the United States, William McKinley. (McKinley was assassinated early on in his second term, which led to Theodore Roosevelt becoming president in 1901.) Born in 1843, McKinley was the seventh of nine children. After returning to Ohio after fighting for the Union in the Civil War, he decided to pursue a career in law, which led to a career in politics. He was a member of the U.S. House of Representatives and then governor of Ohio for four years before being elected to the high office.

The McKinley Presidential Library and Museum is located in Canton (see

PRESIDENT MCKINLEY'S LEGACY IS HONORED IN NILES

Chapter 7). Here in Niles, they celebrate his humble beginnings. The most accessible site is the **National McKinley Birthplace Memorial**. Located on Main Street, it takes up an entire block. McKinley's marble form looms 12 feet at the center of the memorial. The open courtyard is surrounded by a circular colonnade.

The memorial also houses the McKinley Memorial Library (the left wing) and the **McKinley Birthplace Museum** (the right wing). For visitors with a casual interest in the president, the museum will be the more interesting of the two. It contains memorabilia from the Civil and Spanish American wars and materials used in the 1896 presidential campaign when McKinley beat William Jennings Bryan.

For a deeper look, consider scheduling a tour of the **McKinley Birthplace Home**. The original home was destroyed by fire in 1937. This reproduction was built on the site and opened to the public in 2003. Tours depend on staff or volunteer availability, but if the stars are in alignment and you want to know more, it's worth the extra time.

Niles and Youngstown are connected by the Mahoning River. It's quicker to head south on OH 46 to I-680 east, but I prefer a more meandering route east from Niles on OH 169 to US 422 south. This way, you essentially cross the river and then follow its path south.

Youngstown is often portrayed as the poster city for the decline of industry in the United States. This part of the country (from Cleveland to Pittsburgh) was once known as Steel Valley—a place where Republic Steel and U.S. Steel employed thousands of workers. That changed as the city headed into the latter half of the twentieth century and the industry tanked. Today, the city's largest employer is Youngstown State University.

The first stop in Youngstown, however, ignores that recent industrial history. **Mill Creek Park** is one of the most notable MetroParks in the country. The park features three lakes, landscaped gardens, waterfalls, ponds, a nature center, a golf course, and an historic mill. There are 15 miles of footpaths and 20 miles of scenic driving. The park is the work of Volney Rogers. It is said that in 1890, the Youngstown lawyer was enjoying a horseback ride through the country and came across Mill Creek Gorge. Overwhelmed by the scenic beauty, he decided that the land around Mill Creek should be preserved. He began buying lots, which he later gave to the city to be used as a park. He is honored with a statue that stands at the main park entrance.

There are several places you must visit at Mill Creek Park. The first is Lanterman's Mill. Built in the late 1840s, it was the third mill built at Lanterman Falls. The second mill was destroyed by a flood—the millstone can be seen 500 feet downstream in the water. The mill was restored in the 1980s and is maintained and operated as a working mill producing stone-ground flours. At the onsite gift shop, you can buy cornmeal, buckwheat, and whole wheat flour.

A 2-mile trail loop, comprised of the East Gorge Trail and the West Gorge Trail, passes right by the mill. The loop is noted for its sandstone outcroppings and the pure beauty of the gorge itself. The path passes under the famous Umbrella Rock, a gorge-side overhang. In fact, it is this gorgeous scenery that inspired Volney Rogers to make "Mill Creek Hollow" a park in the 1890s.

The other stop is the Fellows Riverside Gardens at the north end of the park, overlooking Lake Glacier. These meticulously maintained gardens spread over 12 acres. The central structure is the Davis Education and Visitor Center, which features a café and gift shop. Various events related to gardening and horticulture are held here throughout the year. Be sure to check out the observation tower for panoramic views of the gardens and the lake.

Back in town, the Mahoning Valley Historical Society has several sites to explore. The main attraction is the **Arms Family Museum**. Visitors with any appreciation for the Arts and Crafts Movement must visit Greystone, the family home of Wilfred and Olive Arms, who lived here from 1905 to 1960. The house has been left much as Olive Arms decorated it. Gallery space is used for showing off rotating exhibitions, which often included artifacts from the Historical Society's collection. From mid-November and into January, the house is decorated for the annual "Memories of Christmas Past" exhibition. Seven period rooms feature vintage holiday decorations, toys, and other Christmas memorabilia.

The **Tyler History Center** is another site. The focus here is the Historical Society's Archives Library, but there are also galleries used to exhibit local history. Often, local historical groups will put on their own exhibitions in the Community History Gallery.

One of the more interesting stories told at the center is that of Harry Burt. From 1893 to 1922, Burt created a small business empire. As a confectionary, he began by opening a small penny candy shop. As the Burt Confectionary grew, he added a restaurant, and then he started making ice cream. His claim to fame was to coat ice cream in specially formulated chocolate, freezing it on a stick. It was called the Good Humor Sucker, and soon he was purchasing refrigerated trucks and hiring smartly dressed drivers to sell these ice cream bars directly to the public.

The more cultured stop in Youngstown is yet another museum, **The Butler Institute of American Art**. Founded in 1919, this was the first museum in the world dedicated to American art. The permanent collection includes the work of Winslow Homer, examples from the Hudson Valley School, and an entire gallery dedicated to work that features American sports. Best of all, there is no cost to visit the museum, though donations are always appreciated.

Finally, the tour of town comes full circle with the **Youngstown Historical Center of Industry and Labor**. The discovery of block coal in Youngstown led to a boom in iron and, subsequently, steel production throughout the twentieth century. This museum has an impressive collection of artifacts from the industries that made Youngstown what it is. A lot of effort has gone into preserving something of the scale of these furnaces and foundries. On display you will find a workmen's locker room and part of a company house. There's also an archive of documents which provide researchers with a wealth of information about the daily work of production and the workers' efforts to organize.

Here we part ways with the Mahoning River for a time. From Youngstown, take Market Street south. It becomes OH 7. You will drive about 23 miles to North Lima. At the center of town, take a right on South Avenue (OH 164) and head south southwest 4.5 miles into Columbiana.

The center of Columbiana is the traffic circle at the intersection of Main Street and Park Avenue. The **Log House Museum** is on the northeast corner. Back in 1809, this was the site of the local post office. Later one of Columbiana's first homes, this fine log cabin, was moved to the site, where it now houses the Historical Society of Columbiana and Fairfield Township. Pio-

THIS LOG CABIN IN DOWNTOWN COLUMBIANA HOUSES THE TOWN HISTORICAL SOCIETY

neer artifacts, quilts, and other items are on display. The museum also holds the bones of a mastodon found nearby.

Columbiana's signature event—the **Shaker Woods Festival**—held over three consecutive weekends (Friday and Saturday) in August, brings a couple hundred craftspeople to Shaker Woods, just east of town. The festival takes place in the woods. The property is divided into seven sections, each named for an historic Shaker community. Vendors, selling everything from Shaker brooms to coconut shell lamps, dress in period attire. There are plenty of concessions, and the organizers even provide live entertainment on two stages.

From Main Street in Columbiana, take Pittsburgh Street east. The road angles southeast as you continue along, and it becomes Columbiana-Waterford Road. At OH 7, turn south and drive 13 miles to US 30. It's little more than a 5-mile drive on US 30 into East Liverpool.

Alternatively, there's a less scenic route to East Liverpool (following OH 11) that brings you closer to two amazing inns. The Courthouse Inn and Restaurant in Lisbon and the **Spread Eagle Tavern and Inn** a bit farther off in Hanoverton are inns of the classic sort. Places where weary travelers shake off the cold in front of a warm fire, dig into a fine meal, and rent a room for the night.

The Spread Eagle dates back to 1837 when Hanoverton was a busy town on the Sandy and Beaver Canal. It is said that Abraham Lincoln once stopped here and gave a speech. With the advent of the railroad, the town went the way of most places that relied on canal traffic. The building was restored, as was the adjacent saltbox that once was the home of the justice of the peace. Meals can be taken in any of the inn's seven dining rooms. Drinks and the like can be had in the Patrick Henry Tavern Room or downstairs in Gaver's Rathskeller. The Spread Eagle offers a very unique experience.

The **Courthouse Inn and Restaurant** in Lisbon was built in 1802 as a hotel and inn. It is, in fact, the oldest brick building in Ohio. While the Spread Eagle preserves a strong historic vibe, the Courthouse is more contemporary. The restaurant, for example, is vegetarian, and the guest rooms are tastefully done up in bright yellows, oranges, and hot lavender. And if that at all sounds tacky, then I've done a bad job of describing it.

The restaurant, Renelee's, has an excellent atmosphere. Funky and eclectic, the space needs no special occasion to inspire a little celebrating. There's a patio with a large fireplace and stone tables and stools. There's also Love's Café, an onsite bakery.

East Liverpool has the questionable distinction of being the place where Charles "Pretty Boy" Floyd was gunned down by the FBI in 1934. His body was eventually embalmed at the Sturgis Funeral Home, where a death mask was made. After a time, the funeral home became a B&B, and a copy of the

THE LISBON COURTHOUSE INN HAS A LOT OF HISTORY AND A SURPRISINGLY FUNKY VIBE

death mask hung in the basement laundry room. The inn is closed now, but visitors can check out another copy of the mask at the **East Liverpool Police Museum** at City Hall on Sixth Street. The police department here goes back to 1882, so a lot of interesting memorabilia and artifacts are on display, in addition to the visage of the infamous gunman.

Now the bit of pottery know-how that was behind the creation of this interesting historical record was not a rare thing in East Liverpool. Once known as the Pottery Capitol of the Nation and America's Crockery City, East Liverpool was once a big player in the ceramics industry. From 1840 to 1930, East Liverpool was responsible for more than half of the country's ceramics production. The list of local potteries in that period boggles the imagination.

This legacy is remembered at **The Museum of Ceramics**. Housed in the old post office—from the day when post offices were built to impress—the museum chronicles 150 years of ceramic production. You don't have to know the difference between Lotus Ware and Fiesta Ware to appreciate the museum's exhibitions. However, those who do know the difference might better appreciate how well curated the museum is. In addition to the history of the industry here in eastern Ohio, the museum also features some exhibitions on the area's social history.

Wellsville and the **Wellsville River Museum** can be found 5 miles west of East Liverpool, off of OH 7. The museum is housed in the old Hammond home. Built in 1870, Dr. Hammond lived here with his family and practiced medicine. It was not uncommon for doctors to set up shop in their homes back in the day. Today the museum features eleven rooms of exhibitions—each a gallery dedicated to a specific aspect of local history. Exhibitions feature model riverboats, artifacts from the Civil War, and the sword of Colonel John Hunt Morgan, of Morgan's Raiders. The museum is owned and operated by the Wellsville Historical Society.

You will pass the town of Toronto, Ohio, on the way to Steubenville. A great dessert spot in town is **33 Degrees, The Shakery**. Located right in town on Franklin Avenue, the Shakery has ice cream and sundaes, but they're known for their shakes. They come in a ton of flavors, and you can mix flavors to create your own custom favorite.

Steubenville, further down on OH 7, is the City of Murals. This is a bold claim in a state full of small towns big on murals, but with 23 so far, it seems they are on solid ground. The town was founded in 1787 with the construction of Fort Steuben, and later it became better known as the hometown of Dean Martin.

The big attraction in town is **Historic Fort Steuben**. The carefully reconstructed fort is the heart of Fort Steuben Park. The fort is stocked with interpreters who recreate the eighteenth century for guests. For two days in June, the experience kicks into high gear with the Ohio Valley

THE OLD FORT IS GREAT FOR FAMILY HISTORY LESSONS

Frontier Days. This event brings all sorts of activity to the fort—from soldiers demonstrating musketry to surveyors explaining their tools. And all the other craftspeople, like blacksmiths and candle makers, are on hand too.

Aside from the fort, the park features an impressive fountain, the first federal land office west of the Alleghenies (built with logs from the original structure), and a visitor center with information about the entire Ohio River Scenic Byway, from East Liverpool to Cincinnati. Continuing south along that scenic byway, that is OH 7, the next stop is Martins Ferry.

The oldest European settlement in Ohio, Martins Ferry overlooks the Ohio River. Since its start in 1779, the town has had many names. The name it has today honors Ebenezer Martin, who established a grid system for the town's streets in 1835. (His father Absalom was one of the city's first settlers.) Prior to that, it was variously called Hoglinstown, Mercertown, Norristown, Jefferson, and Martinsville. The town's fortunes grew in the nineteenth century with the Industrial Revolution and waned as manufacturing waned in the twentieth century.

These days, Martins Ferry and its neighbor to the south, Bridgeport, are overshadowed by Wheeling, West Virginia, across the river. The two towns' combined population of less than 9,000 is surpassed three times over by Wheeling, and if you know anything about economics, businesses follow the population. Still, there is an opportunity for some sightseeing this side of the Ohio.

The **Sedgwick House Museum** is the museum for the Martins Ferry Area Historical Society. Built in 1870, the house became home for the Sedgwicks at the turn of the century. They remained until the 1960s, and then, a hundred years after it was built, the historical society moved in and began displaying artifacts from the region's past. The museum covers a nice swathe of history, from pioneer days to the near-present. Be sure to call ahead before visiting; the hours posted have volunteers on hand on the weekends, but the schedule can vary.

For travelers interested in following the old National Road, it crosses over from West Virginia here in Bridgeport. Main Street, north of I-70, becomes National Road as you continue west. Chapter 8 in this book covers a bit more of this historic route.

Bellaire is on the river, south of I-70. The first of two museums to visit here is the **National Imperial Glass Museum**. Bellaire doesn't feature as largely in the history of glass production as East Liverpool does in the history of ceramics, but the Imperial Glass Company was an important part of local life for several generations. From its founding in 1901 to its dissolution in the 1980s, Bellaire ran on glass.

The museum itself is run by the National Imperial Glass Collectors' Soci-

THE NATIONAL IMPERIAL GLASS MUSEUM PRESERVES AN IMPORTANT PIECE OF BELLAIRE'S HISTORY

ety. As such, it holds an impressive collection of glassware. A tour of the museum begins with a short video about the history of the company and then continues to the glass display rooms. There is an impressive focus not just on the company and its products, but on the men and women who spent good portions of their lives creating this glassware.

At the north end of Bellaire, thus requiring some backtracking, there is a small museum dedicated to a product we all know and love. Unfortunately, the producers of the product keep a tight rein on who can and cannot use the name of their product. So, visitors to Bellaire will not find a LEGO Building Block Museum. They will find, rather, the **Toy and Plastic Brick Museum**. Founded in 2007, this is the largest private collection of LEGO in the world. Filling 36,000 square feet of an old middle school, visitors can spend hours exploring all the creative ways LEGO building blocks can be assembled. This one is a great stop for the kids—but adults may appreciate even more all the work that went into creating this amazing museum.

Bellaire also has a few places to eat. One of those is **The Roosevelt** on Union Street. This Italian eatery is not going to win any awards for curb appeal, but the word in Bellaire is that it's the best food in town. People rave about the marinara sauce. Everything here is made on-site—from the sauces to the pasta. A lot of restaurants save a little time and money and stock the kitchen with frozen meatballs. Not here; it's all fresh. Nothing fancy, but it's all good.

There is one more historic site and museum that I would be remiss to ignore, even though it's over the river in West Virginia. The site is the **Grave Creek Mound Archaeological Complex in Moundsville**, over the bridge from Shadyside, which is about 10 minutes south of Bellaire. Other chapters in this book explore some of the ancient mounds found in Ohio. This mound, just across the river, is a giant cone-shape, 69 feet tall. The mound is over 2,000 years old, and inside it, researchers have found many artifacts that tell us a little about the people who built it and why they built it.

These artifacts are on display at the Delf Norona Museum. The exhibitions here foster a deeper understanding and appreciation of the Adena Hopewell culture.

IN THE AREA

Accommodations

THE COURTHOUSE INN AND RESTAURANT, 116 West Lincoln Way, Lisbon. Call 330-870-4216. Website: thecourthouseinnandrestaurant.com. $$$.

SPREAD EAGLE TAVERN AND INN, 10150 Plymouth Street, Hanoverton. Call 330-223-1583. Website: spreadeagletavern.com. $$$.

Attractions and Recreation

33 DEGREES, THE SHAKERY, 805 Franklin Avenue, Toronto. Website: facebook.com/pg/33degrees.

ARMS FAMILY MUSEUM, 648 Wick Avenue, Youngstown. Call 330-743-2589. Website: mahoninghistory.org/visit/arms-family-museum.

THE BUTLER INSTITUTE OF AMERICAN ART, 524 Wick Avenue, Youngstown. Call 330-743-1107. Website: butlerart.com.

EAST LIVERPOOL POLICE MUSEUM, 126 West Sixth Street, East Liverpool. Website: facebook.com/ELPDMUSEUM1.

GRAVE CREEK MOUND ARCHAEOLOGICAL COMPLEX, 801 Jefferson Avenue, Moundsville, West Virginia. Call 304-843-4128. Website: wvculture.org/museum/GraveCreekmod.html.

HISTORIC FORT STEUBEN, 120 South 3rd Street, Steubenville. Call 740-283-1787. Website: oldfortsteuben.com.

LOG HOUSE MUSEUM, 10 East Park Avenue, Columbiana. Call 330-482-0946.

MCKINLEY BIRTHPLACE HOME AND RESEARCH CENTER, 42 South Main Street, Niles. Call 330-652-1704, ext. 7217 (the number to schedule a tour). Website: mckinley.lib.oh.us/index.php/index3.

MILL CREEK PARK, P.O. Box 546, Canfield, OH 44406. Call 330-702-3000. Website: millcreekmetroparks.org.

MUSEUM OF CERAMICS, 400 East Fifth Street, East Liverpool. Call 330-360-6001. Website: themuseumofceramics.org.

NATIONAL IMPERIAL GLASS MUSEUM, 3200 Belmont Street, Bellaire. Call 740-671-3971. Website: imperialglass.org.

NATIONAL MCKINLEY BIRTHPLACE MEMORIAL & THE MCKINLEY MUSEUM, 40 South Main Street, Niles. Call 330-652-4273. Website: mckin leybirthplacemuseum.org.

NATIONAL PACKARD MUSEUM, 1899 Mahoning Avenue, Warren. Call 330-394-1899. Website: packardmuseum.org.

RIVER ROCK AT THE AMP, CONCERTS AT WARREN COMMUNITY AMPHITHEATRE, 321 Mahoning Avenue, Warren. Call 330-856-7867. Website: riverrockattheamp.com.

SEDGWICK HOUSE MUSEUM, 627 Hanover Street, Martins Ferry. Call 740-633-5046. Website: ohio.org/destination/museums/sedgwick-house -museum.

SHAKER WOODS FESTIVAL, 217 OH 7, Columbiana. Call 330-482-0215. Website: shakerwoods.com.

SUTLIFF MUSEUM, 444 Mahoning Avenue, Warren. Call 330-395-6575. Website: sutliffmuseum.org.

TOY AND PLASTIC BRICK MUSEUM, 4597 Noble Street, Bellaire. Call 740-671-8890. Website: brickmuseum.net

TRUMBULL COUNTY MUSEUM, 303 Monroe Street, Warren. Call 330-394-4653. Website: trumbullcountyhistory.org

TYLER HISTORY CENTER, 325 West Federal Street, Youngstown. Call 330-743-2589. Website: mahoninghistory.org/visit/tyler-history-center.

YOUNGSTOWN HISTORICAL CENTER OF INDUSTRY AND LABOR, 151 West Wood Street, Youngstown. Call 330-941-1314. Website: ohiohistory .org/visit/museum-and-site-locator/youngstown-historical-center-of-indus try-and-labor.

UPTON HOUSE, 380 Mahoning Avenue, Warren. Call 330-395-4633. Website: uptonhouse.org.

WELLSVILLE RIVER MUSEUM, 1003 Riverside Avenue, Wellsville. Call 330-532-1018. Website: facebook.com/WellsvilleHistoricalSociety.

Dining

THE COURTHOUSE INN AND RESTAURANT, 116 West Lincoln Way, Lisbon. Call 330-870-4216. Website: thecourthouseinnandrestaurant.com. $$$.

THE HOT DOG SHOPPE, 740 West Market Street, Warren. Call 330-395-7057. $.

THE MOCHA HOUSE CAFÉ AND EATERY, 467 High Street, Warren. Call 330-392-3020. Website: mochahouse.com. $.

THE ROOSEVELT, 3175 Union Street, Bellaire. Call 740-676-9015. $.

SPREAD EAGLE TAVERN AND INN, 10150 Plymouth Street, Hanoverton. Call 330-223-1583. Website: spreadeagletavern.com. $$$$.

Other Contacts

TRUMBULL COUNTY TOURISM BOARD, 321 Mahoning Ave, Warren. Call 330-675-3081. Website: exploretrumbullcounty.com.

7
AMISH COUNTRY

MANSFIELD, LOUDONVILLE, MILLERSBURG, BERLIN,
CHARM, SUGARCREEK, COSHOCTON, UHRICHSVILLE, NEW
PHILADELPHIA, DOVER, ZOAR, CANTON, KIDRON

ESTIMATED LENGTH: 200 miles

ESTIMATED TIME: 5 hours

HIGHLIGHTS: Historic Mansfield is where we begin this trip, with stops at the Ohio State Reformatory (where *The Green Mile* was filmed) and the Richland Carrousel Park. On the way to Loudonville, you will want to visit the Malabar Farm State Park. In Loudonville, two canoe liveries make it possible to explore the Mohican River, a fine river for paddling. Then it's off to Millersburg, the antiques-shop capital of Amish Country. Farther east we come to Berlin, a tourist trap of a town that capitalizes on the Amish Country aesthetic with quilt shops, antique malls, and lots of food. The next stop is the Guggisberg Cheese Company shop in Charm, and then it's on to Sugarcreek, known as the Little Switzerland of Ohio. Here you can take in a show at the Carlisle Inn or do a little window shopping. Then we head south to Coshocton and the famous Historic Roscoe Village. There you can enjoy the ambiance of history, grab a bite to eat at The Warehouse, visit a museum or two, and ride a canal boat. Leaving the Amish behind for a spell, we now head east to Uhrichsville and the Dennison Railroad Depot Museum, then north to Dover and a tour of the amazing Warthers Museum, where you can explore the many intricate carvings of Ernest "Mooney" Warther. The historic Zoar Village is next. Then it's back into Amish Country for a stop in Wilmot for the Amish Door Restaurant (or Beebops Grill if you feel more like a burger and fries). Nearby Winesburg has an excellent B&B, and there's also the Wendell August Forge Shop. The final bit of our trip takes us north to Kidron, where you can shop at the famous Lehman's Hardware, a sprawling emporium of Amish-friendly tools and household supplies.

GETTING THERE: Begin your trip in Mansfield. Head south on Main Street to East Hanley Road, which you will follow east to Pleasant Valley Road, at which

LEFT: MANSFIELD IS KNOWN AS THE "CARROUSEL CAPITAL OF THE OHIO"

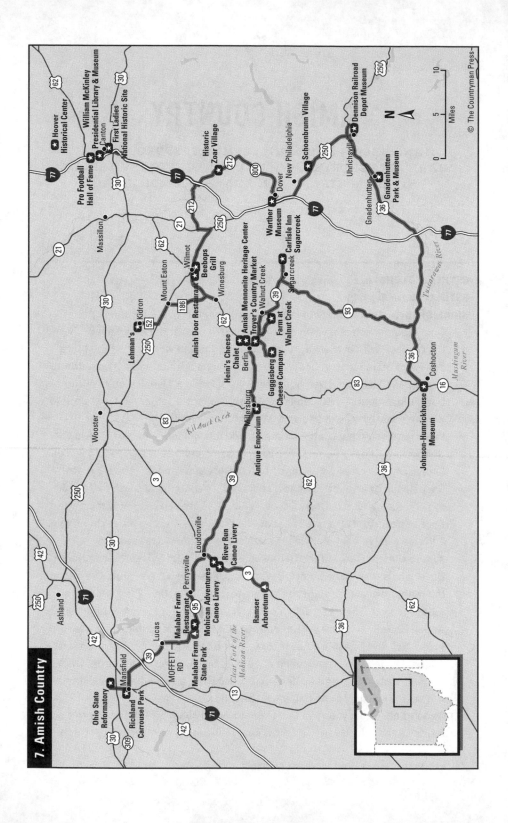

7. Amish Country

© The Countryman Press

N

Miles
0 5 10

Hoover Historical Center

William McKinley Presidential Library & Museum

First Ladies National Historic Site

Canton

62

30

Pro Football Hall of Fame

77

Massillon

21

21

30

250

212

212

Historic Zoar Village

800

Dover

New Philadelphia

Schoenbrunn Village

250

Uhrichsville

Dennison Railroad Depot Museum

250

77

77

Gnadenhutten

Gnadenhutten Park & Museum

36

Tuscarawas River

Warther Museum

62

Wilmot

Beebops Grill

Winesburg

Mount Eaton

186

62

52

Kidron

Lehman's

250

Amish Door Restaurant

Amish Mennonite Heritage Center

Troyer's Country Market

Walnut Creek

Carlisle Inn Sugarcreek

Sugarcreek

Farm at Walnut Creek

39

93

36

Coshocton

Muskingum River

Johnson-Humrickhouse Museum

16

83

36

62

Heini's Cheese Chalet

Berlin

Guggisberg Cheese Company

Millersburg

83

Kill Buck Creek

Wooster

Antique Emporium

39

3

250

Loudonville

River Run Canoe Livery

3

Perrysville

Mohican Adventures Canoe Livery

95

Malabar Farm Restaurant

MOFFETT RD

Malabar Farm State Park

Lucas

39

Ramser Arboretum

Clear Fork of the Mohican River

13

42

71

Ashland

250

42

Ohio State Reformatory

Mansfield

30

309

Richland Carrousel Park

42

71

36

62

Clear Fork of the Mohican River

Mohican River

point you will turn south (right). You will pass Malabar Farm State Park. When you come to OH 603, jog south and then take OH 95 east toward Perrysville. In the center of town, you will come to the intersection of OH 95 and OH 39. The latter is the main road through Amish Country, and you will stay on it, heading east through Loudonville into Millersburg. US 62 joins OH 39 for the trip east to Berlin. From there you will head south (via OH 39 and TR 369) to the town of Charm, then east (back to OH 39 by way of TR 70) to Sugarcreek. OH 93 will take you south from Sugarcreek to Coshocton, after which you will take US 36 east to Uhrichsville. Then follow OH 800 (with all its twists and turns) to New Philadelphia. After the road crosses the Tuscarawas River northeast of New Philly, turn northwest onto OH 212 to reach Zoar Village. From Zoar, take OH 212 west 11.7 miles to US 250, which you will follow west to US 62. The final lap of the journey heads back into the heart of Amish Country, with a visit to Wilmot (on US 62) before heading north to Kidron, which is reached by following US 250 west to TR 52 north.

Many unique Christian sects have called Ohio home. The image of the Amish—and to some extent their Old Order Mennonite cousins—has become a permanent, and at times misunderstood, piece of American culture. But other lesser-known groups have also settled here. The Shakers, Zoarites, and Moravians all built communities in Ohio at one time or another. The history of the Zoarites and Moravians is on display in nearby Zoar Village and Gnadenhutten. The Amish, on the other hand, have an active presence throughout the state.

There are Amish communities that get more press than those in Ohio. The Amish of Pennsylvania's Lancaster County and those around Shipshewana, Indiana, come readily to mind. So it may come as a surprise to some to learn that Ohio is home to more Amish than any other state in the country. Amish and Old Order Mennonites live all over Ohio, but a unique concentration centered in Holmes County makes this region the state's official Amish Country.

Ohio's Amish Country straddles the edge of the Appalachian Plateau, northeast of Columbus. North of OH 39—the state route that connects Mansfield and Loudonville in the west with Sugarcreek and Dover in the east—the terrain is notably more rolling than rugged. South to the Tuscarawas River, however, the hills become steeper, and the roads have more curves than not. Throughout it all, are narrow country roads, farm fields, and small towns.

Capitalizing on the public's fascination with the Amish way of life and their Old World craftsmanship, in particular, the region abounds with restaurants featuring home-style cooking and shops selling handmade furniture and Amish crafts. It's often difficult to determine how much the

THE OHIO STATE REFORMATORY WAS FEATURED IN *THE SHAWSHANK REDEMPTION*

Amish themselves participate in the tourism industry, but their presence in the area is undeniable. Black buggies are common enough that drivers tend to exercise caution, never really knowing what vehicle might be over the next hill or around the next bend. You will see the Amish on their farms, the children playing barefoot in the yard and the men walking behind horses, plowing their fields.

Sitting as it does just outside the border of Holmes County, the gateway to Amish Country is Loudonville. Begin your trip to Loudonville in Mansfield, and take in the sights along the way.

In 1994, Castle Rock Entertainment released *The Shawshank Redemption*, a movie adapted from Stephen King's novella *Rita Hayworth and the Shawshank Redemption*. The plot centers on Andy Dufresne, a banker unjustly sentenced to life in prison for murdering his wife. Though the story takes place in Maine, the film was shot here in Mansfield. The **Ohio State Reformatory** played the role of Shawshank State Prison, and today it is an attraction on the Shawshank Trail. (The "trail" is a self-guided tour of sites related to the filming of the movie.) The former prison is open in the summer as a museum. More than offering just a summary of a movie locale, the prison tells its own history—from the history of the site as a Civil War training camp to the architecture, which was designed to help troubled young men contemplate their offenses and plan for a better future. In the fall, the prison switches gears and becomes a haunted Halloween attraction for folks who like to have the living bejeezus scared out of them.

Later, when you visit Malabar Farm, you can make another stop on the Shawshank Trail. Near the **Malabar Farm State Park** is the hayfield where Andy leaves his note for Red. (Fans of the movie will know what I am talking about.) The tree where the note is found was damaged by a storm in recent years. You can find the tree on the north side of Pleasant Valley Road, just east of the intersection with Bromfield Road.

From the penitentiary, take US 30 west one exit to Main Street. Follow Main Street south to Fourth Street and the **Richland Carrousel Park**. This is the centerpiece of Mansfield's Historic Carrousel District. The charm of an old-fashioned carousel fits perfectly with the downtown area's brick streets and old-time neon signs. The carousel itself is the work of a local company, Carrousel Works. Each of the 52 animals and two chariots is hand-carved, but what makes this merry-go-round especially interesting is that it is the first carousel to be built new since the 1930s. You can ride the carousel any day you like. Except for holidays, it's open daily from 11 to 5.

Just north of the park is a strip of downtown businesses that feel a lot like you're stepping back into the 1930s. First, there's the **Coney Island Diner**, a fantastic eatery. A row of booths lines one wall of the diner, and a row of stools at the kitchen counter runs along the other. The restaurant is well known for its "famous" fresh pea salad and the Coney dog blue plate special, but there is a mess of great dishes here for the hungry traveler. Try the fried bologna sandwich for a diner classic.

Next door to the diner is the City News and Suzy's Smoke Room. There are not many places in the Midwest where you can find a shop like this. Newspapers and magazines, cigars, pipe tobacco, and tobacciana fill the space. Suzy mixes her own special blend of pipe tobacco, readily bagged from large glass jars on the counter.

From Mansfield, head east on Park Avenue East. Two miles out of town, turn right onto Lucas Road (OH 39). To get to Malabar Farm, turn right (south) onto Union Street in downtown Lucas. The road name changes to Moffet Street before you get to Pleasant Valley Road, where you will turn left (east). In about 1.5 miles, you come to Bromfield Road. Signs for the state park will guide you from there.

The Malabar Farm State Park is more than just a historic site. It is a working farm that introduces visitors to a richer understanding of conservation and ecological stewardship. The farm was once the property of Luis Bromfield, a Pulitzer Prize–winning writer. Bromfield hosted many celebrities at Malabar Farm during his time here. Lauren Bacall and Humphrey Bogart, to name two examples, held their wedding and spent their honeymoon on the farm. Bromfield wrote about conservation, but his approach was not simply to call for leaving nature to its own devices. He advocated the restoration of forests and responsible agriculture.

The park offers guided tours of the farm, which includes a peek at work being done to keep the farm running productively. The tours of the Big House look at life on the farm in the early twentieth century. Sitting rooms, bedrooms, guest rooms, and Bromfield's study are all on the tour. The park also has the usual state park activities—trails for hiking, a visitor center where you can learn a little about the area's wildlife, and a primitive campground.

Near the entrance to the park is the **Malabar Farm Hostel**. Part of the Hostelling International USA association of accommodations. For those traveling solo, this is an excellent place to stay. The rooms are cheap, and the setting can't be beat. The hostel is an old farmhouse. Not as grand as Bromfield's Big House, but comfortable enough.

THE MALABAR FARM IS AS INTERESTING AS IT IS BEAUTIFUL

Ramser Arboretum

The **Ramser Arboretum** is a little more than 8 miles south on OH 3 from downtown Loudonville. Unlike many arboretums that feature a visitor center and interpretive signage, the 680-acre Ramser Arboretum is more like a tree preserve. The property is populated with native trees and planted hardwoods. Best of all, there are 6 miles of trails for hiking.

Excellent dining is surprisingly within walking distance. A mile to the east on Pleasant Valley Road is the **Malabar Farm Restaurant**. This historic building was built in 1820 by David Schrack. As such, it's known as the Schrack Place. The stone for the four-foot thick walls was quarried nearby. Bromfield purchased the property in 1941, which is why it is part of the state park today. The restaurant rightly focuses on meals prepared with locally sourced food. In the summer, the deck is the best place to sit.

Where Pleasant Valley Road comes to a T, east of the park, take OH 603 south to OH 95 east. In downtown Perrysville, you will rejoin OH 39, which you will take east to Loudonville. The Clear Fork of the Mohican River flows through the heart of Loudonville, and those who appreciate paddling will want to take advantage of one of the town's two canoe liveries. Just south of Loudonville on OH 3 are the **Mohican Adventures Canoe Livery** and the **River Run Canoe Livery**. Located just down the street from each other, both of these outfits have a huge stable of canoes, which carry thousands of visitors down the river each year.

Traveling down OH 3, you will come to the blink-and-you'll-miss-it town of Jelloway. Just south of town is the split for OH 205 south. Turn left at the intersection, and the arboretum is directly ahead. This is a low-key affair. Park in the grassy lot, grab a map from the kiosk and go exploring.

Continuing east on OH 39, the next stop is Millersburg. It's an easy run-up US 62 to Millersburg from Columbus, and it's even easier to continue north on OH 83 to Wooster. This makes Millersburg a busy crossroads of sorts. A strip of fast food joints south of town attests to that. While many folks are undoubtedly just passing through, antique-lovers will want to schedule some time in Millersburg. The Antique Emporium on West Jackson Street is one of a number of excellent antiques shops. Every shop reflects the local community, and the shops in Millersburg are no exception. The Antique Emporium is stocked with old Amish tools, buggy benches, and baskets—the kind of stuff you would expect in Amish Country.

If your budget can handle it, northeast of Millersburg you will find the perfect spot for dining and upscale accommodations. While the

THE ANTIQUE EMPORIUM IS JUST ONE OF THE ANTIQUES SHOPS IN MILLERSBURG THAT WILL KEEP YOU BROWSING ALL AFTERNOON

Inn at Honey Run is billed as a bed-and-breakfast, it is much better described as a country boutique hotel. The inn lies northeast of Millersburg on County Road 203. The location, extra meeting spaces, and onsite dining make this a popular destination for corporate retreats. Aside from the meeting rooms, these features also make this a great place for a romantic weekend. For more privacy and more room to settle in, there are also cottages with Jacuzzi tubs and wood-burning fireplaces.

The inn's restaurant, called **Tarragon**, boasts a "diverse, upscale casual dining menu." Meals are prepared under the direction of a chef who trained at Le Cordon Bleu in Paris, among other places. The chef's rich culinary experience has influenced the contemporary American menu, and the kitchen makes an effort to use local ingredients. The result is a collection of familiar entrees reflecting the flavor of the region.

As you continue east on OH 39, the next stop is Berlin. In the summer, the streets and parking lots are full of motorcycles and minivans. And why not? If Amish Country tourism has a center, it's here in Berlin. There are places to stay, places to eat, and places to shop. This is also where you will find the Amish & Mennonite Heritage Center, northeast of Berlin on County Road

77. The story of the Amish, from 1525 to the present, is on display at the Heritage Center in the form of a 265-foot mural-in-the-round called the Behalt Cyclorama. The German word *behalt* means "to remember," and the display is intended to help visitors do just that. The cyclorama is a way to remember the history of the Amish people, from their Anabaptist roots in Zurich to the dispersion of the community, in all its forms, around the world. A tour of the exhibition lasts 30 minutes.

Quilters will not want to miss a chance to visit the Helping Hands Quilt Shop on US 62. For generations, quilting was a craft of necessity. Quilters took scrap fabric and put it to good use. Function trumped form. Today, a quilt's appearance—from the creative use of matching colors to the stitching patterns—is every bit as important as the warmth it provides people at night. For more than 40 years, Helping Hands Quilt Shop has been the place to buy everything you need to make a quilt. The shop also carries over a hundred quilts made locally. They even take special orders if you are looking for a quilt you cannot find on the rack.

Across the street from the quilt shop, you will see a sign for the "Home Style Cooking" of the **Boyd and Wurthmann Restaurant**. Serving breakfast, lunch, and dinner, this is where the locals eat. The menu could be used as a catalog of American comfort food. Eggs, bacon, sausage and biscuits, and thick-cut, honest-to-goodness from-scratch bread for breakfast. At lunch and

THE SMALL TOWN OF CHARM IS DUTIFULLY CHARMING

The Big Cheesy

One reason people visit Amish Country is to find wholesome foods straight from the farm. These days, when industrial agriculture and food production has us all reading ingredient lists and scratching our heads, the Amish "brand" brings a sigh of relief. When you see the word *Amish* on a label at your local grocery store, there's always the question of whether you're being sold the real deal or a slick decoy. But when you stop by a farm market or specialty shop in Ohio's Amish Country, the name means something.

This is especially true of cheese. Folks love Amish cheese, and within a short drive of Berlin, there are three shops where you can find honest-to-goodness Amish cheese, farm produce, and canned goods. The first is **Heini's Cheese Chalet**, found a mile north of Berlin, off US 62. Since 1935, the Dauwalder family has been making cheese in Amish Country. The factory itself goes back even further, to a time when it was known as the Bunker Hill Cheese Co-op. Just as they did a hundred years ago, Amish farmers still deliver their milk to the factory in milk cans. The Chalet, as Dauwalder family now calls it, is both a retail space and the front end of their cheese factory. Because the cheese is made here, visitors can get a factory tour to see how it's done.

As you return to Berlin and leave town again, this time by way of East Main Street (OH 39), the next stop is **Troyer's Country Market**, purveyors of fine Troyer Cheese. But cheese isn't all they offer. The market also sells locally sourced meats and canned goods. You can order a feast for a large family or just grab some goodies for the road. The variety is the best thing about Troyer's. They sell cheddar, Swiss, and pepper jack, and the Amish wedding foods are amazing. You can take home apple pie syrup or blueberry jam, brine pickles or pickled beet eggs.

The third place in this dairy-themed trio is the **Guggisberg Cheese Company in Charm**. This one is a bit harder to get to, but it's only 3 miles away. The most direct route is to head south on County Road 367 until the road comes to a T at County Road 120. Turn left and then after a quarter-mile turn left again, onto County Road 557. Travel less than a mile south, and you will land in Guggisberg.

Alfred Guggisberg, the man behind the company, was born in Switzerland and was trained there in the art of cheese making. The most popular cheese here is the Baby Swiss, which Alfred created in an attempt to meet the tastes of his American customers. Baby Swiss is creamier than Swiss Swiss, and it has smaller holes. The shop sells the Baby Swiss and the company's other varieties of cheese.

dinner, diners will see plates piled up with fried chicken, real mashed potatoes and gravy, and pot roast.

Berlin has more lodging options than most towns in the area. There is a
Comfort Inn, as well as the local Berlin Grande Hotel. There are also several
motels. One of the nicer options, however, is to the southeast, toward Walnut
Creek. The **Miller Haus Bed & Breakfast** allows guests to escape town for a
bit and also gives them a quiet night in the country. Located between Berlin
and Walnut Creek on County Road 135, the B&B sits far from the road. Daryl
and Lee Ann Miller operate the inn. Lee Ann shares her favorite recipes as a
regular cooking guest on the local Fox affiliate. The home was originally
built by Daryl and his uncle.

Inside, you will find the inn stocked with Amish-inspired comforts. The
guest rooms feature Amish quilts and hand-crafted furniture. Breakfast
might feature homemade biscuits or a unique egg-and-sausage dish. The
cook's baking expertise is on display nightly, when guests can enjoy a fresh-
baked pie or some other treat. There are nine guest rooms at the Miller Haus,
which is good. If there were fewer, it would be much harder to secure a room
at this popular spot.

THE MAIN REASON TO STOP IN CHARM IS TO PICK UP SOME GUGGISBERG CHEESE

THE MAIN TOURIST ATTRACTION IN SUGARCREEK IS
THE LIFE-SIZED CUCKOO CLOCK

It is exactly 10 miles from Berlin to Sugarcreek via OH 39. Along the way, you will pass Walnut Creek. There's a small detour to a unique attraction there. If you follow County Road 114 west, it will take you to the **Farm at Walnut Creek**. This is not the kind of farm you'd expect to find in Amish Country. In addition to seeing cows, goats, pigs, and sheep, you will also find llamas, camels, kangaroos, and giraffes. Visitors can call ahead (330-893-4200) and reserve an hour-long wagon ride through the property, or you can simply drive through. There are plenty of opportunities for the kids to feed the animals—which come from five continents—and adults will appreciate the produce stand and perhaps a tour of the non-electric farmhouses.

Back on OH 39, continue to Sugarcreek, called "The Little Switzerland of Ohio." At the center of town is the world's largest cuckoo clock. This ornate attraction once resided in nearby Wilmot, but it was installed here in 2012. Every 30 minutes, a small polka band emerges from the works and plays a tune that sets the dirndl- and lederhosen-wearing couple a-dancing.

The Carlisle Inn in Sugarcreek is a unique hotel. Each floor has its own country theme. There's a pool and a sitting room, and every room has a balcony overlooking the farm fields that roll off in every direction. The Theater at Carlisle Inn shows original Amish-themed musicals. One of the most popular in recent years has been *Half-Stitched, The Musical*, which is based on the *New York Times* best-selling book *The Half-Stitched Amish Quilting Club Book* by Wanda E. Brunstetter. The Dutch Valley Restaurant across the parking lot is operated by the same folks who own the hotel (and quite a few other properties). So, with the hotel, restaurant, and theater, you really don't need to go anywhere else. There's even a gift shop and food market next door.

From Sugarcreek, take OH 93 South to US 36 West. For a short time, the itinerary ventures beyond Amish Country to explore some of the sights nearby.

Coshocton sits at the confluence of the Tuscarawas and Muskingum Rivers. In the early 1800s, this village on the western banks of the Muskingum was an important canal town. The Ohio & Erie Canal was a prominent feature of the area until the Flood of 1913 mostly wiped out the local canal system. But during the canal's heyday, Roscoe Village was the place for business. Canal boat captains once tied up their boats behind the warehouse, now **The Warehouse,** and unloaded their goods. Shops on Whitewoman Street did a fine bit of trade.

After the flood, the village began a slow decline—that is, until a group of folks from Coshocton began to buy buildings with the intention of restoring them. The Roscoe Village Foundation saw to the restoration and preservation of all the buildings you see on Whitewoman Street. Many have been converted to other purposes—homes are now antiques shops, warehouses are restaurants and pubs, and a lockkeeper's house is now an acoustic instrument store. Several of the buildings serve as museums commemorating some aspect of life in Roscoe Village during the 1830s. There's Dr. Maro Johnson's House, the Village Smithy, and the Hay Craft Learning Center. Along with a replica canal boat that takes visitors for a ride on the restored section of the old canal, sites feature costumed guides who demonstrate old crafts and answer questions about the village.

The **Johnson-Humrickhouse Museum**, at the south end of the village, predates the restoration of the neighborhood. Opened in 1931, it preserves the collection of David M. and John H. Johnson, who collected Native American and Asian art on their travels. One of the more fascinating displays

COSTUMED INTERPRETERS ARE SCATTERED THROUGHOUT ROSCOE VILLAGE

The Presidential Tour

I t seems you can't throw an egg in Ohio without hitting some former president's birthplace, ancestral home, library, or monument. One of the most impressive of these ubiquitous commemorations is the William McKinley Presidential Library and Museum in Canton.

The centerpiece of the site is the towering McKinley Memorial, the last resting place of the 25th President of the United States. It is a 108-step walk up to the memorial, which is made of concrete, granite, and marble. The interior of the memorial is breathtaking. A bright, airy dome rises 77 feet above the dark granite sarcophagi of McKinley and his wife. Those who suspect that organizations like the Templars, Freemasons, and Illuminati are secretly pulling the strings of power will be excited to note that McKinley was himself a Freemason. His connection to this mysterious society is celebrated at the memorial.

Adjacent to the monument is the McKinley Museum, which features exhibitions from McKinley's life and political career. The museum building is also the home of a small science museum and the presidential library.

While in Canton, you might also want to check out the First Ladies National Historic Site, which explores the role of the country's first ladies.

For non-presidential history, you could visit the Pro Football Hall of Fame and the Hoover Historical Center on the campus of Walsh University.

PRESIDENT MCKINLEY'S DESK

includes the Newark Holy Stones. While these artifacts, found in the Newark Earthworks, may be a hoax, the story behind the attempts to determine their authenticity is fascinating.

Heading east on US 36, ride 27 miles to reach the town of Gnadenhutten. There's an antiques shop or two in town, but the real reason to stop is the **Gnadenhutten Park and Museum**. During the American Revolution, frustrated American militia massacred a band of Christian Delaware who had been part of the Moravian mission. They were suspected of having informed the British and their allies of American military movements. After a "trial" the Lenape were separated into two groups—men were locked in one building, women and children in an another—and given the night to pray. On the morning of March 8, 1782, they were all executed. Each member of the group, which included 39 children, was killed with a scalping knife. Only two young boys lived to tell what happened.

The park in Gnadenhutten is where the massacre occurred. Several years later, a missionary collected the remains of the dead and buried them here. There is also a small museum with Native American artifacts and relics from the frontier era.

Uhrichsville and the **Dennison Railroad Depot Museum** is another 6 miles east on US 36. During World War II, trainloads of troops bound for deployment from the East Coast passed through the Dennison Depot. There was a Red Cross canteen here during the war, and thousands of volunteers kept the troops stocked with free food and coffee, as well as some old-fashioned hospitality, at a time when these young men were likely very anxious about the future. The stop was nicknamed "Dreamville, USA." The museum commemorates that history, as well as the history of the railroad in general.

Just down the street is the **Dennison Yard**. The exterior suggests it's a sports bar, but the menu is pure Italian. The menu has two kinds of pizza. There's the thin crust (a.k.a. The Original Pangrazio's) and the double-crust Godfather. The latter takes a little extra time to cook, but it's worth the wait. The Chicago-style Al Capone doubles up on cheese, sausage, and pepperoni if you're looking to end the day full.

If the story of Gnadenhutten left you wanting to know more about the Moravian missionaries who came to the frontier and the people with whom they shared their faith, head to **Schoenbrunn Village** in New Philadelphia. To get there, follow US 250/OH 800 north to the New Philadelphia exit for East High Avenue. The entrance to the village is just over a half mile north, on your left. Located just southeast of downtown New Philadelphia, it was first settled in 1772 by David Zeisberger, who arrived here with a party of 28 including men, women, and children. Eventually the settlement grew to 400, mostly converts from the Delaware. His accomplishments at Schoenbrunn include building the first school and first church in Ohio. As such, it is considered Ohio's first village.

The community lived here only a few short years before pressures of the ongoing war forced them to resettle closer to Coshocton. The war caused the community to move around quite a bit. During the Gnadenhutten Massacre, Zeisberger was a captive of the British at Fort Detroit. After his release, he led many members of the community to Michigan and Ontario, where they resettled.

The village today is reconstructed on the site of the original settlement. There are log cabins, garden patches, and men and women ambling around in period clothing. Reenactments, colonial fairs, and numerous tours take place throughout the year.

From New Philadelphia, head up US 250 to Dover. The most intricate carvings you will likely ever see in your life can be found at the **Warther Museum**, near the intersection of Tuscarawas and West Slingluff Streets in Dover. Ernest "Mooney" Warther made his living making kitchen knives. (In fact, the company he launched in 1902, Warther Cutlery, is still making some of the finest handcrafted knives around.) Carving was just his hobby, but the detailed miniature railroad engines and train cars he made from wood and ivory are beyond compare. Every nut, bolt, and rivet was hand-carved. For accuracy's sake, Mooney ordered copies of the original engineer's designs for whatever engine he was working on. From those plans and photographs, he cut, carved, and assembled works of art. Many of the carvings are displayed with a motor that shows what the train looks like when it is in motion.

His work was popular enough that his brother took the carvings on the road. He would set up in a town and charge folks admission to see Mooney's collection of carvings. These trains, moving dioramas, and other projects are all on display at the museum.

From Dover, head north on OH 800 to OH 212 north. The route follows the contours of the Tuscarawas River and passes through the Historic Zoar Village. This unique historical site is both an outdoor museum of sorts and a place where people live. The village was an experiment in communal living. In 1817 a group of German separatists settled here. For more than 80 years, the community thrived.

The flower gardens in the town square are a great place to begin exploring. Then begin walking down Main Street toward the Zoar Store. This building serves as an information center, and there you can gather more details to plan your visit. One of the best things about Zoar is that its small size allows visitors to walk everywhere, and no matter where you go there's something interesting to see.

Many of the old buildings in Zoar have been repurposed. There are small shops tucked into all sorts of unexpected places. The old cider mill is now the Cider Mill of Zoar Crafting Retreat. The inn features exposed brick walls, thick hand-hewn beams, and a beautiful mural in the common room and is now dedicated to hosting crafting classes and weekend retreats. A spacious, well-lit crafting room is stocked with what seems like acres of worktop space, table lamps, etc. The inn's four guest rooms feature private baths. While no longer an option for the casual tourist, crafters might want to plan a weekend around a stay at the mill.

From Zoar Village, we return again to Amish Country. Take OH 212 North to OH 21 South. When you get to US 250, head west to Wilmot.

THE GARDENS AT ZOAR VILLAGE ARE BEAUTIFULLY MAINTAINED

Many travelers make the trip to Wilmot for the sole purpose of eating a chicken dinner at the Amish Door Restaurant. Fried chicken dinners have been a staple of rural tourism for generations. Where else can you get fresh chicken with all the sides, served family style, better than Grandma used to make? Window shopping at the neighboring cluster of shops selling antiques, quilts, and baskets is the obvious choice for an after-dinner activity.

Every now and then, a visitor comes to Wilmot who doesn't fully appreciate the joys of a country-style meal with all the fixins. That visitor is in luck. Just down the street from the Amish Door is **Beebops Grill**, a small burger joint that serves some of the best burgers in the state of Ohio. No fooling! The hamburgers are thick and juicy. They are stacked too high to fit in an average person's mouth, but with a little work, it can be done. Sides include hand-cut fries and delightfully substantial onion rings.

Beebops has an open challenge for anyone who enjoys putting away more food than is healthy. The challenge involves eating a burger with a pound of meat, onion rings, pickles, cheese, tomatoes, etc. The end product is an 8-inch tower of intestinal disaster, but more people accept the challenge than you might imagine. Will you be one of them?

From Wilmot, head south to Winesburg. This is not the town in the classic

AN ALTERNATIVE TO THE AMISH DOOR RESTAURANT IS BEEBOPS GRILL, JUST DOWN THE STREET

Sherwood Anderson novel, *Winesburg, Ohio*. It is, however, an amazing historical community. Founded in the early 1800s, a large number of the town's original buildings—many of them log cabins—are still being used. In addition to a small grocery and some antiques shops, Winesburg has an excellent B&B, the Grapevine House on Main Street.

The Grapevine House is a sprawling inn. It includes the original home (built in 1834), an adjacent home, and a barn. The Main House has all the guest rooms, five total. The neighboring Erma's House has two rooms, and the Barn has two rooms. These are typically rented out to larger parties looking for more expansive accommodations.

Heading north, our final stop is in the town of Kidron, a mile north of Winesburg. Take County Road 186 north toward Mount Eaton.

Traveling through Amish Country,

visitors often find themselves asking how the Amish do without many of the things we take for granted. How can they make waffles without an electric waffle iron? How do they light their homes after dark? How do they wash, dry, and iron their clothes? Of course, the answers to these questions don't take long to figure out. But then another set of questions arise. Where can you buy a cast-iron waffle iron? Where do you get quality oil lamps? Where can one purchase washboards, handwringers, and extra-large wash tubs?

The answers to the questions in the second are all in the town of Kidron. That's where you will find Lehman's, the famous nonelectric hardware store. A family could, presumably, find everything it needed here to start a home-stead and live off the grid. Lehman's sells farming equipment, carpentry tools, and wood-burning kitchen stoves, just to name a few of the things you probably won't be taking home. They also have everything a family of tourists might be willing to spend money on. There are hand-carved rolling pins, old-timey toys, t-shirts, books, and oodles of snacks.

This explains why Lehman's becomes the busiest place for miles around during warm summer days and on cool fall weekends. It's a nearly perfect expression of what Amish Country is all about for many people: a meeting of Amish simplicity and American tourism.

IN THE AREA

Accommodations

CARLISLE INN, 1357 Old Route 39, Sugarcreek. Call 330-852-2586. Website: dhgroup.com/inns/carlisle-inn-sugarcreek. $$.

CIDER MILL OF ZOAR CRAFTING RETREAT, 198 East Second Street, Zoar. Call 330-874-6111. Website: cidermillofzoar.com. Call for weekend crafting retreat prices.

THE GRAPEVINE HOUSE, 2140 Main Street, Winesburg. Call 330-359-7922. Website: grapevinehouse.com. $$.

INN AT HONEY RUN, 6920 County Road 203, Millersburg. Call 330-674-0011. Website: innathoneyrun.com. $$$$.

LUCAS MALABAR FARM HOSTEL, 3954 Bromfield Road, Lucas. Call 419-892-2055. Website: hiusa.org/lucas. $.

MILLER HAUS BED & BREAKFAST, 3135 County Road 135, Millersburg. Call 330-893-3602. Website: millerhaus.com. $$.

Attractions and Recreation

DENNISON RAILROAD DEPOT MUSEUM, 400 Center Street, Dennison. Call 740-922-6776. Website: dennisondepot.org.

FARM AT WALNUT CREEK, 4147 County Road 114, Sugarcreek. Call 330-893-4200. Website: thefarmatwalnutcreek.com.

GNADENHUTTEN PARK AND MUSEUM, 352 South Cherry Street, Gnadenhutten. Call 740-254-4143.

GUGGISBERG CHEESE COMPANY, 5060 OH 557, Millersburg. Call 330-893-2500. Website: guggisberg.com.

HEINI'S CHEESE CHALET, 6005 County Road 77, Millersburg. Call 330-893-2131. Website: heinis.com.

JOHNSON-HUMRICKHOUSE MUSEUM, 300 North Whitewoman Street, Coshocton. Call 740-622-8710. Website: jhmuseum.org.

MALABAR FARM STATE PARK, 4050 Bromfield Road, Lucas. Call 419-892-2784. Website: malabarfarm.org.

MOHICAN ADVENTURES CANOE LIVERY, 3045 Ohio 3, Loudonville. Call 419-994-4097. Website: mohicanadventures.com.

OHIO STATE REFORMATORY, 100 Reformatory Road, Mansfield. Call 419-522-2644. Website: mrps.org.

RAMSER ARBORETUM, 24565 Danville-Jelloway Road, Danville. Website: ramserarbor.org.

RICHLAND CARROUSEL PARK, 75 North Main Street, Mansfield. Call 419-522-4223. Website: richlandcarrousel.com.

RIVER RUN CANOE LIVERY, 3070 County Road 3175 (Wally Road), Loudonville. Call 419-994-5204. Website: riverrunfamilycampground.com.

SCHOENBRUNN VILLAGE, 1984 East High Avenue, New Philadelphia. Call 330-663-6610 or 740-922-6776. Website: facebook.com/HistoricSchoenbrunnVillage.

TROYER'S COUNTRY MARKET, 5201 County Road 77, Millersburg. Call 330-893-3786. Website: troyerscountrymarket.com.

WARTHER MUSEUM, 331 Karl Avenue, Dover. Call 330-343-7513. Website: thewarthermuseum.com.

Dining

BOYD AND WURTHMANN RESTAURANT, 4819 East Main Street, Berlin. Call 330-893-3287. Website: boydandwurthmann.com. $.

BEEBOPS GRILL, 108 East Main Street, Wilmot. Call 330-359-5300. $.

CONEY ISLAND DINER, 98 North Main Street, Mansfield. Call 419-526-2669. Website: famousconeyisland.com. $.

DENNISON YARD, 313 Center Street, Dennison. Call 740-922-5748. Website: dennisonyard.com. $.

MALABAR FARM RESTAURANT, 3645 Pleasant Valley Road, Perrysville. Call 419-938-5205. Website: malabarfarmrestaurant.com. $$$.

TARRAGON, THE INN AT HONEY RUN, 6920 County Road 203, Millersburg. Call 330-674-0011. Website: innathoneyrun.com/dining. $$$$.

THE WAREHOUSE, 400 North Whitewoman Street, Coshocton. Call 740-622-4001. Website: warehousesteaknstein.com/coshocton. $$.

Other Contacts

COSHOCTON COUNTY CVB, 401 Main Street, Coshocton. Call 740-622-4877 or 1-800-338-4724. Website: visitcoshocton.com.

HOLMES COUNTY CHAMBER OF COMMERCE AND TOURISM BUREAU, 6 West Jackson Street, Millersburg. Call 330-674-3975. Website: holmescountychamber.com

VISIT CANTON/STARK COUNTY, OHIO! 222 Market Avenue North, Canton. Call 1-800-552-6051. Website: visitcanton.com.

THE WATERFRONT IS A CENTERPIECE OF GAHANNA

8

A NATIONAL ROAD,
A STATE CAPITAL

ZANESVILLE, NEWARK, GAHANNA, GRANVILLE, COLUMBUS,
DELAWARE, MOUNT VERNON, GAMBIER

ESTIMATED LENGTH: 150 miles

ESTIMATED TIME: 4.5 hours

HIGHLIGHTS: The route begins on the Old National Road, east of Zanesville, at the National Road–Zane Grey Museum. Passing through Zanesville, you won't want to miss taking some time to view the work of Alan Cottrill at his Sculpture Studio. Continuing west, make two stops—the Flint Ridge State Memorial and Museum and the Blackhand Gorge State Nature Preserve— before you get to Newark. Just south of town is the Great Circle Earthworks and farther down is the Dawes Arboretum. In nearby Grandville, the grandiose Bryn Du Mansion often features gallery exhibitions, offering visitors a little culture when they come for a tour of the property. Then it's on to the Buxton Inn, where guests can settle for the night in one of the town's most historic landmarks. Arriving in Columbus, you might visit the James Thurber House or tour the Ohio Statehouse before heading to German Village, with its incredible bookstore, coffee shops, and authentic German-American restaurants. Leaving Columbus, the tour heads north to a short visit at the Olentangy Indian Caverns, then winds up in Mount Vernon. Perhaps a stay at the Mount Vernon Inn can be arranged. In nearby Gambier, visitors can tour Kenyon College.

GETTING THERE: This trip begins 10 miles east of Zanesville on US 40, continues west through town to Brownsville Road (County Road 668) North. The next stretch follows OH 16 to Newark and Grandville. Then, by way of OH 161 and US 62, the next stop is Gahanna. Continuing west on US 62 into downtown Columbus, the route tools through town then heads north on OH 315 to Delaware. The last leg of the trip heads east by way of OH 3 to Mount Vernon and Gambier.

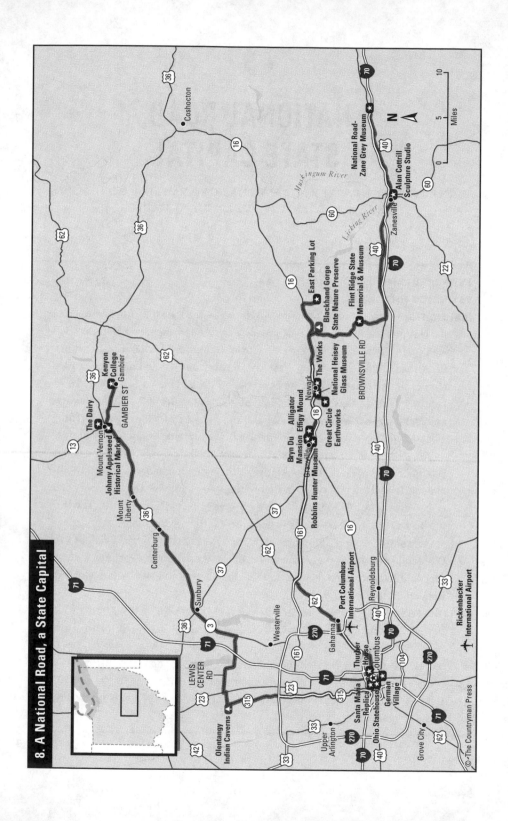

8. A National Road, a State Capital

© The Countryman Press

The earliest overland routes on the Ohio frontier were the trails Native Americans had used for generations. Settlers widened and improved these trails to accommodate horses and wagons. One such route was Zane's Trace. Built by Colonel Ebenezer Zane, by 1797 the road connected Wheeling, West Virginia, with Maysville, Kentucky. The road was a gentle arc that roughly followed the path of US 40 West to Columbus and US 62 South.

In the early 1800s, when the federal government began building its first national road, the plan was to connect the Potomac River in eastern Pennsylvania with the Ohio River. Eventually the road extended westward all the way to St. Louis, on the mighty Mississippi. Zane's Trace made laying the road through a stretch of Ohio easier. The National Road, as it was called, just absorbed the existing route.

Today, US 40 roughly follows the route of the old National Road. In places, you might see signs for Alt US 40. These side roads typically follow the old highway's original path. For cross-country travel, US 40 has largely been usurped by I-70, which 1 mile to the south runs parallel to US 40. But the old route has some charm.

Appropriately enough, a museum commemorating the National Road is found on US 40, just east of Zanesville. The **National Road–Zane Grey Museum** also honors the legacy of Zane Grey, that famous author of western novels who originally hailed from Zanesville. Born in 1872, Pearl Zane Gray (his family later changed the spelling of their last name, and Zane ditched his first name) was the great-grandson of Ebenezer Zane, the founder of Zanesville. Grey was one of the country's first millionaire authors, though he had a heap of critics who found his work lowbrow. Exhibitions tell of his love of fishing—some of his gear is on display—and travel. In addition to telling Grey's life story, the museum shop carries used Zane Grey novels, some of them very rare and very expensive.

Other exhibitions at the museum illustrate the role of the National Road in the history of America's westward push. On it, thousands of early settlers dragged their Conestoga wagons over the Alleghenies and through Ohio, Indiana, and Illinois, seeking a better life on the western frontier. People today lit-

THE CONESTOGA WAGON WAS A LOT BIGGER THAN MANY PEOPLE IMAGINE

THE NATIONAL ROAD WAS A SIGNIFICANT ROUTE FOR PIONEERS TRAVELING WEST

tle realize how truly large these wagons were. Standing beside one at the museum, it becomes easier to imagine how a family could fit an entire life inside it.

From the museum, follow US 40 west to downtown Zanesville. The **Alan Cottrill Sculpture Studio** is on South Sixth Street, a block south of US 40. (In town, it's called Main Street). Sixth is a one-way street, so you will have to cut down a block on Seventh or Fifth Streets and find your way over.

Alan Cottrill has made a life in sculpture. From his studio in Zanesville, he creates large-scale pieces appropriate for public institutions as well as smaller pieces for collectors. When you visit the Alan Cottrill Sculpture Studio, you might get a chance to see the artist at work and ask him about his various projects. Throughout the studio space and upstairs, studies and completed works are on display. The larger pieces typically start out as small models, enlarged before being cast. Many of the original mock-ups can be seen here, along with details as to where to view the final product.

Continuing west, US 40 crosses the Muskingum River on the famous Zanesville Y Bridge. The town straddles the confluence of the Muskingum and Licking Rivers. While other cities might use this as an opportunity to build a few bridges upstream and a few down, the people of Zanesville were crossing the rivers on a Y-shaped bridge as early as 1814. At the center of the original bridge was a tollhouse.

About 13.5 miles after crossing the bridge, our route departs the National

Road and continues onto Brownsville Road (CR 668). The Flint Ridge State Memorial and Museum is on the right, 3 miles north of US 40. For more than 11,000 years, people have quarried flint from this part of Ohio. The stone was used by Native Americans for tools, weapons, and ornamentation—and Flint Ridge flint has been found at archaeological sites all over the eastern United States. Because it's so important to the history of the region, flint is the official state gemstone of Ohio.

Though water has filled most of the ancient quarries scattered throughout the park, the museum was built over the remains of an old pit. Exhibitions illustrate how native peoples extracted flint from the earth and fashioned it to their purposes. There are examples of the tools the Hopewell people would have used to mine flint and shape it into a form that was easy to transport and trade. The property itself takes up more than 500 acres, and two trail loops are open to those who want to hike out and see the various quarry sites.

SCULPTOR ALAN COTTRILL'S WORK IS ON DISPLAY AT HIS STUDIO IN ZANESVILLE

North of Flint Ridge, just off Brushy Fork Road, is the next stop. The **Blackhand Gorge State Nature Preserve** comprises nearly 1,000 acres along the Licking River. The gorge is named for an engraving of a black hand that once appeared on one of its sandstone cliffs. The hand and some other petroglyphs were destroyed when the locks were built, and whatever remained was finished off when crews blasted rock to create a path for the railroad in the 1800s. Blackhand sandstone became the name of the predominant rock formation of the region, a rock especially common in the southwest, in the Hocking Hills.

The nature preserve has three parking lots, each with a trailhead. The 4.26-mile Blackhand Trail connects the main parking lot and the west parking lot. The west parking lot is on Brushy Fork Road. Two side trails along the way could turn this hike into a loop, rather than a 9.5-mile out-and-back. The north parking lot provides access to an excellent 2-mile loop that will guide you through the forest and along a mile of the river.

To get to the north or east parking lots, you will have to go around to the other side of the preserve, taking OH 16 East to Nashport Road and making a quick turn south onto County Road 273. After visiting the preserve, the route continues west on OH 16. Entering Newark from the east, you will see one of the state's most unique architectural displays. The Longaberger Basket Home Office is not easily missed. The company's seven-story HQ is a giant picnic basket—or, more fittingly, a "Longaberger Medium Market Basket," the company's best seller.

Newark organizes itself around a large town square, at the center of which is the Licking County Courthouse. The streets in town are a confusing combination of one-way and two-way thoroughfares. Strangers are as likely to get turned around as not, and yet there's never enough traffic to explain why so many one-way streets are necessary.

East of the courthouse on East Main Street is **Skorpios Gyros**, a small eatery that serves excellent Greek food. There are a couple of tables on the sidewalk, but this restaurant doesn't have a dining room. Most guests walk up to the window, place their order, and take their food to go. The menu offers a nice selection of Greek cuisine, but gyros are the specialty. The gyros are made fresh when you place your order, and the fries come dusted with a special Greek seasoning salt. The cooks can also dress up the fries with feta and olive oil (the Greek Fries) or with gyro meat, onions, and gyro sauce (the Ruble Fries).

Southeast of the courthouse, on First Street, a very unique museum called **The Works** does more than just tell stories about the past. The museum's mission is to engage visitors with technology, the arts, and the history of area industries. It's all about interaction. At The Works, kids as young as nine years old can participate in glassblowing. There are science labs, art galleries, and a print shop. There is a full schedule of classes, camps, and

THIS SPRAWLING GREEN SPACE PRESERVES THE EARTHWORKS IN NEWARK

programs for people of all ages, so if you'd like to learn about something in particular, be sure to time your visit accordingly.

Speaking of glass, a few blocks west of the courthouse, on West Church Street, is the **National Heisey Glass Museum**. Newark was the home of the original A. H. Heisey & Company. For more than 60 years, the company made some of the finest commercial glass products in the country. The quality of Heisey Glass is such that it has become a bit of a collector's item, and the museum here is the property of Heisey Collectors of America, Inc. The company closed in 1957 and sold its molds to Imperial Glass, but when Imperial folded in 1984, Heisey Collectors of America was able to buy most of the original molds. The museum has a full collection of Heisey pieces, from decorative figurines to daily use glassware and serving plates.

The final stop in Newark is a site that harkens back to the period of the Hopewell people. The early culture that quarried flint from the Flint Ridge is also responsible for the **Great Circle Earthworks**, south of Newark off of OH 79. As with most mounds, you need to walk on this one to appreciate it. The circle's diameter is nearly 1,200 feet. After Newark was settled, the community used the mound site as fairgrounds, which in some sense preserved them from being plowed under or pushed aside for building. A small museum on the site shares some of the theories that explain the purpose of the Great Circle Earthworks.

From Newark, follow OH 16 West to the exit for Granville Road. Three miles down the road, you will find yourself in downtown Granville. The New England flavor of Granville is not coincidental. Folks from Granville, Massachusetts, and Granby, Connecticut established the village in 1805. They laid out the town with a distinctly New England sensibility. Roads were centered on a public square, boxed in by churches. The New Englanders, however, were not the first to settle in the area. A group of Welsh immigrants arrived a few years earlier. As you drive around, you may notice many roads named for some of these Welsh families.

The Welsh influence is behind the name of the sprawling estate you will see on your right before you get into town. The **Bryn Du Mansion** was

THE BRYN DU MANSION IS THE CENTER OF A STUNNING PUBLIC ESTATE

originally an Italianate villa built in 1865, but in 1905 it was purchased by John Sutphin Jones, who made a fortune from his ventures in the coal and the railroad industries. Jones had the entire mansion redesigned, and the Georgian-Federal style building you see today is the result. He named the mansion Bryn Du, which means "black hill" in Welsh.

The property passed through the hands of several families before the Village of Granville purchased it in 2002. Since it took ownership, part of the grounds out front has been given over to the township. On Saturday mornings in the summer, these fields are full of kids playing soccer. The mansion itself is used for various events. Polo and field hockey clubs meet here, and a few annual art shows and special art exhibitions take place here as well.

Just west of the mansion is a historic site that significantly predates the nineteenth century. The Alligator Effigy Mound was built sometime between the first century BCE and 400 CE. The people who built the Newark Earthworks may have built this mound as well. No one knows for sure. What is known is that the mound was not a burial site and that it is one of two known animal mounds in the state. The other is **Serpent Mound**, southwest of Chillicothe. The mound sits on a promontory, of sorts, overlooking the Raccoon Valley. To get there, turn north on Bryn du Drive and follow it to the top of the hill.

On your left, as you arrive in town, is one of Granville's most important landmarks: the **Buxton Inn**. This historic hotel has been hosting visitors since 1812 and boasts an impressive list of distinguished guests. Abraham Lincoln, Harriet Beecher Stowe, Henry Ford, and John Philip Sousa all spent a night at the Buxton Inn. The most recent owners have expanded the inn by adding the adjacent property. Today the inn has 25 guest rooms, each decorated with antiques appropriate to the historic setting.

In addition to being the perfect place to stay when visiting the Columbus area, the Buxton Inn has a restaurant and tavern, perfect for an intimate meal or a casual drink. The atmosphere is Colonial, but don't expect pewter flatware. The menu is mainly steak and seafood—classic American dishes done right.

The inn is within walking distance of such sites as the Denison Museum, the Granville Lifestyle Museum, and the **Robbins Hunter Museum**. This last one is a historic property. The museum preserves the Avery-Downer House, a fine example of Greek Revival architecture. Construction on it was completed in 1842, and it was a private residence for about 60 years before it became a fraternity house and then a sorority house for students at nearby Denison University. Over the years, additions were made to the original house, and now the grand abode boasts twenty-seven rooms—though not all of them are open for tours.

The Counting House, at the back of the property, was brought here from nearby Newark by Robbins Hunter to be used for his antiques business.

It was originally a bank. The Robbins Hunter Museum is open to visitors Wednesday through Saturday. The property is closed in the winter.

Downtown Granville is a nice place for a walk. There are a couple of places to grab a bite to eat. For your morning coffee, there's a small diner, a coffee shop, and Whit's Frozen Custard. If you like your coffee extra fancy, stick with the coffee shop. But if you're simply looking for a solid cup of joe, Whit's beats the competition by offering a cup for just fifty cents. Add a muffin to the order, and you're all set to take on the morning. When the weather's good, you can take your order outside to the patio tables. Whit's also hides one of the best places for lunch around.

The narrow staircase to the left of the Whit's cash register leads up to Granville's best-kept secret: The Soup Loft. At the top of the stairs is a small kitchen that is not unlike the kitchen set from *I Love Lucy*. A counter separates the food prep from the masses, and there is little space for dining in. The menu is simple: sandwiches, salads, and soup. The restaurant makes all the food fresh daily. There are a couple of soups you will find every time—regulars love the tomato pesto and goat cheese soup—and daily specials are for more adventurous diners.

From Granville, head west on OH 161 to US 62 South. The road feeds traffic into the heart of Gahanna. This village was founded on the banks of Big Walnut Creek. In Gahanna's early years, the creek powered a local mill, which was a critical part of the settlement's success. The creek still plays a role in the economic health of the community. A large plaza on the water, Creekside Gahanna, features fountains, pools, waterfalls, and flower beds leading down to a paved trail along the creek. The plaza is the centerpiece of an active downtown.

It's just a short walk from this attractive public space to places like the nearby Old Bag of Nails Pub and the **Gahanna Grill**. The Grill is known for its famous Beanie Burger. Now, before you vegetarians rejoice, this isn't a meat-free burger made from black beans. The Beanie Burger is a bacon cheeseburger with sautéed onions and house-made coleslaw. The menu has a lot of variety, from wraps to seafood. Best of all, it's a local establishment that has been serving folks in Gahanna since 1939.

The Gahanna Historical Society owns and operates a bed and breakfast in town. The **Lily Stone Bed & Breakfast** is for everyone who has ever stayed at a B&B and wished the décor featured more floral prints. The walls, curtains, and linens of each of the inn's four guest rooms are tastefully blossoming with that characteristic Victorian flare. The home was built in 1900 and is the only B&B in the country owned by a historical society. Best of all, this is one of the most affordable places in town to stay.

From Gahanna, we turn now to Columbus proper. Following US 62 west just past I-71, turn right onto Jefferson Avenue and subsequently into the heart of the Jefferson Avenue Historic District. From 1913 to 1917, James

THE COLUMBUS SKYLINE OVERLOOKS THE SCIOTO RIVER

Thurber's family lived in the house at the end of the block. Thurber attended Ohio State University during this time.

In recent years, in part because of the marketing surrounding the movie adaptation of Thurber's short story "The Secret Life of Walter Mitty," there's been some renewed interest in Thurber's life and work. Thurber was born in 1894 in Columbus. He attended college here and then moved away to serve during World War I. He returned to Columbus for a short time (1921–1924) and wrote for the *Columbus Dispatch,* after which he moved to New York and got a job writing for *The New Yorker.* That's when his career really took off. By the time he died in 1961, he was a noted essayist, short fiction writer, and illustrator. His cartoons appeared regularly in *The New Yorker.*

The **Thurber House** on Jefferson Avenue is now a museum and nonprofit writing center. Parts of the house are preserved as the Thurbers would have had them. Other rooms are dedicated exhibition spaces. Across the street from the home, a park and a whimsical statue of a unicorn commemorate one of Thurber's most celebrated stories, "The Unicorn in the Garden."

Ohio Statehouse is less than a mile west on Broad Street. The capitol huddles between the city's skyscrapers on a patch of green known as Cap-

ACROSS FROM THE THURBER HOUSE A SMALL PARK COMMEMORATES ONE OF HIS MOST POPULAR SHORT STORIES

itol Square. A statehouse was first proposed for Columbus in 1838, but construction wasn't completed until 1861. Political wrangling and a cholera epidemic, among other obstacles, slowed progress considerably.

The statehouse is more than just the seat of Ohio's state government. Throughout, there are monuments to important moments and people who have shaped the state's history. The Ohio Statehouse Museum Education Center coordinates guided tours of the statehouse. The tours occur daily, and visitors can take the self-guided audio tour as well.

From the statehouse, drive south on Third Street into Columbus's **German Village**. Beginning in the mid-1800s, Germans arrived in Columbus by the droves. Settling in south Columbus, they created a little Germany of their own. German Village was a place where a family could find other German-speaking newcomers. There was a German-language newspaper, and the public schools taught German to keep tradition alive. After Americans fought Germans in both world wars, the vitality of the village waned. Slowly industry crept into the old residential blocks, and the families left. It wasn't until the early 1960s that the German Village Society was established and began to restore the neighborhood.

The historic buildings on Third Street are just an introduction to the neighborhood, but it's where you find most of the shops and restaurants. The **Pistacia Vera Pastry Kitchen and Café**, for example, is a decadent bakery that serves dishes like ratatouille quiche for brunch. French cuisine dominates the menu, with items such as croissant and quiche, and madeleine and almondine.

Just down the street is the best bookstore in town. The Book Loft of German Village is a sprawling maze of a bookstore. The shop has room after room of books. Instead of relying on a central sound system to pipe music throughout the store, each room and nook has its own CD player. It's difficult to browse for any length of time without wondering how to take some of the music home. The entrance to the bookstore is at the end of a long alley. Be sure to grab a map at the counter. It's not inconceivable that someone could get lost in here. On the other hand, maybe that wouldn't be so bad.

One place where the village's German heritage can be experienced is **Schmidt's Sausage Haus Restaurant**. To get there, take Third Street south to Kossuth Street east. The restaurant is right there at the Purdy Alley. Schmidt's serves classic German dishes like chicken spaetzle, wiener schnitzel, cabbage rolls, and knockwurst. The restaurant is the product of a

CELEBRATE THE CULTURE OF GERMAN VILLAGE AT SCHMIDT'S

family of sausage makers, so you will also find unique sausages on the menu. The restaurant is best known for its specialty, the Bahama Mama sausage platter. If this is your first foray into German cuisine, the buffet has a little bit of everything.

From German Village, head west on I-70 (the entrance ramp is at Fourth Street) and take the first exit north, which is OH 315 (the Olentangy Freeway). About 17.5 miles later, turn west onto Home Road in the town of Delaware. The next stop is on your left, 0.5 mile from the turn.

The **Olentangy Indian Caverns** go back quite a few years. Millions, in fact. It took that many years for water to cut through the solid limestone to create the caves visitors tour today. For last couple hundred years, at least, humans have put the caverns to good use. Native Americans made arrowheads in the caves and maybe even buried their dead here. Cattle rustlers hid here from the law. And since the early part of the last century, tourists

THOUGH SMALL, THE OLENTANGY INDIAN CAVERNS ARE A NICE DIVERSION

have been tramping through this geological underworld. Of course, roadside attractions aren't what they used to be—or maybe it's better to say they're not getting the traffic they used to get—and many speculate whether the Olentangy Indian Caverns will be open to the public a decade from now. But while it's still open, the site makes for a nice, if not short, diversion.

Below ground, there are five named chambers. This makes the caverns seem much bigger than they are. Some "rooms" are so narrow that you might have to back out to let others pass. In fact, you can walk the entire map in less than 5 minutes. That's not to say it isn't interesting, but the most interesting piece might be the museum that visitors pass through as they make their way to the cave entrance.

The first white feller on record to visit the caves was one J. M. Adams. Story has it that Adams was just passing through with a westbound wagon train. One of his livestock wandered away from camp and fell to its death at the cave entrance. So what's a guy to do? Well, if you were J. M. Adams, it would only make sense to look around a bit, carve your name and the date on the wall—J.M. Adams—1821—and continue your trip.

From Delaware, make your way east to OH 3 North. The best route is to follow Home Road east to US 23, and there's a short jog north on US 23 before you continue east on Lewis Center Road. After you pass under I-71, the road becomes Big Walnut Road. When you get to OH 3, it will be called North State Street. Turn left. You will pass Sunbury, Centerburg, and Mount Liberty before arriving in Mount Vernon.

Mount Vernon is the birthplace of one of the more influential, though not readily recognized, individuals in American music history. Daniel Decatur Emmett, who was born here in 1815, wrote such recognizable tunes as "The Blue Tail Fly" (a.k.a., "Jimmy Crack Corn"), "Old Dan Tucker," and "Dixie" (a.k.a., "I Wish I Was in Dixieland"). The latter has become the unofficial anthem of the South, and it has contributed to the American lexicon with phrases like "You ain't just whistling 'Dixie.'" These songs and Emmett himself contributed to the development of early minstrel shows.

Mount Vernon is also the home of Mount Vernon Nazarene University. It's a small private college with just over a couple thousand students. As such, the town has a handful of great bed and breakfasts doing a fair trade in housing visiting parents, business travelers, and weekend tourists. One of the nicest is the **Mount Vernon Inn** on West High Street. This B&B is pretty high-end. From the street, Mount Vernon Inn appears to be a quaint brick home with white trim. The inn, however, is much larger than that first impression might suggest. The back of the property features a separate L-shaped hotel. Between the two, paths meander through beautiful gardens, of which all the guest rooms have a view. This is more a boutique hotel than a B&B, but the breakfast is still a gourmet affair.

North of Mount Vernon on OH 3 (a.k.a., North Main Street to Wooster

Johnny Appleseed

Before beer became America's dominant adult beverage, we had cider. Hard cider, that is. To make hard cider, you need apples. The tricky thing is that it takes a long time for an apple tree grown from seed to produce fruit. So when a family moved to western Pennsylvania, Ohio, and Indiana—those lands newly opened to settlement in the early nineteenth century—they either needed to wait many years for cider or find someone with an apple nursery.

That's how John Chapman made his mark. Roaming far and wide along the frontier country, he bought up small plots of land to plant, grow, and sell apple trees. The first recorded landholding of John Chapman, also known as Johnny Appleseed, was here in Mount Vernon, on the Kokosing River. An Ohio Historical Marker on Phillips Drive, just west of Main Street, north of the Aqueduct, commemorates this local connection to the legendary figure.

Johnny Appleseed was known for his gregarious nature and his somewhat unorthodox religious views. In addition to facilitating the spread of apple trees throughout the region, he was a committed Swedenborgian. As such, as he traveled between his many nurseries he acted as a missionary for the New Church—a movement built on the writings of Emmanuel Swedenborg. Among other things, Swedenborg claimed the Last Judgment already took place in 1757.

Johnny Appleseed believed physical deprivation in life earned a soul heavenly riches in death. The classic Swedenborgian image is of a man who wore no shoes and dressed in not much more than decency required. It is unclear if he ever had a home of his own— he stayed with family when he could and otherwise slept outdoors and relied on the kindness of those he met on the road. And even though he put up few barriers to the elements, slept on the floors and porches of farmers he did business with and lived what we would consider a truly grueling nomadic life, he lived to be at least 80 years old.

Road) is **The Dairy**. There are some things on its menu that folks might tend to avoid. Fish tail, pork tenderloin, and breaded veal aren't what you'd expect to see next to nachos and foot-long hot dogs. But if you've come to The Dairy for dinner, you've missed the point. This is a dairy product retailer and wholesaler that makes and serves excellent ice cream on-site. With a ready supply of fresh hard scoop ice cream, the parlor serves all the usual concoctions—from a scoop of your favorite in a waffle cone to a Boston shake. They even have soft serve, if that's your thing.

The next town on the itinerary is Gambier, the home of Kenyon College. To get there, drive east on Gambier Street. Less than 5 miles down the road, you will come to West Wiggins. Turn left (west), and you will soon be at the center of Gambier and on the Kenyon College campus.

For readers of English literature, the mention of Kenyon College immediately brings to mind that most esteemed of publications, the *Kenyon Review*. Founded in 1939 and for the first 21 years of its existence, the *Review* was edited by John Ransom Crowe, the poet, critic, and agrarian theorist. Crowe was also a faculty member at Kenyon. Those were the halcyon days that English majors dream of recreating as they strive for a life of letters. Here on the campus of Kenyon College—one of the finest liberal arts colleges in the country—it's easy to imagine a world where a betweeded professor spends a lifetime mentoring promising students, writing important articles on contemporary literary criticism, and gathering leading writers together to explain the craft. In fact, much of that is still going on.

The Gambier House Bed and Breakfast, at the corner of Gambier and Acland Streets, is an excellent B&B offering guests five rooms and a carriage house. The innkeepers serve a gourmet breakfast every morning, and the location simply cannot be beat. The inn is just a block away from the heart of Kenyon College, and The Village Inn and Gambier Deli are just around the corner.

The food at **The Village Inn** is not exotic or unfamiliar, but the traditional tavern menu has been tweaked to attract a wide audience—from local diners to families in town visiting students. Instead of offering the usual burger (served on white-bread buns) and fries (which go from the freezer to the fryer), burgers are served on a brioche roll, and the fries are hand-cut in-house. Or you can spice up the order with sweet potato fries. The coleslaw is house-made, and the fish and chips are served with a pineapple tartar sauce. A favorite with regulars is the famous VI Mac & Cheese. Swap out the typical macaroni and American cheese with cavatappi (read: fancy macaroni) and the smoked Gouda, and toss with andouille sausage, onions, and peppers, and you have a recipe for gourmet comfort food.

IN THE AREA

Accommodations

BUXTON INN, 313 East Broadway, Granville. Call 740-587-0001. Website: buxtoninn.com. $$.

THE GAMBIER HOUSE BED AND BREAKFAST, 107 East Wiggin Street, Gambier. Call 740-427-2668. Website: gambierhouse.com. $$.

LILY STONE BED & BREAKFAST, 106 South High Street, Gahanna. Call 614-476-1976. Website: gahannahistory.com/stay. $$.

MOUNT VERNON INN, 601 West High Street, Mount Vernon. Call 740-392-9881. Website: themountvernoninn.com. $$.

Attractions and Recreation

ALAN COTTRILL SCULPTURE STUDIO, 110 South Sixth Street, Zanesville. Call 740-453-9822. Website: alancottrill.com.

BLACKHAND GORGE STATE NATURE PRESERVE, 5213 Rock Haven Road, Newark. Call 740-763-4411. Website: naturepreserves.ohiodnr.gov/blackhandgorge.

BRYN DU MANSION, 537 Jones Road, Granville. Call 740-587-7053. Website: bryndu.com.

THE DAIRY, 300 Wooster Road, Mount Vernon. Call 740-393-3156. The Dairy is open year-round, but it closes much earlier in the winter months. Website: thedairyshoppe.com.

GERMAN VILLAGE, 588 South Third Street, Columbus. Call 614-222-4747. Website: germanvillage.com.

GREAT CIRCLE EARTHWORKS, 455 Hebron Road, Heath. Call 1-800-589-8224. Website: ohiohistory.org/visit/museum-and-site-locator/newark-earthworks.

NATIONAL HEISEY GLASS MUSEUM, 169 West Church Street, Newark. Call 740-345-2932. Website: heiseymuseum.org.

NATIONAL ROAD–ZANE GREY MUSEUM, 8850 East Pike, Norwich. Call 1-800-752-2602. Website: ohiohistory.org/visit/museum-and-site-locator/national-road-and-zane-grey-museum.

OHIO STATEHOUSE, 1 Capitol Square, Columbus. Call 614-752-9777. Website: ohiostatehouse.org.

OLENTANGY INDIAN CAVERNS, 1779 Home Road, Delaware. Call 740-548-7917. Website: olentangyindiancaverns.com.

ROBBINS HUNTER MUSEUM, 221 East Broadway, Granville. Call 740-587-0430. Website: robbinshunter.org.

THURBER HOUSE, 77 Jefferson Avenue, Columbus. Call 614-464-1032. Website: thurberhouse.org.

THE WORKS: OHIO CENTER FOR HISTORY, ART & TECHNOLOGY, 55 South First Street, Newark. Call 740-349-9277. Website: attheworks.org.

Dining

GAHANNA GRILL, 82 Granville Streer, Gahanna. Call 614-476-9017. Website: gahannagrill.com. $$.

PISTACIA VERA PASTRY KITCHEN AND CAFÉ, 541 South Third Street, Columbus. Call 614-220-9070. Website: pistaciavera.com. $.

SCHMIDT'S SAUSAGE HAUS RESTAURANT, 240 East Kossuth Street, Columbus. Call 614-444-6808. Website: schmidthaus.com. $$.

SKORPIOS GYROS, 112 East Main Street, Newark. Call 740-322-6292. $.

THE VILLAGE INN, 102 Gaskin Avenue, Gambier. Call 740-427-2112. Website: villageinngambier.com. $.

Other Contacts

CONVENTION AND VISITOR BUREAU OF WORTHINGTON, 579 High Street, Worthington. Call 614-841-2545. Website: visitworthingtonohio.com.

DELAWARE COUNTY TOURISM BUREAU, 34 South Sandusky Street, Delaware. Call 740-368-4748. Website: visitdelohio.com.

9

THE WIDE OHIO RIVER

PORTSMOUTH, IRONTON, GALLIPOLIS, POINT
PLEASANT (WV), BELPRE, PARKERSBURG (WV),
MARIETTA, WOODSFIELD

ESTIMATED LENGTH: 205 miles

ESTIMATED TIME: 4.5 hours

HIGHLIGHTS: Following the Ohio River upstream, this trip begins in Portsmouth with a tour of the Southern Ohio Museum. Heading east on US 52 to Ironton, nature lovers can plan a picnic or hike at the Lake Vesuvius Recreation Area. The route continues out of Ironton on OH 7. In Gallipolis, you will visit the Our House Tavern and the French Art Colony before taking a short side trip to the Bob Evans Farm near Rio Grande. Returning to the Ohio River, brief cross over into West Virginia to visit the Port Pleasant River Museum. OH 7 tends to bypass a few of the towns on the river. If you remain near the water, however, you will always find the way through. After Pomeroy, you have a decision to make. You can either cut straight across to Belpre on OH 7 or take the more scenic route along the river on OH 124. In Belpre, there's the Farmer's Castle Museum Education Center, and across the river in Parkersburg, you can catch a boat out to the Blennerhassett Island State Park. The final town on the route is Marietta, which has the Campus Martius Museum and the Valley Gem Sternwheeler, as well as the quaint Harmar Village. Afterwards, head up the Little Muskingum River. The OH 26 to Woodsfield route is a scenic drive through wooded hills, with a number of covered bridges.

GETTING THERE: The trip begins in Portsmouth, on the Ohio River. US 23 passes through town, and both north and south of the city it has access to interstates. From Portsmouth, the route essentially parallels the Ohio River all the way to Marietta. The route starts on US 52 then follows OH 7. In Pomeroy, OH 7 continues north, but you will jump onto OH 124 heading east. Near Belpre, the path rejoins OH 7, which continues on to Marietta. The final leg of the trip chases a windy route up the Little Muskingum River, along OH 26 to Woodsfield.

LEFT: THIS PLANK WALKWAY CROSSES THE MUSKINGUM TO HARMAR VILLAGE

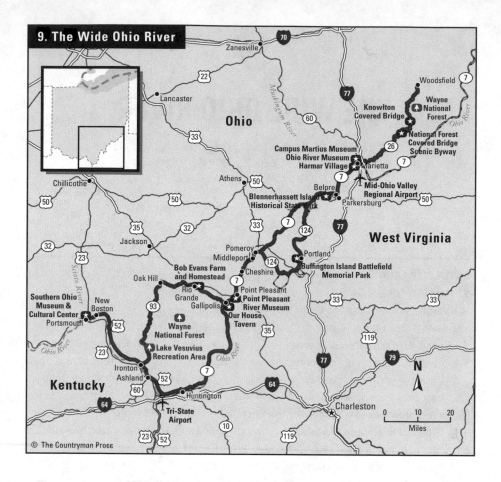

9. The Wide Ohio River

Zanesville

Ohio

West Virginia

Kentucky

Chillicothe

Lancaster

Athens

Woodsfield

Knowlton Covered Bridge

Wayne National Forest

National Forest Covered Bridge Scenic Byway

Campus Martius Museum
Ohio River Museum
Harmar Village

Marietta

Mid-Ohio Valley Regional Airport

Belpre

Parkersburg

Blennerhassett Island Historical State Park

Jackson

Pomeroy
Middleport

Portland

Bob Evans Farm and Homestead

Cheshire

Buffington Island Battlefield Memorial Park

Oak Hill

Rio Grande

Point Pleasant
Point Pleasant River Museum

Southern Ohio Museum & Cultural Center

New Boston

Gallipolis

Our House Tavern

Portsmouth

Wayne National Forest

Lake Vesuvius Recreation Area

Ironton
Ashland

Huntington

Tri-State Airport

Charleston

Kentucky

N

0   10   20
Miles

© The Countryman Press

When the famed birder John James Audubon floated down the Ohio River in 1808, he was traveling along what would become a main route for settlers making their way into the interior of the new nation. From Shippingport, Pennsylvania, travelers floated south and west; the Falls of the Ohio, near Louisville, were all that slowed their progress to the Mississippi. Once in Missouri, they picked up trails heading west.

Audubon and his new wife were traveling the Ohio River, together with his business partner, on their way to make their fortune in Louisville, Kentucky. The travel was easy-going on a river boat—the current simply carried them all the way. With little to do, Audubon's attentive eye was trained on the passing landscape, "gazing all day on the grandeur and beauty of the wild scenery around us." He later recalled, "Nature, in her varied arrangements, seems to have felt a partiality towards this portion of our country. As the traveller ascends or descends the Ohio, he cannot help remarking that alternately, nearly the whole length of the river, the margin, on one side, is bounded by lofty hills and a rolling surface, while on the other, extensive plains of the richest alluvial land are seen as far as the eye can command the view."

While the view has changed somewhat over the past two centuries—now small towns border the river, bridges cross it, and stretches of industry line it—much of the landscape remains the same. The Appalachian Mountains featured so predominantly in nearby Pennsylvania and West Virginia, spill over the Ohio River in the form of the Appalachian Plateau, which consists of rolling foothills that give Southeast Ohio a distinctly more rugged character than the rest of the state. Over the eons, the river-cut path through the plateau has created soaring bluffs and flood-enriched flats along the river's edge. The Ohio River National Scenic Byway begins where the river leaves Pennsylvania, near East Liverpool, Ohio. From there it follows the river, meandering to the south and west. The waterway serves as the southern border for Ohio, Indiana, and Illinois before emptying into the mighty Mississippi.

Towns along this stretch of the Ohio—the eastern two-thirds of the river—do not enjoy the prosperity found in more populous cities like Cincinnati or Columbus. Many of the towns along the river are small and easy to miss, but there are notable exceptions, such as Marietta and Parkersburg (West Virginia), just to name two.

The story of the Underground Railroad features prominently along the western stretches of the Ohio River. The river was the boundary between slave-holding Kentucky and free Ohio. Along the eastern run of the river, much of the history centers on the early republic. Gallipolis, for example, was settled by French aristocrats who were fleeing pre-revolutionary France. The Our House Tavern celebrates this heritage with a gallery of artifacts, much of it chronicling the relationships that these immigrants maintained with the old country. In Marietta, the **Campus Martius Museum** tells the story of the settling of the Ohio River Valley, a process begun with trappers and traders in the decades before the Revolutionary War.

For this route, we will not go with the flow. Rather, we will travel upstream from Portsmouth to Marietta, taking in the sites as they come.

When traveling, there are the usual attractions that simply can't be missed, especially those cultural institutions that tell the story of a community. But to really get a feel for a place as the locals know it requires something else. Some time at the hardware store, perhaps. Or better yet, a visit to the favorite local grub stand. This trip begins with two places to help you achieve these goals.

Portsmouth was born out of necessity. The original settlement in the area, at the confluence of the Ohio and Scioto River, was a town called Alexandria. Its settlers built it a little downstream on lower ground. For more than ten years, the little burg bore the brunt of the river's frequent flooding. With an aim to resettle on higher ground, Portsmouth was founded in 1803 on the east side of the Scioto. Today, there are few buildings near the water west of the Scioto, and the flood plain up the Scioto is now an irregular patchwork of farm fields.

Portsmouth is the county seat of Scioto County. Aside from the structures of county government, portions of downtown are dominated by Shawnee State University. On Gallia Street, you will find the **Southern Ohio Museum and Cultural Center**. The finest museum around, the Center has permanent exhibitions celebrating the work of the twentieth-century painter

PORTSMOUTH HAS A GREAT REGIONAL MUSEUM

Clarence Holbrook Carter. Born in Portsmouth, Carter went on to earn national recognition for his work. Another exhibition showcasing local mastery goes back thousands of years. The Art of the Ancients collection comprises more than 10,000 artifacts produced by the Adena and Hopewell cultures in Ohio.

Heading east from the museum, Gallia Street merges with US 52. About 3 miles away, after US 52 splits into two one-way streets, you will see a popular eatery on the right. **Hickie's Old Fashion Hamburger Inn** may not blow you away with curb appeal, but this place is the place to get a burger. The mailing address says Portsmouth, but Hickie's is actually in the tiny village of New Boston (which is nearly surrounded by its sprawling neighbor). Hickie's is best known for the Big Yogi: three hamburger patties stacked high and topped with cheese, coleslaw, tomatoes, onion, and pickles. They also serve an excellent bean soup.

THE OLD BOB EVANS FARMHOUSE IS A MUSEUM THAT REMEMBERS THE GROWTH OF THE SAUSAGE EMPIRE

From one county seat to another, continue east on US 52 to Ironton, the seat for Lawrence County. The Wayne National Forest is an imposing presence on a local map. The northern half of the county is national forest, and this presents an opportunity for camping and hiking. The **Lake Vesuvius Recreation Area** has four campgrounds and a number of trails for day hikes and overnight backpacking. For a quick visit, the Rock House Trail is a short three-quarters-of-a-mile. In the spring, this is one of the best places to see wildflowers. The recreation area is about 6.5 miles north of Ironton on OH 93. (In town, it's called Park Drive.)

The next stop is near the town of Rio Grande. There are two ways to get there. You can return to US 52 and follow the river around to Gallipolis. Along the way in Sybene, US 52 breaks to the south and hugs the West Virginia side of the West Virginia–Kentucky border. Our route continues along the river, however, on what is now OH 7. Or you can cut your drive time in half and bypass a section of the scenic river drive by taking OH 93 25 miles north to the town of Oak Hill. From town, take OH 279 East to US 35 East. The next exit is for Rio Grande. From there, follow the signs to the **Bob Evans Farm and Homestead**.

This small farming community, 10 miles west of Gallipolis, is where it all started—at least for the folks who enjoy Bob Evans sausage and restaurants. The Evans family lived in the brick farmhouse for 20 years. Bob and Jewell Evans raised their children here, and when Bob had a hard time finding decent sausage for his small diner in Gallipolis, he started making his own, right here on the farm. Pretty soon he opened a small restaurant out front, and what was originally called The Sausage Shop became the first Bob Evans Restaurant. The sausage business and the restaurant business continued to grow, and now you will find their bright red dining rooms all over the Midwest, as far west as Kansas, and south into Florida.

The family home is now the Bob Evans Homestead Museum. Exhibitions throughout explain different aspects of the family and their business—how it all began, the advent of television advertising, and how the restaurant could quickly produce so many biscuits. After touring the museum, visitors often stop for a meal at the original Bob Evans, which now seats 142 guests. The restaurant has a large gift shop up front as well.

TRY THE FRENCH ART COLONY FOR SOME CULTURAL EXPOSURE

The Mothman Cometh

Point Pleasant is home to one of the country's oddest tales: the legend of the Mothman. In the years 1966 and 1967, numerous witnesses reported seeing a large winged man with glowing red eyes in and around Point Pleasant, West Virginia. Sightings reported the local paper, and the story took on a life of its own. In his book *The Mothman Prophecies*, John Keel connects the ominous sightings with the tragic collapse of the Silver Bridge that took 46 lives a week before Christmas in 1967.

The creature defies categorization. Unlike the Yeti, which has a possible (if not implausible) story to explain its existence, the Mothman doesn't appear to be a known species. Sasquatch, at least, could be an undiscovered primate of some kind. The sightings, as well, don't fit the usual pattern for extraterrestrial contact. Some have even raised the supernatural as an explanation, with little traction.

What's left is something quite unexplainable. What did these people see? Was it an unusually husky sandhill crane? An elaborate hoax? An unearthly harbinger of doom for commuters on the Silver Bridge?

Today the story lives on in movies and on television. It's the stuff the tabloids are made of. Point Pleasant has embraced the whole story. From an annual weeklong Mothman Festival and a stainless-steel statue in town to a Mothman research center, this urban legend has become synonymous with this small town on the Ohio River.

Returning to the river by way of US 35 East, the next town you will pull into is Gallipolis. Few towns have as unique a pedigree as Gallipolis (pronounced galli-po-LEECE). Founded in 1790, the town was established by French aristocrats. Some five hundred well-to-do French refugees fled there during the French Revolution and settled on the Ohio River. This expatriate community maintained ties with its families in France for generations. In fact, Napoleon's ex-girlfriend is said to have been a member of the community, and in later years, Gallipolis would host dignitaries from the homeland.

In 1825, the Revolutionary War hero General Lafayette visited Gallipolis and stayed at the Our House Tavern. The original innkeeper is said to have stood on the dock, encouraging new arrivals to "Come on up to our house" as they disembarked from their boats. The name stuck. Built in 1819 by Henry Cushing, the tavern had a dining room and a taproom. There was also a large ballroom for special events.

The tavern is now a museum. Many of the rooms are presented as they may have looked when the tavern and dining room were active. The upstairs ballroom is dedicated to the history of Gallipolis and the French Five Hundred and includes many pieces donated by descendants of the town's founding families.

Continuing the Gallic theme, just down the street from the **Our House Museum** is **The French Art Colony**. What began as a place offering painting lessons has grown into a fully developed institution for the promotion of the arts. Unlike a museum gallery with a permanent collection, the French Art Colony focuses on education, using its gallery space to display a wide variety of art. Check the website for a list of current events. You may find anything from a show by local artists to an exhibition of antiques from a local collector.

Just upstream and across the river, in West Virginia, is the town of Point Pleasant. The area is often remembered for the tragic collapse of the Silver Bridge and possibly for the legend of the Mothman. But these events go back almost fifty years and are not nearly as fresh in people's minds as they once were. Cross the Ohio River on US 35, then jump on WV 2 to cross the Kanawha River. Once off the ramp, turn left onto Third Street and then left onto Main Street. Just before the park with the Point Pleasant Battlefield Monument, you will find the **Point Pleasant River Museum**.

This unique museum explores the river—from its ecology to the history of its navigation. It contains a large tank stocked with the fish and other aquatic life common to the area, offering visitors a chance to see what happens underwater. The water is a cloudy brew that replicates the natural habitat of these creatures. Artifacts from the river's steamboat days, models of old ships, and salvaged relics from the river are all on display.

The museum sits right next to the flood wall at the confluence of two rivers, which protects the town from the rivers' fickle ways. Those not used to living this close to water might find the high concrete barricade interesting. The opening of the wall, through which the road passes, can be closed quickly with a wide stack of slats that fits into the grooves along the sides. Following the flood wall to the right on the outside, you will see a series of murals facing the Ohio River. They extend from the state park all the way up to Fifth Street.

At only four acres, the **Tu-Endie-Wei State Park** is rather modest by state park standards, but there's a lot happening here. Primarily, the park commemorates the battle between the frontier settlers and the forces of Chief Cornstalk. This was the site of a decisive victory for the settlers in 1774. Geographically, the point was an important crossroads. The Wyandot called it Tu-Endie-Wei, meaning "point between two waters." In 1749, a Frenchman named Pierre Joseph de Celoron de Blainville buried a marker here to claim the land for France. In 1796, settlers built the log house you see here as a tavern.

Heading east on OH 7, you will pass through the towns of Addison and Cheshire before arriving in Middleport. (OH 7 bypasses the town, so watch

THE POINT PLEASANT RIVER MUSEUM RECALLS LIFE ON THE OHIO

for the turnoff onto Hobson Drive.) A block from the Ohio River, Second Street is the main route through town. Close to downtown is the stunning **Downing House Bed & Breakfast**. Built in 1859 by a riverboat captain, this painted brick home captures the feel and comfort of nineteenth-century Middleport. The captain, John B. Downing, crossed paths with Samuel Clemens during the famous writer's riverboat days. The rooms of the inn, therefore, reference Mark Twain and two of his more famous characters—Becky Thatcher and Huckleberry Finn. Also on site is a fantastic antique and gift shop, called "by Hearth & Candlelight." This is a great place to visit, whether you're passing through or plan on spending more than a day in Middleport or nearby Pomeroy.

After leaving Middleport and passing through Pomeroy, you have a decision to make. The next stop is in Belpre, and the quickest way there is OH 7, which leaves the winding Ohio River behind and more or less makes a northwesterly beeline. If you choose the back route (OH 2 to OH 68) and stay along the river, you will nearly double your mileage and your time. The small payoff would particularly interest Civil War Buffs. Just west of the small town of Portland is the **Buffington Island Battlefield Memorial Park**.

The Battle of Buffington Island was the largest Civil War battle to take place in Ohio. The conflict was precipitated by the Confederate raider, Brigadier General John Hunt Morgan, who was having a fine time terrorizing communities along the Ohio River in southern Ohio and Indiana in the summer of 1863. When the troops showed up, Morgan tried to steal away and ford the river near Buffington Island. With the ford already defended by local militia, Morgan decided to camp the night and let his men get some rest. The next day, on July 19, the Union and Confederate forces clashed. Morgan's troops took the worst of it. Though Morgan managed to avoid being seized by the Union, he was captured a week later and sent to a federal prison in Columbus—from which he later escaped.

The battle did not take place on the island—thus the memorial, a fieldstone obelisk, is located where the battle did take place, in the hilly country above Portland, northwest of the island.

The town of Belpre sits in the elbow crook of a right-angle bend in the Ohio River. A little downstream, and officially on the West Virginia side of the river, is the historic Blennerhassett Island. Across from town, where the Little Kanawha River feeds the Ohio, is the town of Parkersburg, West Virginia. The two towns are connected by the Memorial Bridge and the Fifth Street Bridge.

Belpre is the smaller of the pair. It is the home to the Middleton Doll Company and describes itself as the "Baby Doll Capital of the World." There is an interesting little museum on Ridge Street, the **Farmer's Castle Museum Education Center**, which shares the history of Belpre.

Across the river, however, there is much to explore. We won't dive too deep—this is a book about Ohio, after all—but it would be a shame to be this close and miss the **Blennerhassett Island Historical State Park**. To get to the island, you need to head to the Blennerhassett Museum in Parkersburg. From there, you buy tickets for the sternwheeler Island Belle. Regular hourly departures are scheduled throughout the summer.

This palatial mansion was built between 1798 and 1800 by Harman and Margaret Blennerhassett, who had recently emigrated from Ireland's County Kerry. At this time, most of the region was still wilderness; the primary settlements clung to the Ohio River. This 7,000-square-foot home—which would have been considered grand even in the more sophisticated East—was simply stunning in its rustic setting. Sadly, the Blennerhassetts got mixed up in post-Revolutionary politics. The home became the headquarters of Aaron Burr's Southwest Conspiracy, which was his alleged attempt to create an independent nation in the middle of the continent with the help of Spanish allies. When the president ordered Burr arrested on conspiracy charges, militia from West Virginia sacked the mansion and the family fled. After being arrested and released, and failing as a cotton grower in Mississippi and a lawyer in Montreal, Harman Blennerhassett returned to Europe. He eventually settled in the Channel Islands, where he died in 1831. Abandoned, the home burned to the ground in 1811. The state reconstructed it and opened it for visitors in 1991.

Today the estate is open for tours. Like the original mansion, the new home sits at the east end of the island, facing upstream. The main part of the home is flanked by two wings, each connected to the house by a covered

THE LAFAYETTE HOTEL OVERLOOKS THE OHIO RIVER IN MARIETTA

walkway. In addition to the sternwheeler ride and the mansion tour, guests can take a horse-drawn wagon ride around the island.

Taking its name from the mansion, **The Blennerhassett Hotel** in downtown Parkersburg may not have the same pedigree as the mansion, but it is quite nice. The hotel dates from 1889. The rooms have an upscale European feel, each decorated individually. The hotel is also a half-mile from the **Julia-Ann Square Historic District** and the adjacent Avery Street Historic District. Julia-Ann Square hosts numerous activities throughout the year and publishes a brochure for a self-guided tour of the district's 126 historic homes.

Twenty minutes north of Belpre and Parkersburg is the last of the big towns on this route. Upstream from Cincinnati, Marietta is the most prosperous of the state's river communities. Numerous museums, festivals, a picturesque riverfront, and great food all combine to make this a place to spend at least a day.

The **Lafayette Hotel** overlooks the meeting of the Muskingum and Ohio Rivers. From the waterfront, you can see both bridges that cross the water to the historic Harmar Village and those that connect Ohio with West Virginia. It was here that General Lafayette landed in 1825 on his tour of the Ohio River. A plaque marks the spot. The current hotel was built in 1925 to replace the burning of the Bellvue Hotel on the same site. Like most hotels of that era, each room seems to have a different shape. If you remember, ask for a room with a river view.

THERE ARE VARIOUS OPTIONS FOR DINING IN MARIETTA. IF YOU LIKE MEXICAN, CHECK OUT TAMPICO ON SECOND STREET

Two nearby museums capture the history of the town and the region. The first to visit is the Campus Martius Museum on Second Street. This sprawling, multistory facility is a gold mine for history buffs interested in the Old Northwest Territory. This museum has it all, from a Conestoga wagon to a birch-bark canoe. There are artifacts from the region's earliest settlements, oil paintings and prints of the men and women who made the history, an old log cabin, eighteenth-century uniforms . . . the list goes on and on. Plan to roam for several hours if you're the type to stop, read, and take it all in. The lower level features a look at Marietta during the twentieth century, with photos and recreated storefronts.

The second museum is the **Ohio River Museum**, which is on Front Street, a block

THE LEVEE HOUSE OFFERS FINE DINING ON THE RIVER

behind the Campus Martius Museum. Outside on the Muskingum River, the museum maintains the sternwheel towboat *W. P. Snyder Jr.* Kids can explore an actual pilot house, and there are numerous models and displays to round out this collection. Both of these museums charge admission. You could buy a pass to both, which would cost just a little more than the price of one.

To continue the theme of paddle boats on the river, you will want to tour the **Valley Gem Sternwheeler**, a block or so down from Campus Martius, on the water. The Valley Gem is a sternwheeler built for the Muskingum River. Its narrow width allows the boat to pass through the river's hand-operated locks. In fact, the boat recently made an overnight trip all the way upstream to Zanesville. The regular schedule includes dinner cruises, lock cruises, and culinary events.

The final historic stop in Marietta proper is **The Castle**. One look and you will understand the sobriquet. With its thick black iron fence and the home's looming octagonal tower, the property gives the impression of being quite defensible. Construction on the building began in 1855, and it has been the home of many a prominent Marietta citizen. Today it's a great place to learn about the town. Docent-led tours last a little less than an hour, and The Castle is open every day in the summer but Wednesday. Check the site for other seasons.

About now, you're getting hungry, so it's time to start thinking about getting a table at **The Levee House**. Right on the water, this eatery is housed in the only waterfront structure in Marietta still standing. You can see the history in the brickwork. An awning covers a stretch of the patio, which faces the river. The menu is a bit upscale, which makes it a great spot for a romantic meal. The crab cakes are very popular, as are their pasta dishes.

Another dining option is the **Tampico Mexican Restaurant** on Second Street. You can't miss the restaurant's sign—a boldly painted mural covering the entire second floor of the façade. The food is less bold. This is not where you find experimental new-wave Mexican fusion cuisine. This is a solid rice-and-beans place with decent burritos and tacos, great chips and salsa, and a really nice price that won't leave you regretting your decision.

Finally, if you can plan your trip to Marietta to coincide with the **Ohio Sternwheel Festival**—always held the weekend after Labor Day—you won't be disappointed. In addition to a mess of riverboats plying the waters of the Ohio and Muskingum Rivers, there are tons of festivities: fireworks, live entertainment, and crowds out having a good time.

Leaving Marietta by way of Greene Road, we finally let the Ohio River find its own way. With a few exceptions, the trip so far has stayed on the narrow strip of level land cut from the surrounding terrain by water. As Green Street turns into Grub Road (both of which are OH 26), we scramble up into the surrounding landscape along a winding scenic drive that ends in the small town of Woodsfield. This is the **National Forest Covered Bridge Scenic Byway**, which traces a 35-mile path that, for much of the route, follows the Little Muskingum River. The drive passes a number of covered bridges. Some are open to vehicular traffic; others are best left for travelers on foot.

Harmar Village

Just southeast of Marietta, across the Muskingum River, is the historic Harmar Village. An old railroad bridge crosses the river at the base of Butler Street, next to the Marietta Harbor. A pedestrian walkway has been added to the side of the bridge, so from the Lafayette Hotel, it's just a short walk to Harmar Village. This little community has a small downtown with some interesting shopping.

Found, an antiques shop, carries antiques, collectibles, and vintage art. More than just your run-of-the-mill antiques shop, Found offers a curated collection of vintage merchandise. It's well worth your visit.

The final stop in Harmar Village is the **Boathouse BBQ**. If you walked from Marietta proper, it's less than a half-mile hike to the restaurant from the bridge. Right on the water and serving up delicious food, this is well worth the walk by itself. However, you could just choose to drive.

The Knowlton Covered Bridge, for example, is the centerpiece of Knowlton Covered Bridge Park—a year-round campground on the Little Muskingum River. The bridge is the second-longest covered bridge in Ohio, and the park serves as a home base for paddling the river or hiking in the national forest.

Woodsfield sits at the intersection of OH 800 (north/south) and OH 78 (west/east). Unless you live quite close, returning home is simply a matter of heading north on OH 800 to I-70 East or West, or taking the same road south to I-77 by way of OH 7.

IN THE AREA

Accommodations

THE BLENNERHASSETT HOTEL, 320 Market Street, Parkersburg, West Virginia. Call 304-422-3131. Website: theblennerhassett.com. $$$.

THE DOWNING HOUSE BED & BREAKFAST, 232 North Second Avenue, Middleport. Call 740-992-9115. Website: thedowninghouse.com. $$.

LAFAYETTE HOTEL, 101 Front Street, Marietta. Call 740-373-5522. Website: lafayettehotel.com. $–$$.

Attractions and Recreation

BLENNERHASSETT ISLAND HISTORICAL STATE PARK, 137 Juliana Street, Parkersburg, West Virginia. Call 304-420-4800 or 1-800-225-5982. Website: wvstateparks.com/park/blennerhassett-island-historical-state-park. The address is for the Blennerhassett Museum in downtown Parkersburg. The sternwheeler departs from Point Park at the river end of Second Street.

BOB EVANS FARM AND HOMESTEAD, 10854 OH 588, Rio Grande. Call 740-245-5324. Website: bobevans.com/aboutus/the-farm.

BUFFINGTON ISLAND BATTLEFIELD MEMORIAL PARK, 55890 OH 124, Portland. Call 1-800-686-1535. Website: ohiohistory.org/buffingtonisland.

CAMPUS MARTIUS MUSEUM, 601 Second Street, Marietta. Call 740-373-3750 or 1-800-860-0145. Website: campusmartiusmuseum.org.

THE CASTLE, 418 Fourth Street, Marietta. Website: mariettacastle.org.

FARMER'S CASTLE MUSEUM EDUCATION CENTER, 509 Ridge Street, Belpre. Call. 740-423-7588.

FOUND, 113 Maple Street, Marietta. Call 740-215-4663.

THE FRENCH ART COLONY, 530 First Avenue, Gallipolis. Call 740-446-3834. Website: frenchartcolony.org.

JULIA-ANN SQUARE HISTORIC DISTRICT, Juliana and Ann Streets between 9th and 13th Streets, Parkersburg, West Virginia. Call 304-422-9861. Website: juliannsquare.org.

LAKE VESUVIUS RECREATION AREA, Ironton. Call 740-534-6500. Website: www.fs.usda.gov/recarea/wayne/recarea/?recid=6204.

NATIONAL FOREST COVERED BRIDGE SCENIC BYWAY, OH 26, Marietta to Woodsfield. Call the Wayne National Forest at 740-753-0101. Website: www.fs.usda.gov/recarea/wayne/recarea/?recid=6216.

OHIO RIVER MUSEUM, 601 Front Street, Marietta. Call 740-373-3750. Website: campusmartiusmuseum.org/river.html.

OHIO STERNWHEEL FESTIVAL, Marietta. Call the Washington County Convention and Visitor Bureau at 1-800-288-2577. Website: ohioriverstern wheelfestival.org. Held annually the weekend after Labor Day.

OUR HOUSE MUSEUM, 432 First Avenue, Gallipolis. Call 740-446-0586 or 1-800-752-2618. Website: ohiohistory.org/ourhouse.

POINT PLEASANT RIVER MUSEUM, 28 Main Street, Point Pleasant, West Virginia. Call 304-674-0144. Website: pprivermuseum.com.

SOUTHERN OHIO MUSEUM AND CULTURAL CENTER, 825 Gallia Street, Portsmouth. Call 740-354-5629. Website: somacc.com.

TU-ENDIE-WEI STATE PARK, 1 Main Street, Point Pleasant, West Virginia. Call 304-675-0869. Website: tu-endie-weistatepark.com.

VALLEY GEM STERNWHEELER, 601 Front Street, Marietta. Call 740-373-7862. Website: valleygemsternwheeler.com.

Dining

BOATHOUSE BBQ, 218 Virginia Street, Marietta. Call 740-373-3006. Website: boathousemarietta.com. $$.

HICKIE'S HAMBURGER, 3800 Rhodes Avenue, New Boston. Call 740-456-9953. $.

THE LEVEE HOUSE INN, 127 Ohio Street, Marietta. Call 740-374-2233. Website: theleveehousemarietta.com. $$.

TAMPICO MEXICAN RESTAURANT, 221 Second Street, Marietta. Call 740-374-8623. Website: facebook.com/tampicomarietta. $$.

Other Contacts

SCIOTO COUNTY VISITOR BUREAU, 342 Second Street, Portsmouth. Call 740-353-1116. Website: ohiorivertourism.org.

GALLIA COUNTY CVB, 441 Second Avenue, Gallipolis. Call 740-446-6882 or 1-800-765-6482. Website: visitgallia.com.

GREATER PARKERSBURG CVB, 350 Seventh St., Parkersburg, West Virginia. Call 304-428-1130 or 1-800-752-4982, Website: greaterparkersburg.com.

MARIETTA–WASHINGTON COUNTY CVB, 119 Greene Street, Marietta. Call 740-373-5178 or 1-800-288-2577. Website: mariettaohio.org.

10

ANCIENT MOUNDS AND THE EVEN OLDER HOCKING HILLS

BAINBRIDGE, CHILLICOTHE, HOCKING HILLS, LOGAN, NELSONVILLE, ATHENS

ESTIMATED LENGTH: 130 miles

ESTIMATED TIME: 3 hours

HIGHLIGHTS: This trip begins with tours of Fort Hill and Serpent Mounds southeast of Bainbridge, travels through Mennonite Country, and then explores a museum dedicated to the origins of dental education. The Seip Mound on US 50 and the Hopewell Culture National Park in Chillicothe are next. The old canal town contains a handful of excellent bed and breakfasts, the Adena Mansion, and a picturesque old cemetery. The tour then dives into the Hocking Hills, one of Ohio's most beautiful landscapes. After exploring canyons and waterfalls, head into Logan for a zip-line tour of the forest or check out the last remaining washboard factory in the country. You will also find a great antiques shop and the cutest little museum in the state. From Logan, head south into Nelsonville, where you can board the Hocking Hills Railway. The tour wraps up in Athens, with great food, the arts, a historic cemetery walk, and an attractive state park.

For those interested in the pre-European history of North America, the scattering of large complex earthworks throughout the Ohio River Valley can become an addiction. The native tribes that resided here when Europeans made their first incursions west of the Alleghenies were not moundbuilders. Working from what evidence remains—many mounds were plowed under by the first farmers, and others were dug up in futile searches for buried treasure—scholars believe there were three mound-building cultures responsible for the sites you find today: the Adena, Hopewell, and Fort Ancient peoples.

GETTING THERE: Begin your adventure on OH 73, southwest of the village of Bainbridge, at Serpent Mound. Continuing east to OH 41 North will take you to Bainbridge, which is on US 50, just east of the OH 41/US 50 intersection.

LEFT: BEGIN YOUR TOUR OF THE REGION AT SERPENT MOUND

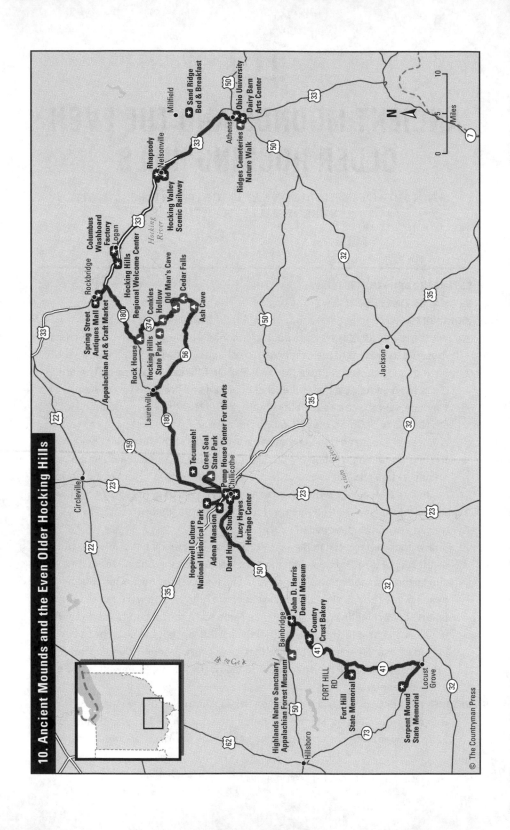

10. Ancient Mounds and the Even Older Hocking Hills

© The Countryman Press

Continuing east on US 50 takes you into the center of Chillicothe. From Chillicothe, you will head northeast toward Logan and the Hocking Hills. The route follows OH 180 through Laurelville. From Logan, continue south on US 33 to Nelsonville and the final destination, Athens.

The first leg of this route explores some of the more substantial mounds in Ohio, beginning with the **Serpent Mound**, southeast of Hillsboro on OH 73. An engaging site, Serpent Mound is the largest effigy mound in the country. (An effigy mound is a raised pile of earth constructed to resemble an animal, person, or religious symbol.) From its tightly wound tail to the mouth stretched wide and ready to eat an egg (or so many believe), the snake-shaped mound is typically a quarter-mile long, though rarely taller than three feet. Serpent Mound captures the imagination in a way you don't necessarily experience at neighboring sites like Fort Hill and the Hopewell Mounds in Chillicothe.

The plateau is brimming with archaeological significance, and excavations have shown that the Adena Culture (800 BCE–100 CE) and the Fort Ancient Culture (1000–1650 CE) occupied the site. So far, however, the snakelike mound itself has not yielded any artifacts, and most of what researchers know comes from surrounding sites, such as the remains of a village near the serpent's tail and a nearby burial mound.

An observation tower on the site gives visitors a hawk's-eye view of the snake, but its creators would have seen the serpent from the ground, so perhaps it makes sense to first wander among the beast's grassy folds before you climb to the observation deck, from which you can see the entire plateau. Along the way, signage marks where the mound seems to record significant astronomical events (max. southern moonrise, for example). If the summer heat isn't sweltering, take some time here—meander the winding path and follow some of the trails for a view of the cave located beneath the "egg" mound. If it is sweltering, you can still look around, but you should take many breaks in the air-conditioned gift shop and museum. The Ohio Historical Society owns the park, but the Arc of Appalachia Preserve System manages the site and grounds. There is a small parking fee.

Another property owned by the Ohio Historical Society and managed by the Arc of Appalachia Preserve System is the **Fort Hill State Memorial**. The turn for Fort Hill Road is on the way to Bainbridge, about 10 miles north of Locust Grove. To get there, take OH 73 south to Locust Grove and follow OH 41 north.

One earthwork at Fort Hill, a wall, surrounds 48 acres of a wooded plateau. All told, the earthen structure stretches for more than 1.5 miles. Built by the Hopewell Culture two thousand years ago, these earthworks were likely not built for protection. (It's really hard to imagine a foe unable to climb up and over the wall without much difficulty.) Rather, it is believed the site had ceremonial significance. Stop by the museum and get an overview of the mounds before you drive into the site. The outline of the place is not readily obvious from the ground, so having a picture in your mind's eye will help sort it all out. Then allow yourself a couple of hours to look around. Aside from the obvious historical charms of the site, the acres of tall trees and rolling expanses of grass make this the perfect place to toss a Frisbee and enjoy a summer picnic.

Continuing north on OH 41, the road to Bainbridge passes through a slice of the old country. From the comfort of their air-conditioned cars, summer tourists pull off to the shoulder to watch farmers work the land with horse and hand. Eventually the cars cluster in the dirt parking lot at the **Country Crust Bakery**, where the smartest of these passersby stop for a delicious break. From cinnamon rolls the size of your head to fresh warm pretzels to a Reuben on pretzel bread that nearly made my heart stop, you can't pass this place by. One thing to take note of: Contrary to the impression you might get from the plain clothes and horses and buggies, this isn't an Amish bakery. These folks are Old Order Mennonites—a sect whose men prefer a clean-shaven face to a beard. A little way south, the community operates JR's General Store, which sells fried chicken, pizza, sheds, and plenty of handcrafts.

Located in the village of Bainbridge is the country's "cradle of dental education." From 1827 to 1830, Dr. John Harris operated a unique venture. He launched a small school that aimed to teach doctors about dentistry. Before Dr. Harris, doctors wishing to specialize in teeth were essentially left to their own devices. By the end of the century, however, dentistry had established itself as a legitimate profession, complete with respectable schools of dentistry. Though quite humble, the school that Harris ran for several years had a surprising impact. Dr. Harris's students went on to found those respectable schools and establish the profession as we know it today. As such, the **John D. Harris Dental Museum** in Bainbridge commemorates a critical moment in the history of dentistry.

THE COUNTRY CRUST BAKERY SELLS AN AMAZING RUEBEN ON A PRETZEL ROLL

The volunteers give a great tour, and it's worth asking the person at the desk to give you one if you have some time to look around. The front of the museum houses the original "school." The rest walks visitors through a history of dentistry—

from Japanese toothbrushes to arcane implements that look a little like torture devices. The back hall takes you through the evolution of the dentist's office. Many of the implements on display can seem quite terrifying, and after a visit, kids might find that their next dental appointment is a breeze.

Take a short detour west on US 50 before returning east toward Chillicothe; make your next stop the **Highlands Nature Sanctuary and the Appalachian Forest Museum**. The museum tells the story of America's eastern temperate forest—highlighting

BAINBRIDGE IS THE BIRTHPLACE OF DENTAL EDUCATION

its importance as the last existing example of the primeval forest once covering the eastern third of North America, most of Europe, and Eastern Asia. Inside the museum, among other displays, you will see a re-creation of an ancient forest grove and have the unique opportunity to really feel the size of old-growth trees. The Nature Sanctuary trails lead into Rocky Fork Gorge. This is a great place to hike and get a better understanding of the local ecology. Returning to US 50, you will drive east, following Paint Creek 20 miles to the town of Chillicothe.

The secret of the success of a town on one of the nation's canals was to get the boats to stop. Heavily loaded barges didn't just tie up on a whim. This was important commercial transportation, after all. So when a crew stopped, they would often take advantage of the break to load up on supplies. That's when local businesses made some money. Rumor has it that the balconies on Water Street in Chillicothe, where the canal once flowed, were used by the town's prostitutes to advertise their services. The prostitutes attracted the clientele and helped Chillicothe become a town of some importance.

The canals that once flowed down Water Street and Canal Street connected points north with the Ohio River to the south, but even before the canals, Chillicothe's location at the confluence of the Scioto River and Paint Creek made it a good meeting place and a strategic site for settlement. American settlers rushing over the peaks of the Alleghenies ran head-on into the resident Native American population. The Shawnee people, in particular, were active here in the Scioto River Valley. Predating the Shawnee were the people of the Hopewell tradition, who took advantage of the Scioto and the Ohio Rivers to tap into trade routes that extended from the East Coast to the Rockies.

Evidence of the prolific Hopewell culture exists throughout the Scioto River Valley. The **Hopewell Culture National Historical Park**, just north of

THERE'S A LOT OF HISTORY BEHIND THE MOUNDS IN CHILLICOTHE

Chillicothe on OH 104, includes five different historical sites. Adjacent to the visitor center, the Mound City Group is 13 acres surrounded by an earth enclosure. Inside are twenty-three individual mounds, all reconstructed. The other sites—the Hopeton Earthworks, the Seip Earthworks, the High Bank Works, and the Hopewell Mound Group—may not interest the casual tourist. Time, weather, or farming have eroded many of these mounds. Others are only partially reconstructed. Start at the visitor center, which has exhibitions and displays of Hopewell artifacts. The collection of effigy pipes is especially interesting. There, you will learn more about what you'll see when you step out to explore the mounds. There is no entrance fee for this national park.

Not many people have heard of Benjamin Henry Latrobe, but he is widely regarded as the father of American architecture. You can see his best-known public works in Washington, D.C., where he designed a humble little project we know as the U.S. Capitol (working alongside Thomas Jefferson). Here in southern Ohio, you can see a stunning example of his private work: The **Adena Mansion**. To get there, follow OH 104 north of Chillicothe to Pleasant Valley Road. The first road on the left, Adena Road, leads straight up the hill to the estate. Built for Thomas Worthington, Ohio's sixth governor, the Adena Mansion sits on 300 acres overlooking Chillicothe. The panoramic landscape—a wide open valley, the meandering Scioto River, and Logan Ridge serving as a backdrop—inspired the image on the Great Seal of the State of Ohio, and it can be a nice photo opportunity, especially when the hills catch the early morning or early evening light. The mansion and the garden, however, are a must-see for anyone visiting Chillicothe. Only 300 acres remain of the 2,000 acres the estate once occupied, but the best was preserved.

The house, which was completed in 1807, has been completely restored. The interior features many pieces of furniture that once belonged to the Worthington family. During regular hours, visitors should be sure to take advantage of one of their guided one-hour tours. Outside, gardens have been added and expanded. The landscaping is stunning in the summer when all the flowers are in bloom.

As mentioned before, the view from the Adena Mansion inspired the Great Seal. This stunning landscape isn't simply for looking. It is preserved as part of the **Great Seal State Park**. The state park is situated on the east side of the Scioto River Valley and offers 23 miles of trails for hiking, biking, and horseback riding. You can also find a disc golf course and picnic shelters if you want to make a day of it.

Heading into town, we come down from the mountain to a humbler setting. Just off Walnut Street on West Sixth Street is the **Lucy Hayes Heritage Center**. It was in this simple clapboard two-story home that Lucy Webb

Adena or Hopewell?

The Adena is a Native American culture dating as far back as 1000 BCE and lasting until about 200 BCE. Most of what we know of the Adena people is that they liked to build mounds. The Hopewell followed the Adena and dated from 200 to 500 CE. Most of what we know of the Hopewell culture is that they perfected mound-building.

Aside from mound-building, however, much remains unknown about these peoples. Did they identify themselves as a unified group? Or were they a loose collection of tribes that shared the tradition of mound-building? Was the Hopewell culture simply a more mature expression of the Adena culture? Are we really talking about one culture, or are these two cultures distinct? What's the relation between the mound-builders and the Native Americans encountered by European explorers? Are they the same people? If so, why did they stop building mounds? If not, where did the mound-builders go? And why did these cultures build mounds anyway?

These are the kinds of questions you will find yourself asking as you tour the mounds of central Ohio. The interpretive sites do a good job of providing some answers, but you will often leave with more questions than you had when you arrived.

FROM ADENA YOU CAN SEE THE VIEW THAT INSPIRED OHIO'S GREAT SEAL

Hayes, the wife of Rutherford B. Hayes, was born. The museum is small and open only on Mondays, but it offers a peek at the woman first referred to as America's "First Lady."

Driving around Chillicothe, the town's charm is evident. There are a number of quality bed and breakfasts to extend your stay into an overnight. One of the best is the **Atwood House**. Years ago, the innkeeper, Bill Hirsch, served as President Nixon's butler. If you ask the right questions, he's certain to regale you with stories of his time at Camp David or the years he spent collecting antiques in New York City. His keen attention to detail is seen in everything from the period décor to the gourmet breakfast.

The inn is one block over from the Lucy Hayes Heritage Center and the Ross County Heritage Center. It's a half-mile to one of the best places to eat in town, the **Old Canal Smoke House**. The Ohio and Erie Canal once flowed right outside. The restaurant is an exceptionally cool barbeque joint. There are exposed brick walls, vintage décor, and a bright open floor plan. The menu offers ribs (baby back or St. Louis style), smoked rib-eye steak, brisket, grilled shrimp, and the catch of the day, among other items. For starters, consider the hefty coconut onion rings or the pig chips. The Smoke House is the perfect start to an evening of entertainment, which should include a visit to the theater—which in Chillicothe means outdoor theater.

Since 1973, Chillicothe has been home to the outdoor drama, *Tecumseh!* The Sugarloaf Mountain Amphitheatre is the venue for this amazingly creative performance, which includes live horses, a pond, and real cannon fire. The performance space is more landscape than stage-dressing and adds a note of realism that fully engages the audience. Performances occur at dusk, and the natural darkening of the night sky adds to the experience, as torches light up and guests gradually forget about the world beyond the Amphitheatre.

The story is that of Tecumseh, the Shawnee leader who brought together a confederacy of tribes to resist the forced settlement of the Midwest. He led his forces in Tecumseh's War and the subsequent War of 1812, dying in 1813 at the Battle of the Thames in Canada. His defeat marked the end of the larger 60-year struggle for dominance of the Great Lakes region of the United States. Noted Native American actor Graham Greene (who has performed in dozens of movies, from Dances with Wolves to The Twilight Saga: New Moon) narrates the performance, with music recorded by the London Symphony Orchestra.

Overlooking Paint Creek, at the southern end of a plateau above Chillicothe, is the very scenic **Grandview Cemetery**. Dard Hunter is buried here, as are veterans of the Revolutionary War. This is an old graveyard, one worth exploring. Not only is a lot of history buried here, but the vistas are also amazing. From the south-facing ridge, you can see Paint Creek below.

The final stops in Chillicothe, before you head into the Hocking Hills, are the Yoctangee Park and the **Pump House Center for the Arts**. The park itself dates back to the early days of the railroad when a portion of the Scioto River was diverted through here. Today, the centerpiece of the park is the

A Walk Around Ohio

If you enjoy a good, long walk, there's a trail you need to know about: the Buckeye Trail, which makes a 1,444-mile loop around Ohio. Many sections of the trail follow the path of Ohio's major rivers—including the Cuyahoga, the Tuscarawas, the Little Miami, and the Great Miami. Other sections pass through state parks and national forests.

One of the most scenic stretches of trail is the Old Man's Cave section, which passes through the Hocking Hills. It gives hikers an intimate look at the Hills, from Ash Cave to Conkles Hollow. For maps and more information about the trail system, contact the **Buckeye Trail Association**.

12-acre Yoctangee Park Lake, crossed by a beautiful stone arch bridge. The old pump house was converted into gallery space, and the Pump House Center for the Arts holds regular shows to inspire and enrich the community.

Southeastern Ohio presents a dramatic change in topography from much of the state. Chillicothe sits on the edge of the flatter and more gently rolling parts of the state and the rugged Appalachian Plateau that continues into West Virginia, eastern Kentucky, and western Pennsylvania. The predominant geological feature here is Blackhand Sandstone. In the Hocking Hills, creeks, streams, and rivers have cut this tough rock, creating terrain marked by deep gorges and waterfalls. The more scenic sites in the area are gathered under the ownership and management of the state as part of the **Hocking Hills State Park**. To get there from Chillicothe, head north on OH 159, then east on OH 180 into Laurelville.

There are several Hocking Hills Visitor Centers in the area. The one in Laurelville is as good a place to start as any. Our whirlwind tour of the dis-

Dard Hunter and the Arts & Crafts Movement

The arts and crafts craze did not start with sellers on Etsy or the make-and-remodel shows of HGTV. And it predates any programming you might have seen on PBS. In America, the Arts and Crafts Movement sprang up in the mid-1800s, on the heels of the Industrial Revolution. While mass production was taking over everything from glass to clothing to furniture, a small community of individuals was coming to lament the loss of these generations-old artisan skills. One such person was Dard Hunter.

Hunter was a native Ohioan who had worked at the famous Roycroft company in Upstate New York. His father ran a printery in Steubenville—that is to say, eastern Ohio—and apparently the print bug bit his son as well. In 1919, Dard and his wife bought the Mountain House in Chillicothe and established a letterpress printing studio. He called it the Mountain House Press. There, he wrote books on papermaking and made books by hand.

The family still maintains the home, which is open by appointment, as well as the **Dard Hunter Studios** in town, which is where Hunter's grandson prints traditional and new Arts and Crafts prints on handmade paper with Dard's letterpress, builds thick oak picture frames, creates jewelry from Dard Hunter designs, and sells Motawi and other unique tiles. When the studio is open, there's a gallery area for browsing, but because this business thrives on mail-order, you should come expecting a more informal experience.

The Mountain House sits on a high plateau overlooking the town. To get there, you will follow High Street south and take it up to West Fifth Street. Highland Avenue, where you will find the house, is on the right.

WATER CASCADES THROUGH THE HOCKING HILLS STATE PARK

persed Hocking Hills State Park will begin at Ash Cave, southeast of Laurelville on OH 56, and continue on with visits to Cedar Falls, Old Man's Cave,
Conkels Hollow, and the Rock House. All of Ohio's state parks are free to
visit, which makes it easy for a park like Hocking Hills. Numerous sites
can be lumped into one park, given that there's no need to create a gated
entrance or prevent unpaid access.

Ash Cave lies at the back of a long gorge. The cave itself is a recess in
the 90-foot-high cliff walls near the head of the gorge. Queer Creek drops
in a thin waterfall into a deep pool before meandering on its way. There are
two trails leading back to the cave. The Gorge Trail is about 0.25 mile long
and follows the creek. The Rim Trail is 0.5 mile long and takes you through
a forest of towering hemlock. You can do one or both—they both connect at
the falls. Turning north on OH 374 takes you to Cedar Falls.

The half-mile loop at Cedar Falls begins in the parking lot and follows
Queer Creek up to a stunning waterfall. It's hard to imagine now, but a grist
mill once sat at the top of the falls. If time is short, park at the east parking
lot and take the stairs directly to the falls, making it an out-and-back hike.
The stairs are unique. Designer Akio Hizume created a series of steps that

are both irregular yet purposeful. Visitors will find that the spacing adds variety and will change what might have been a tiresome slog into a delightful stroll.

Near Cedar Falls is the incomparable **Inn & Spa at Cedar Falls**. Most visitors making an extended stay in the Hocking Hills either camp or rent a cabin. There are cabins for rent everywhere throughout the area—most sited on secluded lots deep in the forest. The Cedar Falls Inn rents cabins as well, but it also offers nine guest rooms. For dining, the inn has a restaurant and tavern. The restaurant, which serves classic American cuisine, comprises two cabins, circa 1840. The menu changes with the seasons. With exposed log walls and tables lit by candlelight, the atmosphere is nearly perfect, and you will not find finer dining in the area.

By far the most popular destination in the Hocking Hills State Park, Old Man's Cave is west on OH 374/664. (Take OH 374 north to the T and turn left.) This is where you will find the Hocking Hills State Park Visitor Center. This stunning stretch of water and rock features two waterfalls (the Upper and Lower Falls), the Devil's Bathtub (an ominously swirling pool), and Old Man's Cave itself. There are a handful of bridges—stone bridges, an A-frame bridge, and a boulder-hopping style bridge—crisscrossing Old Man's Creek. Where the walls were too steep for a trail, long, dark tunnels have been cut into the rock.

Trails from Old Man's Cave overlap the longer Buckeye Trail, or you can take the Gorge Overlook Trail to Cedar Falls. Central to Hocking Hills, it's easy to see why this place is so busy in the summer.

The final two stops in the park are far less busy, though worth a visit. Continue along OH 374 to Big Pine Road and turn right. The hollow is a deep gorge with cliffs towering 200 feet overhead. There is a waterfall at the head of the gorge. You can get there by walking at the base of the gorge, or you can take the high road and make a 2.5-mile loop around the Conkles Hollow Rim Trail. Return to OH 374, and finish up at Rock House. Since it's the only true cave in the park, it is kind of odd that it wasn't named Rock Cave. The cave ceiling rises 25 feet, and the entire cavity is 200 feet long. The sandstone formations are worth the visit. The trail is a relatively short 0.25 mile long, though you will climb or descend 200 steps along the way.

When OH 374 comes to OH 180, head east toward Rockbridge. Just north of Logan, on US 33, this small town boasts the Hocking Hills Canopy Tours and the Hocking Hills Market. The latter is as close to a touristy shopping strip you will find in the Hocking Hills. There are a handful of antiques shops, including the 1,200-square-foot Spring Street Antiques Mall. There are so many antiques here that they pour out onto the shop's front porch. A few doors down is the Appalachian Art and Craft Market, which features the work of more than a hundred different craftspeople.

Travel a few miles south on US 33 and enter Logan. A stop at the Hocking Hills Regional Welcome Center (OH 664 at US 33) yields a special treat. Right on-site they have the famous **Pencil Sharpener Museum**. This small museum is lined with shelves, each stacked with novelty pencil sharpeners. You won't spend a day here—the shed isn't that big—but it's a kitschy diversion worth a few minutes of your time.

About 2 million people come to the Hocking Hills each year. Given that kind of traffic, you might expect nearby Logan to be a town packed with gift shops and restaurants. Not so. Typically, folks that spend more than a day in the area rent cabins and prepare their own meals. Day visitors may hit the shopping center north of town on US 33, but few make it into town. That's a shame, because Logan has some interesting stops, even if they're not necessarily peddling fudge and t-shirts.

Everyone who stops in Logan needs to plan a visit to the **Columbus Washboard Factory**. This is the last washboard factory in the country, and given the need (or lack thereof) for washboards to do laundry these days, it's easy to see why. A factory tour is a real treat. They still make washboards the old-fashioned way, and many of the tools of the trade have been here for generations.

Surprisingly, there is still a call for this classic household implement. Some people, by choice or necessity, live off the grid and still do their laundry by hand. The factory included miniature washboards in care packages they sent to American troops in the Middle East. The limited water supply makes washing machines a luxury in many parts of the region, and the mini-washboards allowed soldiers to have a clean uniform from time to time.

Other people use the washboards as musical instruments. Screw a few bells onto the frame for variety, add a couple of spoons for tapping and dragging, and anyone can be a percussionist. The most popular use for washboards these days, however, is for home décor, and because of that, the factory produces a lot of decorated boards ready for display.

This itinerary concludes in Athens. On the way there, south on US 33, you will pass through Nelsonville. The town is centered on charming Historic Art Square. There you will find Stuart's Opera House and **Rhapsody**, a gourmet restaurant that pairs live music with fine dining.

The other Nelsonville attraction of note is the **Hocking Valley Scenic Railway**. Vintage railcars, pulled by a diesel engine, make regular trips up the Hocking River Valley to Logan. In the summer, a little live-action role-playing—with bandits on horseback—makes the Robber Train really fun for kids. Plan ahead for this one, though, because it often sells out.

Continuing down the Hocking River Valley, the last stop is the city of Athens, the home of Ohio University. The school dates back to the Northwest Ordinance of 1797, which called for the establishment of a public university. The school was eventually chartered in 1804, a year after Ohio achieved statehood. The university stands at the center of Athens, which is nestled in a broad oxbow of the Hocking River and employs more people than any other outfit in town. More than just driving the economy, the annual influx of nearly 20,000 students into Athens defines the local culture.

As with every university town worthy of the name, Athens has a ton of pizza places, bars, and restaurants. There are plenty of dives and a few nice places to eat as well. Right on East Union Street, just east of Court Street is an Athens staple: The Burrito Buggy. This is not your typical Mexican street food, and it bears little resemblance to grub you'd find at the local Mexican restaurant, but the menu is Latin in some sense. They serve up burritos and tacos chock full of beans and veggies. Thirty years worth of alumni have fond memories of grabbing a late night bite at the cart on their way back to the dorms.

Perhaps less healthy, but no less worthy, is **O'Betty's Red Hot**, two blocks north on State Street. Every day but Sunday, this hot dog joint is open from 11 a.m. until 3 a.m. (On Sundays, they open a little later and close a lot earlier.) The French fries are fresh-cut, and the hot dogs come with a variety of toppings. Here you can get the Salome, which is basically a typical Chicago dog, or something more daring like the Dixie, topped with O'Betty's Chili Sauce, aged cheddar, mustard, and onions. You will order near the door and can take your meal to go or head to the back to dine in the kitschy splendor of the onsite Weiner Museum.

A final entry in the Athens dining column takes you a little outside of town, east on State Street to the old mall. Inside you will find **Kiser's BBQ Shack**. The barbeque is much better than the environs might suggest. The chopped pork is a favorite with regular diners, and the restaurant even gets the ribs right.

Of course, Athens is more than a place to grab a bite to eat. Southwest of town, the **Dairy Barn Arts Center** offers regular art exhibitions and a full schedule of lecture, classes, and other events for adults and children. During the holidays, local artists gather for the Holiday Bazaar.

Across the street from the Dairy Barn is the trailhead for the **Ridges Cemeteries Nature Walk**. The Ridges was once known as the Athens Lunatic Asylum and treated the mentally ill from 1874 until it closed in 1993. After a short hike up a long stairway, you will come to the asylum's cemeteries. There are three cemeteries in all, housing the remains of nearly 2,000 patients. The trail makes a loop around the grounds. Most of the gravestones are marked solely with a number, but the first group you will come to has names.

Ghost hunters like to sensationalize the spooky potential of these cemeteries, imagining the doomed souls of the criminally insane wandering this gorgeous piece of property for all eternity. The experience of walking the grounds, however, is quite different. Here it's easy to imagine tortured individuals who suffered a lifetime of mental illness finally released from that burden to find peace and rest.

IN THE AREA

Accommodations

ATWOOD HOUSE, 68 South Paint Street, Chillicothe. Call 740-774-1606. Website: atwoodhousebandb.com. $$$.

INN & SPA AT CEDAR FALLS, 21190 SR 374, Logan. Call 740-380-7489. Website: innatcedarfalls.com. $$$.

Attractions and Recreation

ADENA MANSION & GARDENS (A.K.A., ADENA STATE MEMORIAL), 847 Adena Road, Chillicothe. Call 1-800-319-7248. Website: adenamansion .com. Open April through October.

BUCKEYE TRAIL ASSOCIATION, P.O. Box 254, Worthington, Ohio 43085. Call 740-832-1282. Website: buckeyetrail.org.

COLUMBUS WASHBOARD FACTORY, 14 Gallagher Avenue, Logan. Call 740-380-3828. Website: columbuswashboard.com.

COUNTRY CRUST BAKERY, 4918 OH 41 South, Bainbridge. Call 740-634-2253. Open daily.

DAIRY BARN ARTS CENTER, 8000 Dairy Lane, Athens. Call 740-592-4981. Website: dairybarn.org.

DARD HUNTER MOUNTAIN HOUSE, 8 Highland Avenue, Chillicothe. Website: dardhunter.com/mhhome.htm.

DARD HUNTER STUDIOS, 125 West Water Street, Chillicothe. Call 740-779-3300. Website: dardhunter.com.

FORT HILL STATE MEMORIAL, 13614 Fort Hill Road, Hillsboro. Call 937-588-3221. Website: arcofappalachia.org/fort-hill.

GRANDVIEW CEMETERY, 300 Brookside Drive, Chillicothe. Call 740-774-2230.

GREAT SEAL STATE PARK, 4908 Marietta Drive, Chillicothe. Call 740-887-4818. Website: parks.ohiodnr.gov/greatseal.

HIGHLANDS NATURE SANCTUARY AND THE APPALACHIAN FOREST MUSEUM, 7660 Cave Road, Bainbridge. Call 937-365-1935. Website: arcof appalachia.org/highlands-nature-sanctuary.

HOCKING HILLS STATE PARK, 19852 OH 664, Logan. Call 740-385-6841. Website: thehockinghills.org.

HOCKING VALLEY SCENIC RAILWAY, 33 West Canal Street, Nelsonville. Call 740-753-9531. Website: hvsry.org.

HOPEWELL CULTURE NATIONAL HISTORICAL PARK, 16062 OH 104. Call 740-774-1126. Website: nps.gov/hocu/index.htm.

JOHN D. HARRIS DENTAL MUSEUM, 208 Main Street, Bainbridge. Call 740-634-2228. Website: bainbridgedentalmuseum.org.

LUCY HAYES HERITAGE CENTER, 90 West Sixth Street, Chillicothe. Call 740-775-5829.

PENCIL SHARPENER MUSEUM, 13178 OH 664, Logan. Call 1-800-462-5464 or 740-385-9706. Website: 1800Hocking.com.

PUMP HOUSE CENTER FOR THE ARTS, 1 Enderlin Circle, Chillicothe. Call 740-772-5783. Website: pumphouseartgallery.com.

THE RIDGES CEMETERIES NATURE WALK, Lin Hall, Ohio University Athens. Call 740-593-1304. Website: namiathensohio.org/~oldsite/guide.html.

SERPENT MOUND, 3850 SR-73, Peebles. Call 937-587-2796. Website: arcof appalachia.org/visitserpent-mound.

TECUMSEH! OUTDOOR DRAMA, Sugarloaf Mountain Amphitheatre, 5968 Marietta Road, Chillicothe. Call 1-866-775-0700. Website: tecumseh drama.com.

Dining

INN & SPA AT CEDAR FALLS, 21190 SR 374, Logan. Call 740-380-7489. Website: innatcedarfalls.com. $$$.

KISER'S BBQ SHACK, 1002 East State, Athens. Call 740-594-7427. Website: kisersbbqshack.com. $$.

O'BETTY'S RED HOT, 15 West State Street, Athens. Call 740-589-6111. Website: obettys.com. $.

OLD CANAL SMOKE HOUSE, 94 East Water Street, Chillicothe. Call 740-779-3278. Website: oldcanalsmokehouse.com. $$.

RHAPSODY RESTAURANT, 18 Public Square, Nelsonville. Call 740-753-5741. Website: rhapsody.hocking.edu. $$.

Other Contacts

ATHENS COUNTY CONVENTION AND VISITOR BUREAU, 667 East State Street, Athens. Call 740-592-1819. Website: athensohio.com.

HOCKING HILLS REGIONAL WELCOME CENTER, 13178 OH 664, Logan. Call 1-800-462-5464 or 740-385-9706. Website: 1800Hocking.com.

HOCKING HILLS VISITOR CENTER—LAURELVILLE, 16197 Pike Street, Laurelville. Call 740-332-0516. Website: www.hockinghills.com.

ROSS-CHILLICOTHE CONVENTION & VISITOR BUREAU, 230 North Plaza Boulevard, Chillicothe. Call 740-702-7677 or 1-800-413-4118. Website: visitchillicotheohio.com.

PIKE COUNTY CONVENTION & VISITOR BUREAU, 126 West Second Street, Waverly. Call 740-947-9650. Website: piketravel.com.

11

A COUNTY SEAT TOUR

LONDON, ASHVILLE, CIRCLEVILLE, WASHINGTON COURT HOUSE, WILMINGTON, HILLSBORO, GEORGETOWN

ESTIMATED LENGTH: 150 miles

ESTIMATED TIME: 3.5 hours

HIGHLIGHTS: Meandering south from London and west of Columbus to George-town, southeast of Cincinnati, this itinerary begins at the historic Red Brick Tavern. Skirting around the southeast edge of the Columbus suburbs, folks who enjoy history will have a nice series of stops on this route. There's the Ashville Museum and the World's Oldest Traffic Light in Ashville, and the Clarke-May Museum and Ted Lewis Museum in Circleville. In Washington Court House, the Fayette County Historical Society shares local history as well. As the county seat, the town has a pretty impressive courthouse, with a storied past. The next town on the itinerary is Wilmington. As a college town, there's a lot to see and do—from ceramics at Grandpa's Pottery to the Quaker Heritage Center and the history museum for Clinton County. Five miles west of town you will find Bonnybrook Farms, which offers summer chuck wagon dinner rides. The General Denver Hotel in Wilmington is a great reason to stop as well. If B&Bs are more your style, the next stop should be Woodhaven Farm Bed and Breakfast in Hillsboro instead. There is a winery on the route, Indian Spring Winery in Sardinia. The trip ends in Georgetown, which has plenty of sites specific to Ulysses S. Grant. There are also a number of excellent inns and B&Bs nearby, and if you plan on adding stops from a neighboring chapter's itinerary, this is a great place to refuel and relax before heading out again.

GETTING THERE: This trip begins on US 40, northeast of London (20 miles west of Columbus). Follow US 42 southwest to the center of London. Center Street, south of High Street, heads east and becomes OH 665. You take that east to Darbyville and then turn south on OH 3, which runs parallel to Big Darby Creek, south into Harrisburg. Turn east on OH 762, cross the creek, and continue east on OH 762 to US 23 South. Drive south for 4 miles to the small

LEFT: WILMINGTON HAS A GREAT DOWNTOWN FOR WALKING AND SHOPPING

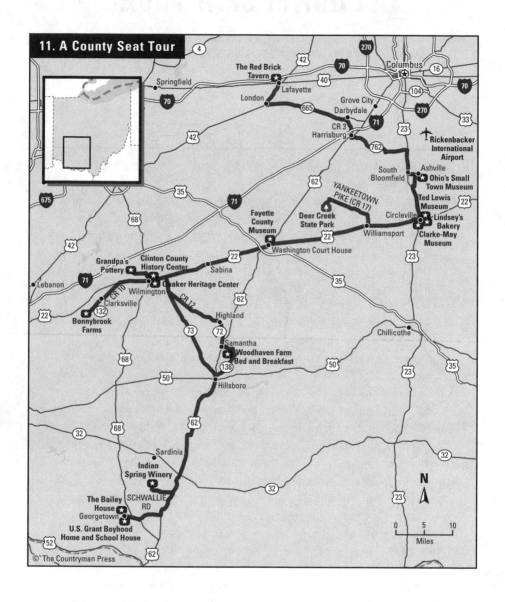

community of South Bloomfield and turn east onto Ashville Road (OH 316). It's 1 mile to Ashville. For Circleville, return to US 23 and head south. Following US 22 west takes you through the next two towns on our itinerary—Washington Court House and Wilmington. OH 73 will take you south from Wilmington to Hillsboro. From there, US 62 takes you to OH 32, and then back along country roads into Georgetown.

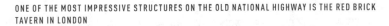

This tour follows a chain of county seats through west-central Ohio. Beginning just outside London (Madison County) and continuing through Circleville (Pickaway County), Washington Court House (Fayette County), Wilmington (Clinton County), Hillsboro (Highland County), and Georgetown (Brown County). As such, be prepared to see some impressive courthouse architecture.

As with many great journeys before this one, we begin on the National Highway. **The Red Brick Tavern** was built in the 1830s, just in time for the National Road to come through the small settlement of Lafayette. It served weary travelers for decades before being repurposed for other uses, and it eventually fell into disrepair. In 1973, after considerable restoration work, the tavern was open once again to diners. Today it's a rather fine restaurant

ONE OF THE MOST IMPRESSIVE STRUCTURES ON THE OLD NATIONAL HIGHWAY IS THE RED BRICK TAVERN IN LONDON

with an excellent heritage. The menu is traditional American fare, not too expensive. Call ahead, though, as table space in the dining room is limited.

The next stop on the route is Ashville. The directions might be a bit too complex to share in paragraph form, but here goes: Follow US 42 southwest from The Red Brick Tavern to the center of London. Center Street, south of High Street, heads east and becomes OH 665. You take that east to Darbyville, and then you turn south on OH 3, which parallels Big Darby Creek as it goes south into Harrisburg. Turn east on OH 762, cross the creek, and continue east on OH 762 to US 23 South. Drive south for 4 miles to the small community of South Bloomfield and turn east onto Ashville Road (OH 316).

As the road enters Ashville, about a mile from US 23, it changes its name to Main Street. Turn left on Long Street, and **Ohio's Small Town Museum** is on the southeast corner of the first intersection. There's a mural on the front wall depicting an Independence Day parade in Ashville. The museum itself, with its collection of local history and lore, celebrates small-town life, from the significant contributions made by industrious residents to the quirky stories, told over and again.

There are some serious exhibitions, such as the World's Oldest Traffic Light. Invented by local inventor Teddy Boor, this light hung at an intersection in Ashville well into the 1980s. It has since been restored to its original glory and is on hand for curious visitors. There is also a stuffed rooster, once known to carry a dime in its beak every day to a nearby store to purchase a handful of corn.

Returning to US 23, head south into Circleville.

The history of Circleville and Pickaway County are on display at the **Clarke-May Museum** on Union Street. The Museum (and the Pickaway County Historical Society) are housed in the 1840 home of Dr. Edward Clarke, a dentist. The house passed to his daughter, who then left it to her housemate, Alice Ada May. (Hence the "Clarke-May" name.) The house is furnished with items belonging to May, and area families have added to the museum from their own collections. The museum offers a glimpse into the daily lives of Pickaway County residents going back 200 years, with a particular look at women in history. There's also a room dedicated to local Native American culture.

The next stop is on Main Street. You don't find a lot of museums dedicated to celebrating the legacy of a single individual unless that individual was elected president of the United States. The **Ted Lewis Museum** in Circleville is unique in that respect. You might be forgiven for not knowing who Ted Lewis was, or why there's a museum in town dedicated to honoring his life and career, but there's no excuse for not stopping by and learning a bit.

Ted Lewis was a local boy who made good. Born Theodore Leopold Friedman in Circleville back in 1890, Lewis went to New York to pursue a career as an entertainer. He began his career playing the clarinet (and not very well, according to many critics), but he knew good music and later as the leader of his own band, he hired the best in the business. Ted Lewis and His Orchestra were a huge hit in the years leading up to World War II, and their run continued for a number of years after the war as well. Songs they recorded with Columbia Records and Decca topped the charts. Lewis became known as "Mr. Entertainment" and liked to close out his shows with the song, "Me and My Shadow."

When Lewis died, his body was brought back to Circleville and buried in Forest Cemetery. His wife Adah helped establish a museum in his honor in Circleville—donating memorabilia from his life as an entertainer. The museum has recordings and film clips of Lewis and his music, as well as the props that came to iconize his act. The museum is open on Fridays and Saturdays, so be sure to time your visit accordingly.

Two doors down from the Ted Lewis Museum, you will find **Lindsey's Bakery.** Gene Lindsey bought the business in 1950, and the bakery has been a hometown favorite ever since. Doughnuts are made fresh in-house, and they rely on the same recipes for decades. Regulars simply devour the pumpkin doughnuts, which are served year-round.

The other big claim to fame here is that Lindsey's Bakery is the "Home of the Original World's Largest Pumpkin Pie." The phrasing of that claim is very specific. The current record, according to the folks at Guinness Book of World Records, is held by the New Bremen Giant Pumpkin Growers (also in Ohio). Their pie clocked in at 3,699 pounds and measured 20 feet across. But for 40 years, Lindsey's baked the largest pie. And even more impressive than that, the bakery recreates the feat every year for the **Circleville Pumpkin Show.**

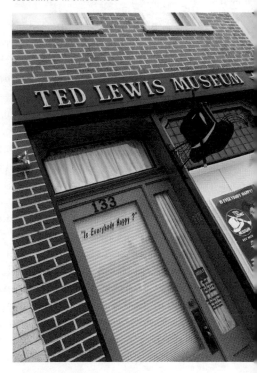

THE OLD ENTERTAINER, TED LEWIS, IS CELEBRATED IN CIRCLEVILLE

Billed as the "The Greatest Free Show on Earth," the Pumpkin Show has been attracting visitors to Circleville since 1903. It begins on the third Wednesday in October and continues through Saturday, and over those four days over 400,000 people come to celebrate October's favorite squash.

A visit to Circleville is not complete without stopping for a treat. **Wittich's Fine Candies and Ice Cream Soda Fountain** on High Street is a temple of confectionary delight. As with many other classic soda fountains, a long counter with stools runs the length of the shop. Across from that is the candy counter. They serve locally produced Smith's Dairy ice cream and the full menu of cool desserts—shakes, ice cream cones, and, of course, sodas. The business was established in 1840, and over the years they've learned a little something. Sundaes feature Wittich's own hot fudge.

US 22 makes a beeline from Circleville west to Washington Court House. The highway skirts south of **Deer Creek State Park**. Like many Ohio state parks, Deer Creek has a lodge with a decent onsite restaurant overlooking the park's lake. Across the water from the lodge is the park's swimming beach. There are trails for hiking and plenty of water for fishing and paddling. The state's website describes the discovery of a campsite first used 4,000 years ago on a ridge that once overlooked the creek. Ancient peoples returned to the camp for generations.

There's a historical marker in front of the Fayette County Courthouse that tells the story of the "Washington Court House Riot of 1894." Not many people know of the riot, its cause, or the aftermath, but there's more to tell than what's found on the sign. On October 9 of that year, Mary Parrett Boyd, a 51-year-old widow, reported being raped by a black man. A few days later, William Jasper Dolby, a local man, 20 years old, was apprehended and brought to Washington Court House; Boyd identified him on October 16. By then a crowd had gathered around the jail, with the expressed intent of lynching Dolby.

The sheriff enlisted the militia to help. As the crowd grew overnight, the governor was asked to send more troops, which he did. The first obstacle on October 17 was moving Dolby the 70 feet from the jail to the courthouse. The militia formed a gauntlet, rifles and bayonets facing the crowd, and officers rushed Dolby through the center. It almost failed, and for a moment, Dolby was in the hands of the mob. But he eventually made it inside the courthouse.

His trial lasted three minutes. Dolby confessed to the assault and was sentenced to 20 years in prison. (There's every indication that the reportedly terror-stricken man's confession was influenced by the howling mob outside and the promise of safety when he was moved to the state penitentiary. Whatever he said at the time, he later denied assaulting Boyd.) The new challenge for the sheriff and the militia was to get Dolby safely to the penitentiary in Columbus.

By then, the crowd was completely out of control—the sheriff's stables were set on fire, rocks were thrown. Unable to sneak Dolby onto a train, they holed up in the courthouse waiting for reinforcements. Then the crowd got their hands on a massive oak timber and began battering the courthouse doors. Colonel Coit, the man in charge of the troops, gave a warning, but they continued to beat at the entryway, and then the troops fired through the doors into the crowd. Five people died; the bullet holes are still there in the doors. Coit was eventually charged and acquitted of manslaughter, the sheriff and the judge both lost their reelection campaigns, and little is known about Dolby after the events of that October.

Of course, a town's history is much more than one event. The **Fayette County Museum** is located 1,500 feet northeast of the courthouse, just behind the antique piece of artillery at the fork where Court Street splits into Columbus and Washington Avenues. The museum is operated by the Fayette County Historical Society. This grand Victorian Italianate home was built in 1875. Even without the historical exhibitions, this is a home worth visiting. As it is, however, there are 14 rooms full of memorabilia donated by Fayette County families. The museum is open on weekends, and they host various special events throughout the year.

To continue, follow US 22 through Sabina to Wilmington.

As the county seat, it makes sense that Wilmington is home to the **Clin-**

THE HISTORY OF WILMINGTON IS ON DISPLAY AT THE CLINTON COUNTY HISTORY CENTER

ton County History Center. The museum is housed in the residence of Brigadier General James W. Denver—the man for whom the city of Denver is named (though he never got around to visiting the place). The museum is described as a "touring museum," which means docents guide visitors through the exhibition space. The museum has a large collection of textiles, Quaker crafts, paintings, and sculpture. In fact, there's too much to display all at once, so the exhibitions rotate. There's also memorabilia from the aforementioned Denver, who was born in Virginia; lived in Kansas, California, and Ohio; and died in Washington D.C.

Matthew Rombach Denver, son of James W., was a moving force behind the **General Denver Hotel**, which was built in 1928 at the corner of Mulberry and Main Streets in Wilmington. In its early years, the hotel featured everything a cultured traveler could want—from a barber shop to a soda fountain. Today, the hotel is just as cultured. The architecture is described as Tudor Revival. Inside, balconies overlook the central lobby. The innkeepers try to maintain the simplicity of an earlier time. There is no pool, and the rooms don't have phones (though they do have televisions).

In addition to fine lodgings, the hotel maintains one of the finest restau-

THE GENERAL DENVER HOTEL ANCHORS ONE END OF DOWNTOWN WILMINGTON

THE WOODHAVEN FARM B&B IS FAR REMOVED FROM IT ALL IN BEAUTIFUL COUNTRY SURROUNDINGS

rants in town. Prices are not outrageous, and the menu is classically American (burgers, steaks, chicken fingers).

Wilmington College is a private liberal arts college, founded by the Society of Friends (i.e., the Quakers) in 1870. The rich cultural contribution of Quakers is celebrated on campus at the **Quaker Heritage Center**. Located in the Boyd Cultural Arts Center, this small museum features a traditional Quaker meetinghouse and exhibitions that explore the history of the Religious Society of Friends, especially how it plays out here in southwest Ohio. There's a special focus on Quaker peacemaking, and the way Quakers engage and influence American culture. With rotating and traveling exhibitions, the visitor experience is continually changing.

Northwest of Wilmington, about 3 miles from the center of town on OH 73, there's a white farmhouse on the right side of the road. Behind the house is a large white barn, and out front, there's a sign that tells guests they have arrived at **Grandpa's Pottery**. If you're lucky, someone will be on hand tossing pots. If you're extraordinarily lucky, Ray "Grandpa" Storer will have time to help you throw your own. The shop produces fine work and anyone with

GRANT'S BOYHOOD HOME STRIVES FOR AUTHENTICITY, BUT WE CAN BE PRETTY SURE THIS BOOK WASN'T A PART OF HIS CHILDHOOD READING

an appreciation of ceramics will want to stop in. The hours can be a little tricky, however, so do call ahead.

The next stop is Hillsboro, but if you have the time, there's a spot a little west of Clarksville that is worth the detour. The destination is **Bonnybrook Farms**, which specializes in making your time on the farm entertaining. On Saturdays in the summer, the farm offers chuck wagon dinner rides. The experience begins with family-fun time around the farm—petting livestock, feeding or catching fish, taking a ride on the 80-foot underground slide. Then gather at the barn for dinner and wrap up the evening with a wagon ride. In the fall, things kick into higher gear with nightly lantern-lit wagon rides, a corn maze, and pick-your-own pumpkins.

To get there, you will follow US 22 west out of Wilmington. Close to 5 miles from the center of town you will come to C.R. 10. Bonnybrook Farms is less than 7.5 miles from the highway, 3 miles past Clarksville.

The best route to Hillsboro is OH 73, but north of Hillsboro is an excellent little B&B, and if that is on your itinerary, it's better to leave Wilmington by OH 73 to C.R. 12 (southeast). When you come into Highland, leave town heading south on OH 72. In Samantha, turn east on Fall Creek Road. The inn is less than 3 miles up the road.

The **Woodhaven Farm Bed and Breakfast** is situated on a 40-acre farm. The inn has two rooms. The Rose Room features a queen-sized bed and a private entrance on the main floor. The Loft is more for groups. There is room for four in a large dormitory-style room. Both have access to common areas, including the galley kitchen and the great room.

On the way to Georgetown, travelers might want to stop at the **Indian Spring Winery** south of Sardinia. From Hillsboro, take US 62 south past OH 32 to Schwallie Road (C.R. 17C) west. Less than 4 miles from US 62, you will turn right on Fite-Hauck Road. The winery is a social destination. People come from all around to try a new wine, but they stay for the live music on the weekends, or the Saturday farmers' market held all summer. Now, visitors are free to stop by any time. Monday through Thursday, however, it is wise to call ahead to make sure someone is on hand to serve you.

Georgetown is our final stop. It's the boyhood home of Ulysses S. Grant, Commanding General of the Union Army during the Civil War and the eighteenth president of the United States. His parents named him Hiram Ulysses Grant, but when nominating the 16-year-old Hiram Grant to a spot at the United States Military Academy at West Point, the family's representative in Congress mistakenly wrote, "Ulysses S. Grant," and the name stuck.

Brown County and the surrounding environs are informally known as the Land of Grant. There's a lot of history here related to the Grant family, the Civil War, and the abolitionist movement.

ULYSSES S. GRANT WASN'T BORN IN GEORGETOWN, BUT HE GREW UP HERE

THE SCHOOL U.S. GRANT ATTENDED AS A BOY

Here in Georgetown are the **U. S. Grant Boyhood Home and School-house.** The home is located, appropriately enough, on East Grant Avenue, two blocks north of State Street and two blocks east of Main Street. (You can't miss Grant Avenue. The U. S. Grant Native Son Statue overlooks the intersection.) Grant was born in a small wood-framed home in Point Pleasant (see Chapter 12). The following year, his family moved to Georgetown and built this two-story brick "cottage." Grant lived here from 1823 until 1839, when he went off to West Point.

Two blocks south of State Street and two blocks east of Main Street is the "Dutch School." This simple two-room schoolhouse was built in 1829 and served the community over 20 years. The school contains appropriate furnishings for the early 1800s, many items coming from the Grant family. It's a great place to learn about nineteenth-century education—the games children played, the curriculum they were taught, and the punishments they received.

There's not a lot of fine dining right in Georgetown, but for good food, you won't go amiss with the **Cherry Street Eatery.** Right in the heart of Georgetown's historic district, the restaurant is easy to find. You can't go wrong with a burger and fries, but you might want to mix it up with that classic of comfort food, the hot open-faced sandwich. There's also an on-site bakery with fresh pies. It's a family operation, and visitors come away feeling like they've been treated like family friends.

A block north of Grant's home on Grant Avenue is **The Bailey House**. This classic Greek revival home was built in 1832 for Dr. George Bailey. The Baileys and Grants were close, and the young Ulysses is said to have visited the home often. The only alteration to The Bailey House from its original design is an 1876 addition. The best thing about this historic home, however, is that it is operated as a bed and breakfast, one of the finest in the area.

The inn features three guest rooms. Two have a shared bath; one has a private bath. There's a train display in the attic and plenty of Civil War memorabilia and books about Grant in the library. This is a great place to stay on any tour of the area, but it's a particularly apt spot for travelers with a yen for history.

IN THE AREA

Accommodations

THE BAILEY HOUSE, 112 North Water Street, Georgetown. Call 937-378-3087. Website: baileyhousebandb.com. $.

GENERAL DENVER HOTEL, 81 West Main Street, Wilmington. Call 937-383-4141. Website: generaldenver.com. $$.

WOODHAVEN FARM BED AND BREAKFAST, 9228 Fall Creek Road, Leesburg. Call 937-403-6485. Website: woodhavenfarmbedandbreakfast.com. $$.

Attractions and Recreation

BONNYBROOK FARMS, 3779 State Route 132, Clarksville. Call 937-289-2500. Website: bonnybrookfarms.com.

CIRCLEVILLE PUMPKIN SHOW, 159 East Franklin Street, Circleville. Call 740-474-7000. Website: pumpkinshow.com.

CLARKE-MAY MUSEUM, 162 West Union Street, Circleville. Call 740-474-1495. Website: pickawayhistory.org.

CLINTON COUNTY HISTORY CENTER, 149 East Locust Street, Wilmington. Call 937-382-4684. Website: clintoncountyhistory.org.

DEER CREEK STATE PARK, 20635 State Park Road 20, Mount Sterling. Call 740-869-3124. Website: parks.ohiodnr.gov/deercreek.

FAYETTE COUNTY MUSEUM, 517 Columbus Avenue, Washington Court House. Call 740-335-2953. Website: fayette-co-oh.com/museum.html.

GRANDPA'S POTTERY, 3558 West OH 73, Wilmington. Call 937-725-3402.

INDIAN SPRING WINERY, 10862 Fite-Hauck Road, Sardinia. Call 937-446-9463. Website: indianspringwinery.com.

LINDSEY'S BAKERY, 127 West Main Street, Circleville. Call 740-474-3871. Website: facebook.com/LindseysBakery/.

OHIO'S SMALL TOWN MUSEUM, 34 Long Street, Ashville. Call 740-983-9864. Website: ohiosmalltownmuseum.org.

QUAKER HERITAGE CENTER, 1870 Quaker Way Wilmington. Call 937-481-2456. Website: wilmington.edu/the-wilmington-difference/qhc.

TED LEWIS MUSEUM, 133 West Main Street, Circleville. Call 740-477-3630. Website: tedlewismuseum.org.

U. S. GRANT BOYHOOD HOME, 219 East Grant Avenue, Georgetown. Call 937-378-3087. Website: usgrantboyhoodhome.org.

U. S. GRANT SCHOOLHOUSE, 508 South Water Street, Georgetown. Call 937-378-3087. Website: usgrantboyhoodhome.org.

WITTICH'S FINE CANDIES AND ICE CREAM SODA FOUNTAIN, 117 West High Street, Circleville. Call 740-474-3313. Website: wittichscandy shop.com.

Dining

CHERRY STREET EATERY, 112 East Cherry Street, Georgetown. Call 937-378-0130. $.

GENERAL DENVER HOTEL, 81 West Main Street, Wilmington. Call 937-383-4141. Website: generaldenver.com. $$.

THE RED BRICK TAVERN, 1700 Cumberland Road, London. Call 740-852-1474. Website: historicredbricktavern.com. $$.

Other Contacts

BROWN COUNTY TOURISM, 103 North Main Street, Georgetown. Call 937-378-4784. Website: browncountyohiotourism.com.

FAYETTE COUNTY TRAVEL AND TOURISM, 101 East East Street, Washington Court House. Call 1-800-479-7797. Website: fayettecountyohio.com/travel-tourism.

PICKAWAY COUNTY VISITOR BUREAU, 325 Main Street, Circleville. Call 740-474-3636. Website: pickaway.com.

VISIT CLINTON COUNTY, Ohio, 13 North South Street, Wilmington. Call 937-382-1965. Website: clintoncountyohio.com.

VISIT MADISON COUNTY. 730 Keny Boulevard, London. Call 740-852-2250. Website: madisoncountyohio.org/visit.

VISITOR BUREAU OF HIGHLAND COUNTY, 130 South High Street, Hillsboro. Call 937-763-7012. Website: visithighlandcounty.com.

12

THE QUEEN CITY
CINCINNATI AND ITS NEIGHBORS

POINT PLEASANT, NEWPORT, CINCINNATI, FAIRFIELD,
HAMILTON, OXFORD

ESTIMATED LENGTH: 100 miles

ESTIMATED TIME: 4 hours

HIGHLIGHTS: This trip begins in Point Pleasant with a visit to the Ulysses S. Grant Birthplace. Heading west on US 52, you can make stops at Woodland Mound Park and the old-school amusement park Coney Island. After crossing the border into Kentucky via I-471, you can tour the Newport Aquarium before diving into the heart of Cincinnati, where there are countless museums, parks, and restaurants. Not to be overlooked are the Taft Museum of Art, the Harriet Beecher Stowe House, and the American Sign Museum. Heading to the northern suburbs, you next visit the Vinoklet Winery and Jungle Jim's International Market. Continuing to Hamilton, the route includes the Butler County Soldiers Monument, Pyramid Hill Sculpture Park, and the Robert McCloskey Museum at Heritage Hall Museum. Winding your way south and north, you will pass through Shandon, with its excellent used bookstore, and Okeana, with the Pioneer Village at the Governor Bebb MetroPark. To the north in Oxford, you can tour the campus of Miami University, visit the McGuffey Museum, or take a hike at nearby Hueston Woods.

GETTING THERE: The trip begins in Point Pleasant on the Ohio River. The town is 25 miles east of Cincinnati on US 52. Following US 52 to I-275, the route crosses into Kentucky before entering Cincinnati on I-475. From downtown, the route continues north on Vine Street, then cuts over to I-75 North and then I-275 West, exiting at Dixie Highway for Fairfield. After Fairfield, there are stops in Hamilton, then it's south on OH 128 to Ross. A series of county roads takes you north to Oxford and the end of the tour.

LEFT: THE VIEW FROM RANKIN HOUSE LOOKS ACROSS THE RIVER INTO KENTUCKY

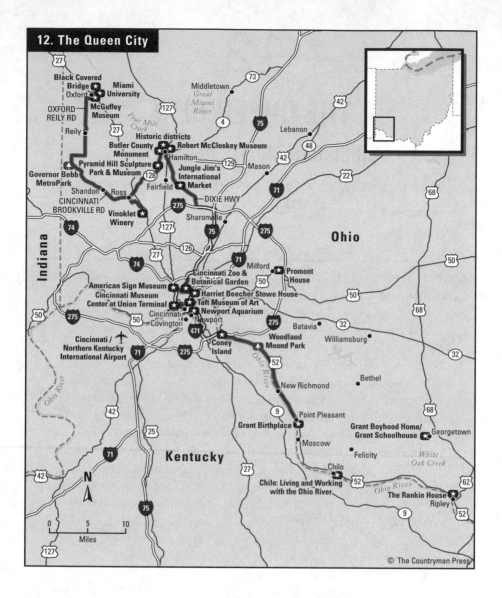

12. The Queen City

Ohio suffers an embarrassment of U.S. presidents. From the ill-fated presidency of William Henry Harrison to the election of Warren G. Harding, eight Ohioans (seven of them natives of the state) have sat in the nation's top seat. One of the most prominent native sons to claim the privilege was Ulysses S. Grant, commanding general of the Union army during the Civil War and president of the United States from 1869 to 1877. In 1822, on the country's wild frontier, Grant was born in a ramshackle cabin on the Ohio River. The Grant family lived in Port Pleasant for only a year before packing up and moving to Georgetown, Ohio, a small town to the east on White Oak

Creek. After Grant died, the Grant Birthplace became part of a traveling exhibition to honor the famous Civil War general.

For a time, the cabin was on display in Columbus, but in 1936, it was returned to its current location in Point Pleasant. The home is small—it has only three rooms—and takes a short time to tour. Along with the home, several other associated buildings have become part of the historic district. To explore more of Grant's past, take a short side trip to Georgetown to visit the Grant Boyhood Home and the Grant Schoolhouse.

Point Pleasant overlooks the Ohio River 25 miles upstream from Cincinnati. Following US 52 north, you will pass through New Richmond before leaving rural Clermont County and entering the metropolitan Hamilton County.

To really appreciate the natural beauty of this stretch of the Ohio River, drive up to the Breezy Point Pavilion in **Woodland Mound Park**. Aside from stunning views, the park has a campground on the river, a water park called Parky's Wetland Adventure, and an 18-hole disc golf course. There are numerous picnic shelters, and those with an inclination toward the outdoors will want to take advantage of the park's nature trails. The park property straddles US 52 northwest of New Richmond, so it's hard to miss.

Continuing along US 52, the road eventually merges with I-275. Ignore the merge and continue along the river on Old Kellogg Road. About 1.5 miles up the road, before you join I-275, is one of the oldest amusement parks in the Midwest. **Coney Island** dates back to the late 1800s, and its story is tied to an apple farmer and his orchard on the Ohio River. James Parker bought 400 acres along the river in 1867, but it wasn't long before he realized that this attractive location had the potential to offer a much more profitable harvest—one that could potentially pay all summer long. He began renting the property and adding amenities, like a dance hall and a bowling alley. Later, he sold the property, and the new owners named it Ohio Grove, The Coney Island of the West. Riverboats brought visitors to picnic, dance, and enjoy the park—which over the years became a full-fledged amusement park with roller-coasters, rides, and a large swimming pool.

In the 1970s, the park was purchased, and most of the rides were moved to a new location, the site of the new King's Island, north of Cincinnati. For a while, it looked like Coney Island had closed for good, but a couple of years later, the park was reopened to the public.

The Sunlite Pool and Classic Rides are the two halves of this classic theme park. The Classic Rides side includes a Ferris wheel, giant slide, and classic steel roller-coaster. Given that this section lacks the all-out insanity of other parks, parents will have an especially fine time. When you are weary of the rides, take a paddleboat or canoe onto Lake Como and enjoy the water. The Sunlite Pool will change your idea of what a "pool" can be. Spanning 400 feet by 200 feet, with four amazing slides and over an acre of shallow water, it's the largest such pool in North America (and the largest recirculating swimming pool in the world).

The route to Cincinnati crosses the Ohio River, and for a time passes through Kentucky. To arbitrarily separate the Greater Cincinnati Metro Area along state lines denies the region's obvious connectedness. Some might even argue that much of what makes Cincinnati a great town is found across the river in Covington or Newport. For certain, if you want to explore the local flavor, you need to experience both.

One of the most popular destinations on the Kentucky side of the water is the **Newport Aquarium**. Taking I-275 to I-471 north, take Exit 5 for Dave Cowens Drive. Follow OH 8 south and west less than a mile to the aquarium, which is on East Third Street. From the outside, it's hard to imagine the million gallons of water that are home to thousands of animals. As you tour the facility, five acrylic tunnels will take you "inside" the tanks, and there is always something exciting swimming by. *Surrounded by Sharks* is perhaps the exhibition that generates the most anticipation with kids, but it's just the tip of the iceberg.

The aquarium is part of the larger retail and dining complex called **Newport on the Levee**. There's a Barnes & Noble and tons of restaurants—even some top-notch seafood if seeing all those fish left you hungry. Parking around the aquarium can be a bear. The Newport Travel Lodge charges a few bucks for visitors to park in the hotel parking lot, and it's close to the aquarium.

Its location on the Ohio River made Cincinnati what it is today. In the early 1800s, riverboats took over the Ohio River, and these steam-powered paddle boats connected Cincinnati with ports as far as New Orleans. What better way, then, to see the city than on board a riverboat. A short way from the aquarium, on just the other side of Central Bridge, is **BB Riverboats**. Sightseeing tours last about an hour. The most straightforward is the Harbor Cruise, but the schedule also includes the fun Pirates of the Ohio Cruise on Fridays. There are also dining cruises—brunch, lunch, and dinner—for a different experience on the water. Photographers should note that no picture of the Cincinnati skyline from the river is complete without a riverboat in the foreground. The dock is across the water from Great American Ballpark, where the Cincinnati Reds play, and on game day, you can see the stands fill as the boat pulls out into the current.

Next up: Cincinnati!

The Queen City, Porkopolis, the Queen of the West, Chilitown USA, and the Blue Chip City. Cincinnati is known as all of the above, but its friends just call it "Cincy." The city proper sits on the northern bank of the Ohio River, but the larger metro area straddles the river and spreads out into three states. This is where the North meets the South, where East Coast meets the

Midwest—an important stop on the trade route that once connected the Ohio River Valley with the Mississippi River and the rest of the world.

This blend of cultures expresses itself in many ways. Take, for example, the local cuisine. Cincinnati is the home of Skyline Chili and Gold Star Chili, where a uniquely seasoned chili is ladled over spaghetti noodles and covered in shredded cheddar. Cincinnati is also the only place in the world where diners can order goetta with their greasy-spoon breakfast (and Cincinnatians eat tons of this stuff!).

The city came into its own in the late eighteenth century, a time when Americans were drawing all sorts of comparisons between their new republic and the Classical period of Greece and Rome. Admirers characterized George Washington as Cincinnatus, the Roman leader who saw his country through a difficult time and then gave up his authority in order to return to his life as a farmer. The Society of Cincinnati was established to preserve the ideals of the American Revolution, and it was members of this club who named the city. Cincinnati's terrain also echoes descriptions the founders read of Rome, the City of Seven Hills. Drawing on these parallels, it seemed that Cincinnati was destined for greatness from the start.

The tour of Cincinnati begins at Fountain Square, at the corner of Vine and East Fifth Street. If not the geographical center of the city, **Fountain Square** is certainly its symbolic center. Dedicated in 1871, the Tyler Davidson Fountain has seen the city grow from a bustling nineteenth-century city to a burgeoning metropolis. The fountain itself celebrates the founding element of the city's success: water. Looking down from 43 feet, the fountain's central figure, the Genius of Water, looks on as rain flows from her hands. The four bas-relief tableaus illustrate the four economic uses of water: the power generated by steam, the power generated by flowing water, the transportation uses of rivers and seas, and the fish that live in water. Though all of these have played a diminishing role in the economy over the years, all four were central to the region's growth.

Across the street at Vine and Sixth, you will find a local treasure. **Batsakes Hat Shop** has been serving the behatted men of Cincinnati for well over 100 years. There are few places like this left anymore. Guss Miller, who began working at the shop for his uncle Pete Batsakes at age 17, now runs the place. There is any number of buy-and-wear lids for the average customer—from fedoras to cowboy hats—but the real connoisseur will ask about having a custom hat made.

A block south of the hat shop is the impressive **Carew Tower**. A dedicated elevator and a short flight of stairs take visitors to the top, where you can experience a grand view. In addition to the eagle-eye perspective on the city, you can see a fair share of Kentucky, Ohio, and Indiana. The observation deck is in the open air—it is quite exhilarating—so consider your ability to deal with the weather conditions before heading up.

On the ground floor of Carew Tower is a real jewel. **Hathaway's Diner** may serve the best breakfast in town. It is a classic 50s greasy spoon that simply never changed, and if you have never tried goetta, this is the place to start. A combination of oats, pork, and spices, goetta is first made into a cold loaf and then sliced and fried on the grill. If the server realizes you're ordering goetta for the first time, the cook will leave it on the grill a bit longer, giving it a nice crunch. The texture can make or break this dish, and general wisdom suggests it is best to start crunchy and begin ordering it softer as appreciation grows.

The dish has roots in the German-American community, and you simply cannot find it outside the Cincinnati area. The world's largest producer of goetta, Glier's Goetta, rolls out over a million pounds a year, which is a lot considering it's mostly distributed locally. If you really come to appreciate goetta, two festivals on the Kentucky side of the border celebrate this local treat—the "Original Goettafest" in MainStrasse Village and Glier's GoettaFest. At these events, they mix it up quite a bit, serving goetta sliders and goetta dogs, all the while basking in the hallmarks of German-American culture.

Navigating Cincinnati like a local would require some time learning all the neighborhoods. There are many. We will only visit a few. Just north of downtown is the famous Over-the-Rhine neighborhood (OTR for short). Here, 943 buildings sit in what is believed to be the largest urban historic district in the country. After exploring the neighborhood's fabulous Italianate nineteenth-century architecture, be sure to stop for a bite at **Senate**. Exposed brick walls, the clean line of the bar that stretches the length of the restaurant, and a small, open kitchen work together to balance a classic sensibility with a contemporary feel. The menu does the same. They are best known for their hot dogs, like nothing you've tried before. The Korean is topped with kimchi. The Trailer Park is wrapped in bacon and covered in coleslaw, cheese, and BBQ potato chips. And the hot dog of the day is always an adventure.

There are quite a few excellent museums in Cincinnati. Close to downtown, at Pike and Fourth Streets, the **Taft Museum of Art** is an unassumingly elegant space for viewing art. The museum resides in the precisely named Baum-Longworth-Sinton-Taft House, which was built in 1820 in the Federalist style. From the beautifully manicured grounds to the imposing pillars, the site itself would be worth a tour even if it weren't the home of one of the most delightful small art galleries in the country. Charles and Anna Taft bequeathed the core of the collection, along with the home itself, to the city in 1927. On its historic walls are paintings by masters such as Rembrandt and Sargent, and the foyer features a landscape mural painted before the Civil War by African-American artist Robert S. Duncanson.

Northwest of downtown, just off Central Avenue, is a museum with a historical angle. Built in 1804, the **Betts House** is the oldest surviving brick building in Cincinnati. Back in the early nineteenth century, people were transitioning from less permanent homes. Brick structures suggested permanence and said something about the way people who lived here perceived the region. Of course, it makes sense that the Betts would have built their home from brick. William and Phebe Betts had a brickyard here and kept feeding the growing city the blocks it needed. The museum itself captures this period of Cincinnati history with a focus on the urban environment.

A few blocks west of the Betts House is a destination for museum lov-

CINCINNATI'S OLD TRAIN STATION IS PERHAPS MORE STUNNING INSIDE THAN OUT

ers. **Cincinnati Museum Center at Union Terminal**, as its name suggests, is located in the city's historic Union Terminal. The center houses a host of museums: the Cincinnati History Museum, the Duke Energy Children's Museum, and the Museum of Natural History & Science. The center also contains the Cincinnati Historical Society Library and an Omnimax Theater. You simply have to set aside more than one day if you hope to explore all of the museums. Of special note is the Cincinnati History Museum, which illustrates the city's past with an impressive recreation of the Cincinnati Public Landing from the mid-nineteenth century. Visitors can climb aboard a 94-foot side-wheel steamboat here. Even if you don't have a day to spend, be sure to visit Union Terminal. Fully restored, the old train station is a breathtaking piece of architecture.

Finally, north of the Museum Center there's a special place you won't want to miss. The **American Sign Museum** has one of the best exhibitions around: a collection of vintage signs. This place is a shrine to commercial culture and the Holy Grail for design enthusiasts. There are pieces of all sizes from all over. As you pull up to the museum, you are greeted by a 20-foot genie who used to hock carpets in Los Angeles. Now he holds a welcome sign. Once you're inside, the world explodes into neon-lit reds, blues, yellows, and greens. There are signs here from famous chains—like McDonald's, Kelly Tires, and HoJo's—and local businesses. All of it is laid out along an indoor Main Street, USA.

Finally, no trip to Cincinnati would be complete without a visit to the zoo. Several years back, the creation of the Historic Vine Street Village changed the way visitors enter the **Cincinnati Zoo & Botanical Garden**. Now guests are greeted by a simple pavilion that provides places for shopping, dining, or just resting your feet. Beyond the entrance, you will find the full collection of animals you come to expect from a decent city zoo: lions, tigers, bears, elephants, giraffes, armadillos, foxes, cheetahs, red pandas, and North American river otters, just to name a few. More intimately, you will see zookeepers wandering around with friendly animals, allowing visitors a chance to see a few of the zoo's residents face to face.

What really makes this zoo stand out, however, is its area of gardens. The botanical gardens blend into the park with exquisite plant beds tucked in between more traditional zoo exhibitions. For a closer look and another opportunity to rest your feet, the zoo's railroad makes a scenic loop through the middle of the property and is worth a ride, if only for the route it takes across Swan Lake. You will find the zoo really deserves its reputation as one of the best zoos in the country for kids, and there's a lot here for adults who might appreciate the historical nature of the place—the Reptile House, for example, is the oldest zoo building in the United States.

There are dozens of places to stay if your plans include a night in or around Cincinnati. One of the finest of these is the **Cincinnatian Hotel**.

A HAWK AT CINCINNATI ZOO & BOTANICAL GARDENS

When it was built in 1882, Cincinnatians witnessed the completion of the city's tallest building, then called the Palace Hotel, which stood eight stories tall and offered 300 rooms. When renovated in the 1980s, the hotel's small-ish nineteenth-century spaces were enlarged, and today the Cincinnatian offers 146 rooms and a handful of suites. Right in town, just a block from Fountain Square, the hotel offers the usual amenities.

Away from the city, you might consider the **Six Acres Bed & Breakfast**. This home, built by Zebulon Strong in the mid-1800s, was a stop on the Underground Railroad. Today, the 6,500-square-foot mansion is a stunningly decorated B&B. The inn offers nine rooms and a two-bedroom suite.

Leaving the city behind, our route—through Hamilton and Butler Counties on the way to Oxford—heads more or less in a northwesterly direction. Ignoring back roads for a moment, from the zoo, take I-75 north to I-275 west. Exit the interstate at Dixie Highway and continue north to Fairfield and the only grocery store you're likely to find mentioned in a travel guide. **Jungle Jim's International Market** is a sprawling village of a grocery store, with amenities you don't find anywhere else—a cigar humidor and tobacco shop, a state liquor store, a cheese shop, and gift shops—and it's all under one roof. Even with all this, what really sets Jungle Jim's apart is the food.

Slavery, Abolition, and the Underground Railroad

Literally on the frontline in the slavery fight, Cincinnati boasted a strong abolitionist sentiment before the Civil War and was a key corridor for the Underground Railroad. Due to the Fugitive Slave Act of 1850, requiring the return of escaped slaves to their masters, escaped slaves who made it across the Ohio River were not safe until they reached Canada. As such, many locals aided in these clandestine journeys north. Throughout the city, museums and monuments commemorate abolitionists, the Underground Railroad, and the men and women who risked everything for a chance at freedom.

When she was only 21, Harriet Beecher moved with her family from Connecticut to Ohio. Her father, Rev. Lyman Beecher, was the first president of Lane Theological Seminary in Walnut Hills, north of Cincinnati. He also taught there and was the pastor of the Second Presbyterian Church of Cincinnati. Harriet lived in the house off and on for a number of years.

Though she wrote *Uncle Tom's Cabin* mostly in Maine after marrying Calvin Ellis Stowe, she probably developed a keen appreciation for the antislavery argument while in Ohio. The **Harriet Beecher Stowe House**, in the Walnut Hills neighborhood, was her father's house; visitors can learn about this impressive family, the history of abolitionism, women's rights, and the Underground Railroad, as well as the history of Lane Theological Seminary.

For a more comprehensive look at slavery, the **National Underground Railroad Freedom Center** does more than simply chronicle the stories of those who took great risks—and often paid dearly—to secure others' freedom. It also teaches visitors about the reality of slavery and human trafficking today. The Freedom Center sits downtown, south of the interstate, directly in line with the Roebling Suspension Bridge.

With aisles and aisles of specialty and international items, many foods that people only see on shelves when they travel overseas, this is a treasured destination for people who find joy mixing food and adventure. The grocery store has been around since 1971. It began as a produce stand run by one Jim Bonaminio. The current space, around 6.5 acres, features animatronic displays and a real tongue-in-cheek sense of style. (The restrooms, for example, are disguised as port-a-potties.)

Continuing up Dixie Highway, the road merges with Central Avenue and drops you off on High Street in downtown Hamilton. As they do all over the Midwest, rivers define the human geography. Hamilton straddles the Miami River, a 160-mile tributary of the Ohio River, which connects towns as far north as Piqua with Dayton, Hamilton, and Cincinnati. In the late eighteenth century, the terrain near present-day Hamilton made this a relatively easy place to ford the river. The water was shallow, the bottom smooth. To take advantage of this, the Army built Fort Hamilton here in 1791 to help supply troops farther west. A year later, General "Mad" Anthony Wayne expanded the fort.

The fort was built on the east side of the river on a site just south of the High Street–Main Street Bridge. Today, what stands on the site is an impressive commemoration of the historical contributions of Butler County, the **Butler County Soldiers, Sailors, and Pioneers Monument**. Inside you will find two floors of exhibitions. The crux of the museum is its collection of Civil War weapons, though historical weapons from other American military conflicts are also on display. The building itself is part of the exhibition. Two stained-glass windows depict the traditional role of women during past wars. In one, two nurses care for Civil War wounded. In the other, three women sit at home, faithfully waiting for the men to return. Atop the monument is the figure of a victorious Civil War soldier, waving his hat in victory. He's come to be known as Billy Yank (the symbolic match for Johnny Reb).

Next door to the monument, still on the site of the old Fort Hamilton, sits an ancient building. This monumental cabin is not original to the site. The four-room log cabin was built across the river from the old fort in 1804, about four years after Fort Hamilton had been abandoned by the army. The cabin's journey from Rossville (the name of the community on the west side

JUNGLE JIM'S IN FAIRFIELD IS A FOODIE PARADISE

of the Great Miami, before it was absorbed into Hamilton) is a fascinating one. Apparently, it sat hidden from view for decades. Years of additions and remodeling disguised the old home within. In 1964, the home was almost demolished, but the log cabin was discovered inside the frame of the house and was preserved, donated to the city, and moved to its present site. Many have commented on the workmanship—such as the cabin's lack of nails.

Kitty-corner to the monument is the **Robert McCloskey Museum at Heritage Hall Museum**, where a hometown favorite is remembered. A permanent exhibition looks at the life and work of Robert McCloskey, the famous author and illustrator of children's books, best known for *Make Way for Ducklings*, which follows a family of ducks all over Boston. The exhibition includes displays of the various awards and honors McCloskey received during his lifetime, original artwork, and the doughnut machine that featured so prominently in the first of McCloskey's Homer Price books.

Hamilton has two notable historic districts. The nine blocks behind Heritage Hall along the river are part of the **German Village Historic District**. While driving through, you will have a chance to appreciate some stunning residential architecture, including the Benninghofen House and the Lane Hooven House. The latter is an impressive octagonal home built in 1863. Interestingly, many of the homes predate the influx of German immigrants in the 1940s that gave the neighborhood its name. The other place to see a piece of Hamilton history is across the river in the **Rossville Historic District**. Founded in 1804, Rossville merged with Hamilton in 1854.

West of the river, our route heads south on Pyramid Hill Boulevard. A half-mile down, you come to the **Pyramid Hill Sculpture Park and Museum**. The park's 335 acres comprise a variety of exhibition spaces. A handful of hiking trails gives visitors a chance to view the artwork displayed around the property. The Ancient Sculpture Museum gives the art of sculpture some context with more than sixty monumental pieces, all over a thousand years old. While the park and museum are open year-round, you can best appreciate all Pyramid Hill has to offer during the warmer months.

Continuing south on OH 128 (which was Pyramid Hill Boulevard), drive a little over 6 miles, passing through the small town of Ross. Turn left onto Cincinnati Brookville Road, which becomes Colerain Road as it crosses the Miami River. Turn left and then right at the fork onto Colerain. About 2.5 miles later, you will come to the **Vinoklet Winery**, which sits on a hill overlooking the Miami River Valley. Catawba grapes have grown in this region for nearly 200 years and are behind one of Vinoklet's more popular wines, Sunset Blush. This far north, it's hard to imagine that you've crossed back into Cincinnati. Vinoklet remains the only winery in Cincinnati located on its own working vineyard. The winery is as popular for its restaurant as it is for its wines. With this hillside location and the potential for stunning sunsets, it's easy to imagine why.

Returning north to Ross, we will continue on Cincinnati Brookville Road north for 11 miles, pulling up just short of the Indiana border. The Governor Bebb MetroPark is named for the state's nineteenth governor, William Bebb. This 264-acre park has trails for hiking and primitive campsites, but the day visitor will not want to miss the park's Pioneer Village. The centerpiece of the village is the boyhood home of William Bebb, but other log cabins have been transplanted here from around the area—all dating from the early to mid-1800s.

The village makes a play at offering a more complete look at an early Ohio

BEBB PARK HOUSES MANY HISTORIC STRUCTURES FROM THE AREA

community; in addition to homes, you will find a blacksmith's shop, a trading post, a school, a village green, and stocks for punishing miscreants. Another unique structure brought to the property is one of two remaining original covered bridges in the county. You can't miss it as you drive into the park. The bridge was brought from the Oxford area and erected over the Dry Fork of the Whitewater River. It is open only to foot traffic. Because the road dips below the grade of the bridge, visitors have a unique opportunity to take a peek at the undercarriage—something that usually gets your feet wet.

From the park, backtrack 0.2 mile to California Road. Take that north to Hamilton Scipio Road East, and continue to Sample Road. Follow that north into Reily. A jog east over Indian Creek and north on Oxford Reily Road will land you, 5 miles later, in Oxford.

The trip winds up in the northwest corner of Butler County, in the beautiful town of Oxford, Ohio, the home of Miami University. The historic campus alone is worth the visit, especially in the fall, when the leaves are turning colors. The school also means that Oxford enjoys a number of great restaurants and is able to support a handful of excellent bed and breakfasts for visiting parents and educators.

Miami University is named for its locale, the Miami River Valley. Four Mile Creek, which marks the eastern boundary of the campus, is a tributary of the Great Miami River. (Four Mile Creek flows into Seven Mile Creek, which subsequently empties into the Miami, just north of Hamilton.) The university can trace its history back to George Washington, who wanted a school in the Northwest Territory. The first classes were held in 1824—that first year, three faculty (including the president) and 20 students made up the school—but the university had been in the planning stages since 1803.

Interestingly, Miami University closed for a time in the late 1800s. Declining enrollment led the board of trustees, in 1873, to close up shop and lease the campus. By 1885, however, the university was granted a second life. Today nearly 15,000 students flock to Oxford for school each year.

One of the school's most lasting legacies comes from one of its earliest professors: William Holmes McGuffey, who came to Miami University in 1826. While he taught here in Oxford, he began writing the now famous McGuffey Readers. These graded primers were used as textbooks throughout the country. Henry Ford often referenced the importance of the McGuffey Readers to his own education.

On the school's campus, there is a museum dedicated to McGuffey and his eclectic readers: the aptly named **McGuffey Museum**. Located in the McGuffey House, exhibitions preserve memories of the period with special attention to the good professor's work as a textbook author.

One of the finest places to spend the night in the area is the **Presidio Pines Bed & Breakfast**, east of town on Oxford-Trenton Road. The inn is an old farmhouse that has been fully remodeled to accommodate guests. Tari

PRESIDIO PINES IS ONE OF THE FINEST B&BS IN A TOWN THAT BOASTS OF QUITE OF FEW EXCELLENT INNS

and Scott Spurlock had been living in the home until they lost it to a fire in 2000. Instead of simply rebuilding and moving back in, they used the insurance money to build another home on the property and began the hard work of turning their farmhouse into a B&B.

Since the original house was made of brick, the shell survived the fire. Inside, you will find a spacious dining area, a comfortable living room, and beautifully appointed guest rooms. There are hardwood floors and exposed brick walls throughout, giving the place a sense of old-world charm. And the kitchen is fully stocked with snacks for those who appreciate a late-night treat.

For dining, the best place in town, hands down, is **Paesano's Pasta House**. The restaurant is located on South Campus Avenue on the site of Oxford's legendary Mary Jo's Cuisine. Paesano's took over the location in 2004. Any new restaurant on the spot was sure to draw comparisons with its popular predecessor, but this eatery has forged its own path and gained quite a reputation for serving the best Italian food around.

For even more casual eats, you should try the **Bagel & Deli Shop** on High Street. Seriously, how can anyone resist a sandwich shop with a "Tonya Harding Club" on the menu?

North of town, you might consider visiting the **Black Covered Bridge**. Heading north on Morning Sun Road, before it crosses Four Mile Creek, you will see Corso Road on the left. This is the old road, and it takes you to the only extant covered bridge still in situ in Butler County. (You might recall that the covered bridge at the Governor Bebb Metropark was moved from its original location.) Built in 1869, the bridge was restored in 2000. There is a small turn-around at the bridge. You can park your car in the circle and walk the entire 206-foot span. The bridge dead-ends at a farm field, so there's no need to worry about traffic.

For a final bit of local history, visit the two-story **DeWitt Log Homestead**, east of Four Mile Creek, off Trenton Oxford Road, down a gated drive. Dating from 1805, the cabin was constructed by early settlers who came from New Jersey by way of Kentucky. It is currently the oldest structure in Butler County. Open daily; it's worth a quick stop.

IN THE AREA

Accommodations

CINCINNATIAN HOTEL, 601 Vine Street, Cincinnati. Call 1-800-942-9000. Website: cincinnatianhotel.com. $$$.

PRESIDIO PINES BED & BREAKFAST, 3152 Oxford-Trenton Road, Oxford. Call 513-967-4603. Website: presidiopinesbedandbreakfast.com. $$$.

SIX ACRES BED & BREAKFAST, 5350 Hamilton Avenue, Cincinnati. Call 513-541-0873. Website: sixacresbb.com. $$.

Attractions and Recreation

AMERICAN SIGN MUSEUM, 1330 Monmouth Avenue, Cincinnati. Call 513-541-6366. Website: americansignmuseum.org.

BATSAKES HAT SHOP, 1 West Sixth Street, Cincinnati. Call 513-721-9345.

BB RIVERBOATS, 101 Riverboat Row, Newport, Kentucky. Call 859-261-8500. Website: bbriverboats.com.

BETTS HOUSE, 416 Clark Street, Cincinnati. Call 513-651-0734. Website: thebettshouse.org. The house is open Tuesdays through Thursday and two Saturdays a month.

BLACK COVERED BRIDGE, 5401 Corso Road, Oxford. Call 513-523-8005 for the Oxford Museum Association. Website: oxfordmuseumassociation .com/black-covered-bridge.

BUTLER COUNTY SOLDIERS, SAILORS AND PIONEERS MONUMENT, One South Monument Avenue, Hamilton. Call 513-867-5823. Website: butler countyohio.org/monument.

CAREW TOWER, 441 Vine Street, Cincinnati. Call 513-579-9735.

CHILO: LIVING AND WORKING WITH THE OHIO RIVER, US 52, Chilo. Call 513-732-2977 or 513-876-9013. Website: parks.clermontcountyohio.gov/ Chilo.aspx.

CINCINNATI MUSEUM CENTER AT UNION TERMINAL, 1301 Western Avenue, Cincinnati. Call 513-287-7000 or 1-800-733-2077. Website: cincy museum.org.

CINCINNATI ZOO & BOTANICAL GARDEN, 3400 Vine Street, Cincinnati. Call 513-281-4700 or 1-800-944-4776. Website: cincyzoo.org. Open daily 9–6.

CONEY ISLAND, 6201 Kellogg Avenue, Cincinnati. Call 513-232-8230. Website: coneyislandpark.com. In the summer, the Sunlite Pool opens daily at 10. Classic Rides opens daily at 11.

DEWITT LOG HOMESTEAD, State Route 73, Oxford. Call 513-523-8005 for the Oxford Museum Association. Website: oxfordmuseumassociation.com/ dewitt-homestead-oxford-ohio.

FOUNTAIN SQUARE, 520 Vine Street, Cincinnati. Website: myfountain square.com. The best parking in town, if you don't stumble upon an open spot on the street, is underneath Fountain Square. You can enter the under-ground garage from Vine and Walnut Streets, between East Fifth and Sixth Streets.

GERMAN VILLAGE HISTORIC DISTRICT, 131 Village Street, Hamilton. Call 513-844-8080. Website: hamilton-city.org.

GRANT BIRTHPLACE, 1551 Route 232, Point Pleasant. Call 1-800-283-8932. Website: ohiohistory.org/visit/museum-historic-site-locator/us-grant -birthplace/. Open April through October.

HARRIET BEECHER STOWE HOUSE, 2950 Gilbert Avenue, Cincinnati. Call 513-751-0651. Website: stowehousecincy.org. Open in the summer Friday–Sunday noon–4. (Open fewer days other times of the year, so call ahead or check the website.)

JUNGLE JIM'S INTERNATIONAL MARKET, 5440 Dixie Highway, Fairfield. Call 513-674-6000. Website: junglejims.com.

MCGUFFEY MUSEUM, 410 East Spring Street, Oxford. Call 513-529-8380. Website: miamioh.edu/mcguffeymuseum. Open afternoons, Thursday through Saturday.

NATIONAL UNDERGROUND RAILROAD FREEDOM CENTER, 50 East Freedom Way, Cincinnati. Call 513-333-7500. Website: freedomcenter.org

NEWPORT AQUARIUM, 1 Aquarium Way, Newport, Kentucky. Call 859-261-7444. Website: newportaquarium.com.

NEWPORT ON THE LEVEE, 1 Levee Way, Newport, Kentucky. Call 859-291-0550. Website: newportonthelevee.com. An outdoor shopping mall with a view of the Cincy skyline and a full calendar of free events.

PROMONT HOUSE MUSEUM, 906 Main Street, Milford. Call 513-248-0324. Website: milfordhistory.net. The museum is open Fridays and weekends.

PYRAMID HILL SCULPTURE PARK AND MUSEUM, 1763 Hamilton-Cleves Road, SR 128, Hamilton. Call 513-868-1234. Website: pyramidhill.org.

THE RANKIN HOUSE, 6152 Rankin Road, Ripley. Call 937-392-1627 or 937-392-4044. Website: ohiohistory.org/rankin. Open regular hours from May through October. Call or visit website for off-season hours.

THE ROBERT MCCLOSKEY MUSEUM AT HERITAGE HALL MUSEUM, 20 High Street, Hamilton. Call 513-737-5958. Website: hamiltonheritagehall .org.

ROSSVILLE HISTORIC DISTRICT, B Street, Hamilton. Call 513-844-8080.

TAFT MUSEUM OF ART, 316 Pike Street, Cincinnati. Call 513-241-0343. Website: taftmuseum.org.

VINOKLET WINERY, 11069 Colerain Avenue, Cincinnati. Call 513-385-9309. Website: vinokletwines.com. Closed on Mondays.

WOODLAND MOUND PARK, 8250 Old Kellogg Road, Cincinnati. Call 513-474-3005. Website: greatparks.org/parks/woodland-mound.

Dining

BAGEL & DELI SHOP, 119 East High Street, Oxford. Call 513-523-2131. Website: bagelanddeli.com. $.

HATHAWAY'S DINER, 441 Vine Street, Cincinnati. Call 513-621-1332. Website: facebook.com/hathawaysdiner. Located on the first floor of Carew Tower. $.

PAESANO'S PASTA HOUSE, 308 South Campus Avenue, Oxford. Call 513-524-9100. Website: paesanospastahouse.com. Open for dinner. Closed on Mondays. $$$.

SENATE, 1212 Vine Street, Cincinnati. Call 513-421-2020. Website: senate-pub.com. $$.

Other Contacts

BUTLER COUNTY VISITOR BUREAU, 8756 Union Centre Boulevard, West Chester. Call 1-888-462-2282. Website: gettothebc.com.

CINCINNATI USA REGIONAL TOURISM NETWORK, 50 East Rivercenter Boulevard, Suite 810, Covington, Kentucky. Call 859-581-2260. Website: cincinnatiusa.com. (Also visit: cincyusa.com.) The Cincinnati USA Convention & Visitor Bureau operates a visitor center on Fountain Square (between Rock Bottom Brewery and Chipotle). The center is open Thursday through Sunday 11–5.

CLERMONT COUNTY CONVENTION & VISITOR BUREAU, 410 East Main Street, Batavia. Call 513-732-3600. Website: visitclermontohio.com.

OXFORD VISITOR BUREAU, 14 West Park Place, Suite C, Oxford. Call 513-523-8687. Website: enjoyoxford.org.

13

AROUND THE GREAT AND LITTLE MIAMI RIVERS

DAYTON, MIAMISBURG, LEBANON, OREGONIA,
WAYNESVILLE, YELLOW SPRINGS, URBANA

ESTIMATED LENGTH: 130 miles

ESTIMATED TIME: 4 hours

HIGHLIGHTS: This trip begins on a high note, with a tour of the National Museum of the U.S. Air Force, just east of Dayton. Heading into the city, you will have a chance to visit the Dayton Aviation Heritage National Park, the Boonshoft Museum of Discovery, the Dayton Art Institute, and several historic sites, including the impressive Carillon Historical Park and the SunWatch Indian Village. Descending down the Great Miami River, the itinerary takes you south into Miamisburg, where you will visit the Miamisburg Mound and the Gebhart Tavern. After passing through Franklin, the route turns southeast and enters Lebanon. There, you can tour the Glendower Mansion and grab a bite (or a room) at the Golden Lamb (the oldest hotel in Ohio). Next, is the Workshops of David T. Smith, after which you will begin to creep east and then north, with stops at the Fort Ancient State Memorial and Caesar's Creek Pioneer Village. In Waynesville, there is a day's worth of antiques shops to visit on Main Street, after which you drive north to Xenia, where you will pick up US 68 and go into Yellow Springs.

GETTING THERE: Dayton is less than an hour north of Cincinnati on I-75. Beginning downtown, the route follows Dixie Avenue south to Miamisburg and then Franklin. Heading east on OH 123, the trip continues to Lebanon, the Fort Ancient State Memorial, Oregonia, and Waynesville. From there you will turn north, passing south of Caesar Creek Lake on the way to Xenia, after which you will follow US 68 through Yellow Springs, Springfield, and Urbana.

LEFT: THE AIR FORCE MUSEUM INCLUDES HANGARS FULL OF FULL-SIZED HISTORIC AIRCRAFT

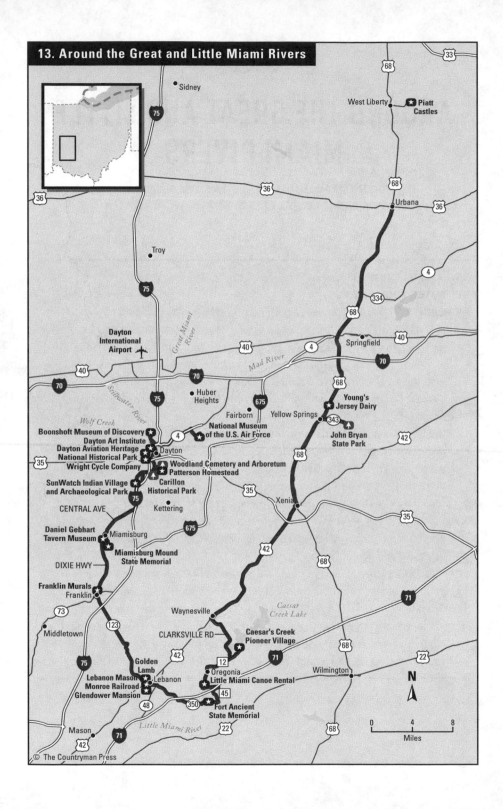

13. Around the Great and Little Miami Rivers

Sidney

West Liberty • ★ Piatt Castles

Urbana

Troy

Dayton International Airport

Huber Heights

Fairborn

National Museum of the U.S. Air Force

Yellow Springs

Young's Jersey Dairy

John Bryan State Park

Boonshoft Museum of Discovery
Dayton Art Institute
Dayton Aviation Heritage National Historical Park
Wright Cycle Company

Dayton

Woodland Cemetery and Arboretum
Patterson Homestead

SunWatch Indian Village and Archaeological Park

Carillon Historical Park

CENTRAL AVE

Kettering

Springfield

Xenia

Daniel Gebhart Tavern Museum

Miamisburg

Miamisburg Mound State Memorial

DIXIE HWY

Franklin Murals
Franklin

Waynesville

Caesar Creek Lake

Middletown

CLARKSVILLE RD

Caesar's Creek Pioneer Village

Golden Lamb

Lebanon Mason
Monroe Railroad
Glendower Mansion

Lebanon

Oregonia
Little Miami Canoe Rental

Wilmington

Fort Ancient State Memorial

Mason

Little Miami River

N

0   4   8
Miles

Great Miami River

Mad River

Stillwater River

Wolf Creek

© The Countryman Press

Dayton dates to 1796, but the region didn't become a destination for settlers until a year later when the Mad River Road connected the settlement to Cincinnati. The city was founded at the confluence of several rivers. The Great Miami River flows north to south through town, and along the way, it is joined by the Stillwater and Mad Rivers, as well as Wolf Creek. The heart of Dayton still straddles these watercourses.

There are several ways to explore Dayton. A chronological approach would begin with the reconstructed native settlement at SunWatch Indian Village and follow with a look at the history of American settlement with a trip to Carillon Historical Park. Rounding out the 1800s and landing solidly in the twentieth century, this tour would explore the history of flight with a visit to the Wright Cycle Shop and the U.S. Air Force Museum. Another approach would be to divide the sites into categories, exploring natural features of the city at various MetroParks, industrial heritage at the Packard Museum and the aviation museums, and area culture at the Dayton Art Institute.

Since this book is all about the journey, our approach will take a geographical approach: beginning east of town at the Air Force Museum and finishing south of town at SunWatch Village, stopping along the way at museums, restaurants, historic homes, picturesque cemeteries, and whatever else makes Dayton special.

The entrance to the **National Museum of the U.S. Air Force** is off Springfield Street. The museum is located on the Wright-Patterson Air Force Base, and because it's a national museum, admission is always free. The large museum is laid out like a series of hangars housing well over 300 planes, helicopters, and missiles—a treasure trove of flight. Exhibitions explore both the history of flight and its military applications.

A series of exhibitions organized according to the country's major conflicts, beginning before World War II, explores the role of the Air Force. The first hangar looks at World War II and how the advent of human flight led to incredible changes in the execution of warfare. The center hangar dedicates itself to the wars in Southeast Asia and Korea, and the final hangar looks at the Cold War. One can only imagine how the museum might someday expand. An unmanned drone represents current events. What's next? The museum has a nice café, bookshop, and museum store. There is also an IMAX theater, opposite the main entrance.

The museum is part of the larger **National Aviation Heritage Area**, comprising 15 sites as widely scattered as the Armstrong Air & Space Museum in Wapakoneta and the Wright B Flyer south of Dayton. There are also some nice sites in downtown Dayton, which we will get to later. For now, it's off to the **Boonshoft Museum of Discovery**.

Families traveling with children will find the Boonshoft Museum an especially fun stop. The museum's mission is to provide "interactive science learning experiences" for children and adults. This includes a small indoor

YOUR TRIP BEGINS AT THE NATIONAL MUSEUM OF THE UNITED STATES AIR FORCE IN DAYTON

zoo, a space dedicated to the role of water in the Miami River Valley, and the always-impressive Science on a Sphere—a 68-inch globe onto which images of earth are projected, creating visually engrossing animated exhibitions.

A really neat space at the museum is the Tree House (officially the "Mead Westvaco Treehouse"). Accessed at the end of a long hall that takes you beyond the traditional walls of the museum, the room overlooks the adjacent woods, sits on stilts, and is wrapped around with windows. The museum uses the room for various classes and presentations. The tree house makes a great perch for bird-watching in all kinds of weather.

From the Boonshoft, take the Deweese Parkway south to Ridge Road south, cross the Stillwater River, and turn left (south) onto Riverside Drive. Turning right again onto Great Miami Boulevard, you will follow the road until it ends at Riverview Avenue. Then take another right. On your right, you will see the Dayton Art Institute. Take the next turn for Belmont Park North to find the parking lot.

The Dayton Art Institute is scenically located on a hill overlooking the Great Miami River. The museum is laid out in the shape of a diamond. The outer rooms encircle a space divided down the middle by a large auditorium. Two cloisters—open spaces surrounded by covered walks—are used for various events. The Hale Cloister features a landscaped lawn, a fountain, and ornamental trees. The Shaw Gothic Cloister is a large atrium the museum rents out for events year-round.

This layout creates a series of intimate gallery spaces on two levels. The upper level—where most guests enter the museum—is dedicated to art in the Western tradition. This is where you find the European masters and early American masterpieces. It's all here, from paintings by the ancient Greeks to American modernism. The lower level reflects the Eastern traditions and also includes work from pre-Columbian South America and Africa. While comprehensive, the museum is in no way overwhelming.

Across the river from the museum is the best place in town for seafood. Located on East Sixth Street, **Jay's Seafood Restaurant** has deep roots in Dayton. The restaurant is located in the old Dayton Corn and Grist Mill. The mahogany bar was built in 1882 for the Pony House Restaurant—a famous institution in its day. Best of all, a visit to Jay's puts you smack dab in the middle of the Oregon Historic District. South of Fifth Street to US 35, bounded to the west and east by Patterson Boulevard and Wayne Avenue, the Historic District is a nice combination of residential neighborhood streets, small shops, and excellent restaurants. The old brick streets and the old homes are worth some undirected roaming by themselves, but for a more purposeful visit, check out the shopping and dining along Fifth Street.

Heading north to Third Street and then west, the Wright-Dunbar Interpretive Center and Visitor Center is about a half mile past the Great Miami River. This is the place to begin a tour of the **Dayton Aviation Heritage National Historical Park**, which includes several sites that commemorate the Wright brothers' connection to Dayton, as well the legacy of the writer Paul Dunbar. The Interpretive Center starts you off with some excellent exhibitions. Here visitors get an overview of Orville and Wilbur Wright's work—from their experience as printers (they designed and built their own press) to building bikes to the breakthroughs they made in advancing human flight. The brothers' first flight may have been at Kitty Hawk, North Carolina, but the groundwork was all laid here in Dayton.

Adjacent to the interpretive center is the **Wright Cycle Company**. Between 1892 and 1908 the Wrights' bicycle business occupied five differ-

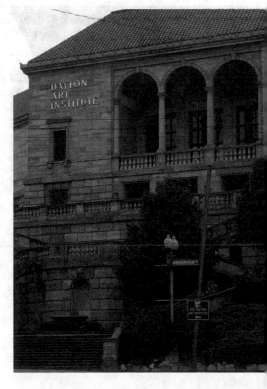

THE DAYTON ART INSTITUTE OVERLOOKS THE GREAT MIAMI RIVER

ent buildings. One of these buildings was purchased by Henry Ford and moved to Greenfield Village in Dearborn, Michigan. The one here on South William Street, the company's home from 1895 to 1897, is the only surviving building that remains at its original location on its original foundation. They used the second story of the shop for their printing business.

Many people don't realize that the Wright brothers were rather successful printers. Orville went to high school with Paul Laurence Dunbar, and for a short time (about six weeks) the brothers published the Tattler—Dayton's first African-American newspaper, which Dunbar wrote and edited. Dunbar went on to become a highly respected poet, novelist, and playwright.

Writing in both the dialect of the African-American community where he was raised and the English of the classicists, Dunbar was the first African-American poet to gain national prominence. He wrote poetry, short stories, novels, and plays. His life was shortened, tragically, by tuberculosis. He died in 1906 at the age of 33 in the home that he shared with his mother, Matilda. Matilda lived out the rest of her days in the home, and in 1936 the house was sold to the state of Ohio.

An important historical site, the **Paul Laurence Dunbar House** is now part of the Dayton Aviation Heritage Park. The site is open for tours on Thursdays, Fridays, and Saturdays with a reservation, so be sure to call ahead to secure your spot before you visit.

THE WRIGHT CYCLE COMPANY WAS HOUSED HERE FROM 1895 TO 1897

Paul Dunbar is buried with other notable figures in Dayton's historic **Woodland Cemetery and Arboretum**. Opened in 1843, the cemetery's original 40 acres were chosen for their hilltop views. The property has expanded to 200 acres as the city has expanded around it. At one time, this was a busier place. Families often visited these "garden cemeteries" for picnics and to tarry awhile with their deceased loved ones.

Today the cemetery is no less beautiful. In fact, the expansive park setting, with its numerous varieties of mature trees, is as scenic as any arboretum. More than 165 species of trees thrive here, and the gravestones beneath the high canopy of leaves give the property a bittersweet poignancy. Even if you don't have loved

MANY CHILDREN VISIT THE WOODLAND CEMETERY TO LEAVE TOKENS AT THE GRAVE OF JOHNNY MOREHOUSE

ones interred here, there are some graves you might want to visit. The columnist Erma Bombeck is buried here, as are the Wright brothers.

A popular gravesite is that of young Johnny Morehouse. In the late 1800s, the five-year-old Johnny drowned in the Miami and Erie Canal. After he was buried at Woodland Cemetery, his dog began keeping vigil. The dog spent every day at Johnny's graveside until it, too, died. The stone figure of a boy with his dog was erected to commemorate the companion's loyalty, and children still leave gifts and treats for the pair.

From the cemetery, take Brown Street south to Springhouse Road. Across the street from each other are two very different Dayton institutions. On the west side of the street is the **Patterson Homestead**. The farmhouse was built by Colonel Robert Patterson, a Revolutionary War veteran. The homestead stayed in the Patterson family for generations. At one point, the farm covered more than 2,000 acres. There was a sawmill and sugar camp, as well as a gristmill and stone mill. Patterson's grandsons firmly established the family legacy; they created the National Cash Register Company after purchasing the National Manufacturing Company and the patent for the first mechanical cash register.

The other institution is the famed **Pine Club**—a local steakhouse with a national reputation. The classic steak-and-potato menu has not changed much since the restaurant's founding in 1947. In fact, very little has changed, from the menu to the wood-paneled décor. This commitment to tradition earned The Pine Club a place on *T Magazine*'s list of "10 of the World's Greatest Old Dining Institutions." (That's the supplemental magazine pub-

THE WOODLAND CEMETERY WAS CREATED AT A TIME WHEN CEMETERIES WERE A PLACE FOR FAMILIES TO PICNIC AND SOCIALIZE

lished by the *New York Times*.) For old-school dining, few places compare.

There are two more stops before we head south of Dayton. The first is the **Carillon Historical Park**. To get there, head north on Brown Street and then take Stewart Street west. One block over, turn south onto South Patterson Road. Less than a mile down, turn right onto Carillon Boulevard. Travel a little way down, and you will see the entrance to the park on your left.

If you only have time for one historic site while in Dayton, the Carillon Historical Park should be at the top of your list. The park is named for the famed Deeds Carillon. With 57 bells, this is the largest carillon in Ohio. Once operated by an electric keyboard, the bells are now played with the more traditional baton keyboard. In the summer, the park's carillonneur plays the instrument on Sunday afternoons.

THE CARILLON HISTORICAL PARK PRESERVES A NUMBER OF DAYTON'S HISTORIC PROPERTIES

The historical park gathers together some of Dayton's most important buildings to tell the history of the city's founding and growth. The Newcom Tavern, for example, is Dayton's oldest standing building. It was built in 1796 and moved in the 1960s to Carillon Park from Main Street. In all, there are twenty-five historic buildings set around a central green. Costumed interpreters are on hand to tell some of the stories behind these structures.

Crossing the river to West River Road, our route continues south to the road's end at **SunWatch Indian Village and Archaeological Park**. Evidence of a Fort Ancient settlement was discovered at this site in the 1960s. The Dayton Society of Natural History sponsored archaeological digs that provided enough information for the village to be reconstructed as an open-air museum.

A tour of SunWatch begins at the Visitor and Interpretive Center. There's a short movie, and some exhibitions fill in the big picture. Then visitors step outside to tour the village as it would have looked 800 years ago. You can explore the mud-walled shelters, with their thatched roofs. Inside, raised beds and a central firepit would have helped to warm those who lived here. Small gardens planted throughout the property shows how the Fort Ancient people may have grown their crops.

The museum offers special events throughout the year, like the SunWatch Native Flute Gathering. Some of these events offer guests an introduction to Native American culture and present debates in modern archaeology. SunWatch is open year-round, and each season reveals a unique perspective on the lives of the people who once called this village home.

You may not find a lot to do in Miamisburg, but there are some interesting historical sites, a handful of great places to eat, and an excellent bed and breakfast. Let's start with the lodgings. **The English Manor Inn Bed and Breakfast** is a stunning Tudor, originally built in the 1920s when Linden Avenue was known as "Millionaires' Row." It can be found just east of town on Linden Avenue. The home features hardwood floors, stained glass windows, and six guest rooms furnished with antiques. The home's original owner was William Schieble, the founder of Dayton's Schieble Toy & Novelty Company.

For dining, there's a longtime favorite: **The Hamburger Wagon**. For more than a hundred years, this rolling vendor's cart has been dishing burgers in downtown Miamisburg. The menu is as simple as can be. You can order a single or double, and those come with pickle, onion, salt, and pepper. The wagon's trademarked slogan makes it clear what's not available: "No Stinkin' Cheeses or Sloppy Sauces!" This is a pretty tight constraint for customers used to getting it their way, but it doesn't seem to have hurt business. The Hamburger Wagon burgers are consistently ranked on the best-in-Ohio lists of great burgers.

The **Daniel Gebhart Tavern Museum**, at the corner of Old Main Street and West Lock Street, is usually open only on Sundays. For weekend travelers, this means there's a 50/50 chance it will be open when they pass through town (unless they hit on the odd Saturday the museum is open). A couple hundred years ago, travelers had better luck with the tavern. Built in 1811 by one Daniel Gebhart, the tavern was a welcome sight on the frontier. Here travelers could find a warm meal and a dry bed. The tavern itself is a great big two-story log building the Miamisburg Historical Society has decked out with authentic furnishings. Behind the tavern is the Kercher Pioneer Home. Also owned by the Miamisburg Historical Society, this additional log cabin gives visitors a twofer when they visit the site.

From Main Street, take Mound Avenue east. As the road makes a sweeping turn south, the name changes to Mound Road. It is 1 mile from Main Street to the **Miamisburg Mound State Memorial**. An earthen mound is not the most durable of monuments. Even the pyramids have eroded over time, and they were made of stone. In order to preserve the site, the Miamisburg Mound is surrounded by a fence. To accommodate those who wish to scale this diminutive peak, there is a staircase to the top, which is also fenced in.

There used to be 10,000 mounds in the Ohio River Valley, and there is a lot of speculation about the how and why of these grand markers. Evidence suggests the Miamisburg Mound may have been the burial place for important leaders. Mound experts say that when a leader died, his or her body would have been laid here in a makeshift hut that was subsequently burned to the ground and covered with **earth**. Later leaders would be honored in the same way, each on top of a predecessor, while the mound grew.

Head back to Main Street and head south. Between Miamisburg and Franklin, the road name changes to Dayton-Cincinnati Pike, then to North Dixie Highway, and back to Main Street. Among other things, Franklin is known for the **Franklin Murals**. The downtown area is full of murals. Some of them are decorative, adding character to otherwise bland architecture. Others capture a piece of Franklin history. To find them, your best bet is to just head down Main Street and keep your eyes open. There are two murals on either side of Main on Third Street, for example. You'll also see them tucked into strange places, like on the side of the VFW Hall. Most are the work of local artist Eric Henn.

TOUR FRANKLIN FOR A LOOK AT THE NUMEROUS MURALS

It's an easy drive from Franklin to Lebanon. Take East Sixth Street (OH 123) east. OH 123 takes you all the way, but it's not a straight shot. To stay on the state route, you will turn left when the road comes to a T at OH122. Six hundred feet away is a five-way intersection. Take the second road on the right, Franklin Road. Once in Lebanon, take any street (West Silver Street, West Mulberry Street, or Main Street) east to Broadway.

Driving to Lebanon, you've crossed the watershed between the Great Miami River and the Little Miami River. The first stop on any visit to Lebanon has to be the **Golden Lamb**. From its humble beginnings as a tavern housed in a two-story log cabin, the Golden Lamb has seen much change in 200-plus years. The original building, from 1803, was replaced by a brick building in 1815, and over the years, the inn has expanded up and out. For more than 50 years of its history, the place was called the "Lebanon House." Through it all, the inn has welcomed guests to Lebanon. As such, it is the oldest continuously operating business in Ohio.

The Golden Lamb today is a great place for both a meal and a bed for the night. Various rooms of the hotel are named for the eminent personages who have stayed here in the past, such as the Charles Dickens Room, the Samuel Clemens Room, and the Harriet Beecher Stowe Room. Less literary guests have included John Quincy Adams, Rutherford B. Hayes, and James Garfield. And if you think these illustrious guests only hail from the nineteenth century, more recent visitors have included Ronald Reagan and George W. Bush. All of these rooms have the low-key elegance you might expect.

The restaurant is on the first floor and opens daily for lunch and dinner, as well as for Sunday brunch. In addition to eating at the dining room, guests can grab a drink at the Black Horse Tavern. The restaurant and the inn itself feel less like places decorated with antiques and more like antique places properly dressed for the period. The menu is a bit pricey, but regulars rave about the lamb meatloaf.

The other place to see while you are in town is the **Glendower Mansion**. Built in 1845, the Glendower Mansion is considered one of the finest examples of Greek Revival architecture in the Midwest. A proper tour would highlight the architectural details that make this home so special, such as the fluted Ionic and unfluted Doric columns. Inside, there are thirteen rooms to explore. The museum is open in the summer from Wednesday through Sunday, and around Christmas time, when the house is decorated with a Christmas carol theme.

The final big attraction in Lebanon is the **Lebanon Mason Monroe Railroad**, which makes scenic excursions through southern Ohio. The office is on Mechanic Street, but you will find the replica Victorian train station at the corner of Broadway and South Streets. There are themed trips throughout the year as well, including the popular North Pole Express.

Before leaving Lebanon, be sure to grab a treat at the Village Ice Cream Parlor on Broadway. This is a classic old-timey parlor that serves sodas, sundaes, and banana splits. Downtown Lebanon in general and the ice cream parlor, in particular, have a "Small Town USA" feel, and a handful of movie producers have taken advantage of that. The **Village Ice Cream Parlor** appeared in both the 1970s classic *Harper Valley PTA* and the 1990s movie *Milk Money*.

Continuing east on OH 123 (Main Street, in town), just after passing under I-71, turn left onto OH 350. After about 3 miles, the road drops quickly to cross the Little Miami River and then rises just as quickly to the high plateau overlooking the river's eastern bank. This is the site of the **Fort Ancient State Memorial**. Archaeologists have named the Fort Ancient people for these grand earthworks. Enclosing 100 acres with 3.5 miles of earthen walls, Fort Ancient is the largest prehistoric hilltop enclosure in the country. Interestingly, the "fort" was built by the Hopewell people more than 2,000 years ago. The Fort Ancient people lived nearby during a much later period in history.

Your tour should begin at the on-site museum. Like most of these interpretive centers, it offers an overview of the site and puts history in context. This is especially important here. Once you're out in the park, the earthworks themselves are not terribly compelling. Only when considering how and why they were built do they become fascinating. In addition to being an important piece of American history, the property is a decent park—a great place for a walk, for rollerblading, or for just sitting on a blanket for a picnic.

On the way to the next stop north of Oregonia, you can take a short detour into town for lunch at the **Little River Cafe**. The menu is none too fancy—they serve pizzas, salads, sandwiches, etc.—but it's a great location, right on the Little Miami Bike Trail. There's outdoor dining and a large stone fireplace outside for chilly days. The original café burned down several years ago, so the current restaurant is brand new.

To get there, head east on OH 350 to the first intersection and turn north onto County Road 45. When the road ends at Wilmington Road (County Road 7), turn west. The road drops down to the Little Miami River, becomes County Road 47, and follows the contours of the river north to Oregonia. The restaurant is on your left as you pull into town.

The Little Miami River is a great river for canoeing and kayaking. There is an excellent canoe livery here in Oregonia—you passed it on your way in. Little Miami Canoe Rental—Oregonia Base offers paddlers a number of trips. You can paddle a short 2 miles down the river or commit to a full 18-mile trek if time permits. High banks and thick woods make this one of the most scenic stretches of water in southern Ohio.

Continuing north on County Road 47, you will come to a fork just after

THE CAESAR CREEK PIONEER VILLAGE IS CLOSE TO CAESAR CREEK LAKE

passing Oregonia Road on your left. Take the right prong for County Road 12 (Oregonia Road). After 4 miles you will come to Pioneer Village Road on your left. Turn left and follow the road to Caesar's Creek Pioneer Village.

Caesar Creek Lake was borne of an act of Congress in 1938. The Flood Control Act of 1938 called for the construction of a dam on Caesar Creek. Of course, the lake itself is a flood of sorts, and to save some of the historic buildings that would otherwise now be underwater, they were moved to what is now **Caesar's Creek Pioneer Village**. There are more than fifteen log cabins and other structures from the late 1700s and the early 1800s. The buildings are open when the village puts on special events—camping weekends, rendezvous, and holiday events. There are often a host of re-enactors who give the village a sense of historic immediacy. The camping weekends are an especially fun way to enjoy the park.

Backtrack on Oregonia Road a short way to Clarksville Road, and then turn north to travel through part of the Caesar Creek Wilderness area. Then go west on OH 73, which leads into downtown Waynesville, which, by most estimates, is the antiques capital of Ohio. Coming in from the south on Main Street, there are antiques shops almost everywhere you look. The **Winsome**

Cottage, for example, has a finely curated inventory of unique vintage items, carrying everything from furniture to jewelry. Right down the street from that is the **Waynesville Antique Mall**, where more than 50 dealers hock their wares.

At the corner of Main Street and North Street, the **Cobblestone Village and Cafe** is a nice spot for a little shopping and lunch. The gift shop is full to the brim with home décor and decorative accessories. The café is touted as a gourmet café—the menu is pretty upscale. Start with the brie en croute (that is, "brie in crust"), then move on to any of the café's sandwiches. It's all good.

Every year Waynesville hosts a few excellent events. The **Second Saturday Street Faire**—held on the second Saturday of the month from June through September—is one of them. A portion of downtown is closed off to car traffic, and dozens of antique dealers, artists, and craft folks set up on the street. There's food and live entertainment, to boot. The other event is the **Ohio Sauerkraut Festival**, held the second full week of October to celebrate sauerkraut. They put it on hot dogs, pizza, and in doughnuts. If it wasn't so much fun, it might sound kind of gross. There's a ton of food, lots of craft booths, and plenty of entertainment.

One of the best finds in Waynesville is **The Hammel House Inn**, which is both a B&B and a restaurant. There has been a building on this site since the late 1700s when a log tavern was built here. The current structure dates back to 1817 (with remodeling and additions). The food is described as "come-as-you-are casual gourmet" (which also means you can bring your dog to lunch). The kitchen specializes in simple fare, done extremely well. The lodgings are excellent too. The inn has five guest rooms, decorated with fine cherry furniture (four-posters and the like). Rooms are large with private baths and seating areas, and the breakfast will keep you coming back.

Before leaving Waynesville, head over to the **Museum at the Friends Home** for a look at the region's history. Housed in the Friends Boarding Home, built in 1900, the museum offers three floors of exhibitions. There are rooms that are decorated with furnishings from different periods, as well as spaces dedicated to different aspects of Waynesville's history and the history of neighboring communities. There is even a chaise lounge said to have been reclined upon by Abraham Lincoln!

From Waynesville, head up US 42 to Xenia. For beautifully appointed rooms in an elegant home, make reservations at **Victoria's Bed & Breakfast**. The inn is located on Second Street in a neighborhood that once housed the town's gentry. There are mansions everywhere you look. Victoria's Bed & Breakfast is one of them. The 25-room brick Eastlake-style Victorian has five guest rooms. The inn's décor complements the home's hardwood floors and high ceilings. Breakfast is more of a continental affair at this particular B&B, but there are plenty of nearby places to eat if bagels and cereal are not substantial enough to fuel your engines in the morning.

Continuing north, now on US 68, our next stop is the artsy enclave of Yellow Springs. This community has everything you need for a weekend away. There are shops, restaurants, and amazing bed and breakfasts. All of it within walking distance of one another. Mature trees throughout the village create a shade-providing canopy that makes it a nice place to get out of the car, even on the hottest days.

At the south end of town, on West Limestone Street, is the Arthur Morgan

VICTORIA'S B&B IN YELLOW SPRINGS IS HOUSED IN A NINETEENTH-CENTURY HOME

MORE THAN AN ICE CREAM JOINT, YOUNG'S JERSEY DAIRY IS A COMPLETE FAMILY ENTERTAINMENT COMPLEX

House Bed & Breakfast. The rooms here have a lot of light. Rather than creating a dark and brooding atmosphere like many historic homes of its era, this bed and breakfast has walls painted in white, with bright accents, and windows that let in the sun. Each guest room has a private bath, though all are not en suite. It's just a block or so from the B&B to the restaurants in town.

Less than 3 miles east of Yellow Springs on OH 343, the Clifton Gorge has excellent hiking. The site is at the northern end of the **John Bryan State Park**. There's a small parking area off of OH 343 with a trailhead that will lead you back to the gorge. The trails take you down to the Little Miami River—it's much narrower here than it is down near Oregonia—where the walls of the gorge rise steeply. The property is not too big, so you don't have to commit hours for a visit, but you could extend the trip by driving around to the main entrance and exploring the rest of the park.

Just north of Yellow Springs on US 68, families flock to **Young's Jersey Dairy** in the summer. This working dairy has a restaurant, a bakery, and a cheese shop. They sell a mess of ice cream. Once a family pulls in for a simple scoop, they simply cannot leave. There are batting cages, miniature golf, a playground, and seasonal attractions like a corn maze (or would that be a maize maze?). This would all seem like crass commercialism if the ice cream weren't so darn good, and if its adjacent restaurant, the **Golden Jersey Inn**, didn't knock your socks off with buttermilk fried chicken or chicken and dumplings.

Any mini-vacation that ends in Yellow Springs can be considered a success. But for those who love the open road, the final hurrah of this road trip is a race north through Urbana and a visit to the unique castles near West Liberty.

Continue north on US 68 around the west side of Springfield to Urbana. In downtown Urbana, on Main Street, is a great little sandwich place that is as well, or better, known for its potato chips as for its food. It's **Mumford's Potato Chip & Deli**. The ham-and-cheese sub, the Rueben, the hoagie—they're all good. Be sure to include a bag of potato chips. Locally made potato chips like these are a rare gem for any community that still has an outfit like this.

IN THE AREA

Accommodations

ENGLISH MANOR INN BED AND BREAKFAST, 505 East Linden Avenue, Miamisburg. Call 937-866-2288. Website: englishmanorohio.com. $$.

GOLDEN LAMB, 27 South Broadway, Lebanon. Call 513-932-5065. Website: goldenlamb.com. $$.

THE HAMMEL HOUSE INN, 121 South Main Street, Waynesville. Call 513-897-3779. Website: thehammelhouseinn.com. $$.

VICTORIA'S BED & BREAKFAST, 209 East Second Street, Xenia. Call 937-374-1202. Website: victoriasbnb.com. $$.

Attractions and Recreation

BOONSHOFT MUSEUM OF DISCOVERY, 2600 DeWeese Parkway, Dayton. Call 937-275-7431. Website: boonshoftmuseum.org.

CAESAR'S CREEK PIONEER VILLAGE, 3999 Pioneer Village Road, Waynesville. Call 513-897-1120. Website: caesarscreekpioneervillage.org.

CARILLON HISTORICAL PARK, 1000 Carillon Boulevard, Dayton. Call 937-293-2841 or 1-877-234-4786. Website: daytonhistory.org/visit/dayton -history-sites/carillon-historical-park/.

DANIEL GEBHART TAVERN MUSEUM, corner of Old Main Street and West Lock Street, Miamisburg. Website: miamisburg.org/daniel_gebhart_tavern_museum.htm. Open Sunday afternoons and one Saturday per month.

DAYTON AVIATION HERITAGE NATIONAL HISTORICAL PARK. Call 937-425-0008. Website: nps.gov/daav.

FORT ANCIENT, 6123 OH 350, Oregonia. Call 513-932-4421. Website: fortancient.org.

FRANKLIN MURALS, downtown Franklin. Call 937-746-8457 (Franklin Chamber of Commerce).

GLENDOWER MANSION, 105 Cincinnati Avenue, Lebanon. Call 513-932-1817 or 1-800-283-8927. Website: wchsmuseum.org.

JOHN BRYAN STATE PARK, 3790 OH 370, Yellow Springs. Call 937-767-1274. Website: parks.ohiodnr.gov/johnbryan.

LEBANON MASON MONROE RAILROAD, 127 South Mechanic Street, Lebanon. Call 513-933-8022. Website: lebanonrr.com.

MIAMISBURG MOUND, East Mound Road, Miamisburg (a mile south of Route 725). Call 937-866-4532. Website: miamisburg.org/miamisburg_mound_park.htm.

MUSEUM AT THE FRIENDS HOME, 115 South Fourth Street, Waynesville. Call 513-897-1607. Website: friendshomemuseum.org.

NATIONAL AVIATION HERITAGE AREA. Call 937-443-0165. Website: aviationheritagearea.org.

NATIONAL MUSEUM OF THE U.S. AIR FORCE, 1100 Spaatz Street, Wright Patterson Air Force Base, Dayton. Call 937-255-3286. Website: nationalmuseum.af.mil.

OHIO SAUERKRAUT FESTIVAL, Waynesville. Call 513-897-8855. Website: sauerkrautfestival.com.

PATTERSON HOMESTEAD, 1815 Brown Street, Dayton. Call 937-222-9724. Website: daytonhistory.org/events/private-event-rental/patterson-homestead/.

PAUL LAURENCE DUNBAR HOUSE, 219 North Paul Laurence Dunbar Street, Dayton. Call 937-313-2010. Website: daytonhistory.org/visit/dayton -history-sites/paul-laurence-dunbar-house-historic-site.

SECOND SATURDAY STREET FAIRE, Waynesville. Website: facebook .com/SecondSaturdayStreetFaire/.

SUNWATCH INDIAN VILLAGE AND ARCHAEOLOGICAL PARK, 2301 West River Road, Dayton. Call 937-268-8199. Website: sunwatch.org.

VILLAGE ICE CREAM PARLOR, 22 South Broadway, Lebanon. Call 513-932-6918. Website: villageicecreamparlor.com.

WAYNESVILLE ANTIQUE MALL, 69 South Main Street, Waynesville. Call 513-897-6937. Website: waynesvilleantiquemall.com.

WINSOME COTTAGE, 93 South Main Street, Waynesville. Call 513-897-0667. Website: winsomecottage.net.

WOODLAND CEMETERY AND ARBORETUM, 118 Woodland Avenue, Dayton. Call 937-228-3221. Website: woodlandcemetery.org.

WRIGHT CYCLE COMPANY, 22 South Williams Street, Dayton. Call 937-225-7705. Website: nps.gov/daav/learn/historyculture/wright-cycle -company-complex.htm.

YOUNG'S JERSEY DAIRY, 6880 Springfield-Xenia Road, Yellow Springs. Call 937-325-0629. Website: youngsdairy.com.

Dining

COBBLESTONE VILLAGE, 10 North Main Street, Waynesville. Call 513-897-0021. Website: cobblestonevillageandcafe.com. $$.

GOLDEN JERSEY INN, 6880 Springfield-Xenia Road, Yellow Springs. Call 937-324-2050. Website: youngsdairy.com. $.

GOLDEN LAMB, 27 South Broadway, Lebanon. Call 513-932-5065. Website: goldenlamb.com. $$.

HAMBURGER WAGON, 12 East Central Avenue, Miamisburg. Call 937-847-2442. Website: hamburgerwagon.com. $.

JAY'S SEAFOOD RESTAURANT, 225 East Sixth Street, Dayton. Call 937-222-2892. Website: jays.com. $$$$.

LITTLE RIVER CAFE, 5527 Oregonia Road, Oregonia. Call 513-932-4770. Website: thelittlerivercafe.com. $$.

MUMFORD'S POTATO CHIP & DELI, 325 North Main Street, Urbana. Call 937-653-3491. $.

THE PINE CLUB, 1926 Brown Street, Dayton. Call 937-228-5371. Website: thepineclub.com. $$$$.

Other Contacts

CHAMPAIGN COUNTY CHAMBER & VISITOR BUREAU, 107 North Main Street, Urbana. Call 937-653-5764 or 1-877-873-5764. Website: champaignohio.com.

DAYTON/MONTGOMERY COUNTY CONVENTION & VISITOR BUREAU, 1 Chamber Plaza, Suite A, Dayton. Call 937-226-8211 or 1-800-221-8235. Website: daytoncvb.com.

GREENE COUNTY CVB, 1221 Meadow Bridge Drive, Beavercreek. Call 937-429-9100. Website: greenecountyohio.org.

LOGAN COUNTY VISITOR BUREAU, 100 South Main Street, Bellefontaine. Call 937-599-5121. Website: logancountyohio.com/visitors-bureau.html.

14

THE WIDE WESTERN PLAINS

VAN WERT, DELPHOS, LIMA, WAPAKONETA, GRAND
LAKE ST. MARY'S, NEW BREMEN, VERSAILLES, PIQUA,
TROY, GREENVILLE

ESTIMATED LENGTH: 175 miles

ESTIMATED TIME: 4 hours

HIGHLIGHTS: This itinerary begins at the Brumback Library in Van Wert, then heads east to explore the Canal and Postal Museums in Delphos. In downtown Lima, stop at the Kewpee Hamburger before visiting the Allen County Museum. Continue south to Wapakoneta, where you will find the Armstrong Air & Space Museum. Be ready for some recreation, since the next stop is the Grand Lake St. Mary's State Park. Then it's off to New Bremen for the excellent Bicycle Museum of America and a tour of the old Miami and Erie Canal. Continuing south to Versailles, a stay (and perhaps a meal) at the Inn at Versailles is a must. The next day, you can search for the graveyard where Annie Oakley is buried and tour the Winery at Versailles. East of Versailles in Piqua, you will visit the Johnston Farm and Indian Agency and then continue on to Troy to visit the Brukner Nature Center and the Overfield Tavern. Now heading west, in Greenville, you must stop at Bear's Mill before heading into town for a tour of the KitchenAid Factory and some shopping at the KitchenAid Experience.

GETTING THERE: This trip begins in Van Wert, 33 miles west of I-75 on US 30. From Van Wert, follow the Lincoln Highway to Delphos and then Elida Road to Lima. South Dixie Highway parallels I-75 down to Wapakoneta. From there, take US 33 to Grand Lake St. Mary's. OH 66 leads south through New Bremen, Minster, and Fort Loramie, but then at the junction with OH 47, the route heads southwest to Versailles. From there, OH 185 heads south and east into Piqua. Following the Great Miami River for a stretch, we take CR 25A down to Troy. Take OH 41 and US 36 to the end of the trip in Greenville.

LEFT: THE JOHNSTON FARM WAS A CONNECTION TO INSTITUTIONAL ORDER ON THE FRONTIER

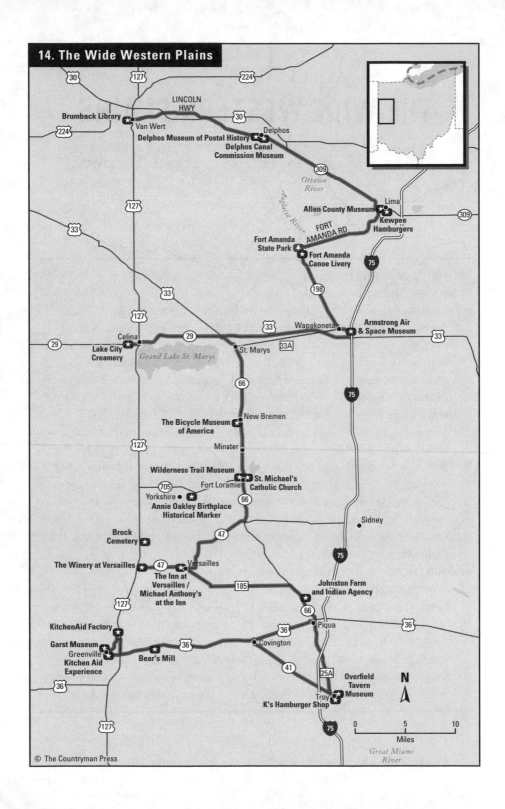

14. The Wide Western Plains

Brumback Library

LINCOLN HWY

Van Wert

Delphos

Delphos Museum of Postal History
Delphos Canal
Commission Museum

Ottawa River

Auglaize River

Allen County Museum

Lima

Kewpee
Hamburgers

FORT
AMANDA RD

Fort Amanda
State Park

Fort Amanda
Canoe Livery

Armstrong Air
& Space Museum

Wapakoneta

Celina

Lake City
Creamery

Grand Lake St. Marys

St. Marys

The Bicycle Museum
of America

New Bremen

Minster

Wilderness Trail Museum

Fort Loramie

St. Michael's
Catholic Church

Yorkshire

Annie Oakley Birthplace
Historical Marker

Sidney

Brock
Cemetery

The Winery at Versailles

Versailles

The Inn at
Versailles /
Michael Anthony's
at the Inn

Johnston Farm
and Indian Agency

KitchenAid Factory

Garst Museum

Greenville

Kitchen Aid
Experience

Bear's Mill

Piqua

Covington

Overfield
Tavern
Museum

Troy

K's Hamburger Shop

N

0   5   10
Miles

*Great Miami
River*

© The Countryman Press

Strangers to driving through the western counties of Ohio might be excused if their first impression is that Ohio is as white-bread Midwest as they had imagined. This is the part of the country that faces on TV derisively call the "fly-over states." It is true that much of western Ohio is flat, lightly peopled, and blanketed in a quilt of farm fields, but those of us who have come to appreciate the back roads—those precious slices of life in America—will find a wealth of history and culture here. It's the kind of place people overlook as they drive down I-75, the eastern edge of a route that takes us from US 30 south to US 36 and includes all points west to the Indiana border.

The town of Van Wert is the backdrop to the first stop, the **Brumback Library**. Built around the turn of the century, the library was a gift from the estate of John Sanford Brumback. The bequest called for the establishment of a countywide library. This was a new idea in 1897 and required the state to change the law and make such tax-supported institutions possible. Thus, the Brumback Library was a first, launching the county-library movement. Designed in a Romanesque style and built from Bedford limestone, most kids just say it looks like a castle. And it does. Surrounded by a dry moat, the library's front entrance is a large stone arch and sports two large towers on each side.

The building was dedicated in 1901 and has been expanded and remodeled, but the interior retains its original glory: High, arched ceilings and marble columns give the space a sense of grandeur not always found in small-town libraries. The Library Journal regularly ranks the Brumback as one of the best libraries in the country—so it clearly has more going for it than its history and fascinating architecture. It's that history and architecture, however, that out-of-town visitors will want to appreciate.

The library is just west of downtown, on the Lincoln Highway. Heading east on the old highway will take you to the heart of Delphos. In town, turn south onto Main Street, and drive one block to the **Delphos Canal Commission Museum**. Running through downtown Delphos, between Canal Street and Main Street, is an original stretch of the Miami and Erie Canal. In 1987, some kids got the idea to raise the hull of a canal boat that had been submerged in the canal since the turn of the century. The project took $5,000 and required the group to locate special equipment, but they eventually got the hull out of the water and into storage. From there, a historical foundation was established to take care of the boat, and the Delphos Canal Commission was born.

The centerpiece of the museum's collection is the *Marguerite*, the canal boat that started it all. Though not much is left of the old craft—just the hull, really—there is a model of the canal boat and artifacts from the canal boat days. The mission of the museum, however, has grown larger than just the preservation of a single boat. Curators have put together exhibitions that tell the story of the early years in Delphos and the industries that have sustained the town. An old schoolhouse classroom and an indoor log cabin exemplify what you can expect when you visit.

Just north of the Canal Museum on Main Street, across from Fourth Avenue, is the **Delphos Museum of Postal History**. This little museum is stocked with exhibitions borrowed from the Smithsonian. The museum describes the history of the U.S. Postal Service, how it has changed over the years as transportation and technology have changed, and how mail has kept Americans connected. The World War II exhibition uses correspondence between individuals to tell deeply moving stories. The kind of intimacy revealed in these letters is particularly unique to the age of letter writing—something those growing up with texting and e-mail will have to reinvent in some other way.

The next stop is the setting for the wildly popular show *Glee*. This television musical takes place in the fictional William McKinley High School in the small city of Lima, Ohio. To get to Lima, follow the Lincoln Highway east from Delphos, then turn southeast on Elida Road (OH 309) to make a beeline to town.

The state route heads south and becomes Jameson Avenue just before town. Two blocks after you cross North Street, turn east onto Market Street. A half mile down is the **Allen County Museum**. The museum commemorates the county's history. Right next door, the museum maintains the MacDonell House, a grand Victorian home built in 1893. This stretch of Market Street used to house the city's wealthiest citizens. The MacDonell House is a great way to recapture some of that architectural and cultural elegance.

For a less highbrow look at Lima, locals know that the best place in town for a burger is one of the town's three **Kewpee Hamburgers**. The oldest is the downtown 1930s diner on North Elizabeth Street. The parking lot was once so narrow that a large lazy Susan had to help drivers exit the lot. The Kewpee chain may not be as familiar today as it once was, but it lives on in many different places. There are Kewpees all across the Midwest, from Wisconsin to Michigan to Ohio. One early offshoot of the chain is the popular Halo Burger, found in and around Flint, Michigan.

Common to all these manifestations of Kewpee Hamburgers is the famous olive burger—a burger with the works, loaded with a pile of chopped green olives. If you haven't tried an olive burger, you need to add it to the list. It's especially tasty with cheese. Lima isn't thriving the way it did early in the last century, and the downtown is a bit run-down, but the Kewpee burgers are still delicious and a great break from the usual fast food.

The river that flows through Lima is the Ottawa, and farther west is the Auglaize River. From Market Street, follow Collett Street south. The road crosses the Ottawa River and then follows its southern bank. Eventually becoming Fort Amanda Road, it will take you out to the Fort Amanda Memorial Park.

The Ottawa River joins the larger Auglaize River farther north, and the

THE ARMSTRONG AIR & SPACE MUSEUM EXPLORES NASA'S LUNAR PROGRAM

waters of both mingle and then empty into the Maumee River in the town of Defiance. When exploring the Auglaize River, head over to the **Fort Amanda Canoe Livery** near Fort Amanda State Park. The outfitter offers five trips of varying lengths on the Auglaize, and they provide everything you will need: canoes, paddles, life preservers, and, most importantly, transportation.

Fort Amanda Road continues about 10 miles southwest of Lima to **Fort Amanda State Park**. The Ohio Historical Society owns the site, and the Johnny Appleseed Metropolitan Park District manages it. Built in 1812, Fort Amanda kept troops supplied during the War of 1812. The fort is gone, but the site makes for a great picnic spot on the Auglaize River.

From the park, OH 198 beats a conveniently direct path to the center of Wapakoneta. Just east of downtown, off Bellefontaine Street and within sight of I-75, is the next stop: a museum that commemorates a pivotal moment in human history.

On July 20, 1969, Neil Armstrong became the first human to set foot on the moon. Buzz Aldrin followed close behind, and together they spent about two and half hours collecting moon rocks before packing up and returning to earth. Though Neil Armstrong grew up all over Ohio—his family lived in 20 different towns—he was born near Wapakoneta and returned to the town for high school. When he took that historic lunar step, he became a hometown hero back on Earth. It makes sense, then, that Ohio decided to honor him with a museum here in town.

The **Armstrong Air & Space Museum** tells the story of America's journey to the moon, with special attention to the role played by this famous Ohioan. Exhibitions begin with the space race and continue with the history of the Gemini space program and the *Apollo* missions. There are artifacts from the missions—Armstrong's spacesuits, a moon rock, a Gemini space capsule—as well as the Astro Theater and several space-flight simulators. The museum is part of the **National Aviation Heritage Area**, which includes another fourteen sites, most of which are located in and around Dayton.

To continue the route and go to Grand Lake St. Mary's, take OH 67 west out of Wapakoneta. There are two options for reaching the lake. You can continue on OH 67, which becomes CR 33A, and heads directly into the heart of the town of St. Mary's. Or you can jump on US 33, which provides almost the same trip, except there are no lights. The state park on Grand Lake St. Mary's is at the northeast corner of the lake, but in recent years toxic algae blooms have been making the water deadly for fish and mighty unsafe for people. It's gotten so bad that beaches have been closed and signs warn against coming into contact with the water.

ST. MICHAEL'S IN FORT LORAMIE IS A STUNNING LANDMARK

All of this, of course, is bad news for the families who make a living catering to tourists. Look at any map of western Ohio, and Grand Lake St. Mary's is the region's most readily recognizable feature. That said, the area hasn't ever been as touristy as you might imagine. There are a handful of small restaurants and businesses that cater to fishing and boating, but it's not a place to buy made-in-China moccasins and pounds of maple-walnut fudge. Okay, that's not entirely true. On the far side of the lake in Celina, there's a great spot for ice cream, roasted nuts, and, you guessed it, fudge. It's the Lake City Creamery, west of town on OH 29. From the outside, it's not much more than a pole barn. Inside you will find the state's best ice cream.

THE HISTORY OF THE BICYCLE, FROM ITS EARLIEST INCARNATIONS, IS ON DISPLAY AT THE STELLAR BICYCLE MUSEUM OF AMERICA

Sometimes it's in a cone, sometimes on a banana split, and if you want it slapped between two cookies, they can do that too.

The next town on the itinerary is New Bremen. From the east side of the lake, take OH 66. In fact, we will stay on OH 66 all the way to Piqua, with a handful of stops along the way. But first, let's make for this unique museum in a small town on the old Miami and Erie Canal.

Small-town museums can sometimes be disappointing. Pulling off a top-notch exhibition space often takes more funds than the local historical society can raise. The **Bicycle Museum of America** is something special. Very special, in fact. It contains the private bicycle collection of Jim Dicke, and it's one of the largest private bicycle collections in the world. The museum used to be located in Chicago on Navy Pier, but Dicke moved it back to his hometown of New Bremen. Bike history runs in the family; his grandfather used to work at the Dayton Bicycle Company.

The bikes themselves are amazing. Early in the history of cycling, the two-wheel conveyance took on many forms. Bike builders experimented with different designs and used every material available to put them together. From the first coasters with wooden wheels to a high-tech monocycle used in the 2008 Olympics, this museum tells the history of bicycling. There are bikes used by the military. Space-age inspired bikes of the 1960s. Even the BMX

THE INN AT VERSAILLES EXUDES A RUSTIC TUSCAN VIBE

bikes so ubiquitous in the 1980s. You can even see Pee-wee Herman's bike from *Pee-wee's Big Adventure*. In addition, there is a ton of memorabilia—head badges, posters, jerseys, and more. The entire museum could be toured in a half-hour, but visitors with any appreciation for cycling and the history of the bike will want to plan a couple hours to really take it all in.

From New Bremen, continue south on OH 66 toward Piqua. As you drive south, the road passes through the small towns of Minster and Fort Loramie. Just east of OH 66 on Elm Street in Fort Loramie, you will want to stop and take a look at **St. Michael's Catholic Church**. Consecrated in 1881, the church architecture has been described as Tuscan-Gothic. The bell tower is 200 feet high, projecting the sound of the church's four bells for miles. Inside, the center vault of the sanctuary soars 55 feet above the pews. There are twenty-two stained glass windows and the woodwork exemplifies Old World craftsmanship.

If you are passing through on a Sunday afternoon in the summer, you might want to visit the Wilderness Trail Museum on Main Street (OH 66). The museum is housed in a nineteenth-century boarding house. There are collections of Native American artifacts as well as bits and pieces of the town's canal history. During the first two weeks of December, the Fort Loramie Historical Association—the folks who run the museum—host the Williamsburg Christmas Dinner. Guests dine on a colonial menu and are entertained with period music.

From Fort Loramie, you will drive about 4 miles south on OH 66 to the intersection with OH 47. Turning to the right (west), the town of Versailles is less than 9 miles away.

The village of Versailles (pronounced locally as ver-SALES) was originally called Jacksonville. The community, however, was well-stocked with people of French descent, and so the name was changed in 1837 to call to mind the old country. Versailles is like many small communities in the Midwest. There's not a lot of commerce downtown. Many storefronts are empty, and retail seems to have made a full retreat. This village stands out because no other town in the Midwest has **The Inn at Versailles** and **Michael Anthony's at the Inn**.

Both the inn and the restaurant share a commitment to an Old-World sensibility. The inn is a boutique hotel with twenty-two uniquely decorated rooms. Some rooms have Jacuzzis; others have fireplaces. All are luxuri-

JUST WEST OF VERSAILLES IS A POPULAR LOCAL WINERY

Little Sure Shot

Phoebe Ann Moses was born in 1860 in a log cabin in Darke County. She went by the name Annie. After her father died of pneumonia, the young Phoebe took to hunting small game in order to supplement the family's meager income. She became quite proficient with the rifle. In 1875, when a sharpshooter named Frank Butler offered a $100 prize to anyone who could outshoot him, she stepped up and won the contest, hitting 25 of 25 targets compared to Butler's 24. A year later, the two were married.

ANNIE OAKLEY IS BURIED NEXT TO HER HUSBAND NORTH OF VERSAILLES

Annie would eventually join Frank's sharpshooter act on the vaudeville stage, billed as Annie Oakley. At only five-feet tall, Annie wasn't an imposing figure—that is, until she pulled out her rifle. She would go on to perform in Buffalo Bill Cody's Wild West show. Her association with Buffalo Bill and the subsequent exposure secured her reputation as one of the most impressive figures of the late nineteenth and early twentieth centuries.

To explore the Annie Oakley story, begin at the Garst Museum in Greenville. The museum is the home of the National Annie Oakley Center and does a great job of introducing visitors to the life and times of this local hero.

North of Versailles, two sites commemorate the sharpshooter. Drive north from Greenville on US 127, and take Greenville–St. Mary's Road when it branches off to the right. (The intersection is about 10 miles north of the junction of US 127 and US 36.) About 1.5 miles up the road on your right is the

Brock Cemetery, the final resting place of Annie Oakley and Frank Butler. There's a historical marker at the site.

Continue north on Greenville–St. Mary's Road, and turn right onto North Star–Fort Loramie Road. Drive about 3.5 miles—passing through Yorkshire on the way—to Spencer Road, and turn right again. South on Spencer Road, along the side of the road, is a large stone with a plaque that marks the location of Annie's birthplace. The log cabin is gone, but the farm field behind the marker hints at the scenery that must have been the backdrop to her early years.

ously appointed with ornate European-style furniture, soft beds, and comfortable linens.

It might be said that **Michael Anthony's** on the first floor comprises a number of small dining rooms. In one corner, windows look out on downtown Versailles. A nearby nook is warmed by a fire in the fireplace. The effect is that the restaurant can be crowded and diners can still leave with a sense of having enjoyed a fine meal in an intimate setting.

The menu reflects the seasons—much of the produce is grown on the restaurant's Sycamore Bridge Farm. Many other ingredients are locally sourced. All these go into a menu that features European and American cuisine. In addition to classic French and Italian dishes, you will see familiar fare, such as southern fried chicken and wood-fired pizza.

West of Versailles on OH 47, east of US 127, **The Winery at Versailles** has carved several acres of vineyard out of a landscape dominated by fields of soybeans and corn. The winery has been here since 1994. In addition to their wines, there's a kitchen that serves up excellent meals. Take a look at their website for special events (wineryatversailles.com).

From Versailles, take East Main Street east to Versailles-Southeastern Road and turn right (south). The road heads southeast for a bit, and then it turns to the south. Soon after the turn, you will see Ballinger Road on your left. Turn and follow Ballinger east. Continue east all the way to OH 66 and then turn right (south). Downtown Piqua is about 4 miles away, but about 2 miles before you arrive, turn left onto Hardin Road. The farm fields on your right are part of the historic Johnston Farm and Indian Agency. The three-story brick farmhouse was both the Johnston family home and the only Federal Indian Agency in Ohio. Furnished throughout with period antiques, the building is a perfect example of Federal-style architecture and looks today as it would have in the late 1820s.

Other restored or recreated structures on the property include the Cider House, the Springhouse, and the Double-Pen Barn. There is also a restored portion of the Miami and Erie Canal. Guests can float down the canal on the site's replica canal boat, the *General Harrison*, which is pulled by mules.

Throughout the historical park, costumed interpreters are available to answer questions, discuss pertinent history, and add a splash of color to your visit. The **Johnston Farm and Indian Agency** is closed November through March, presumably because the canal freezes over and the buildings are not easily heated. In the summer, the park is open Thursday through Sunday. Call before visiting during the colder months, as hours change.

After visiting the Johnston Farm, you have a decision to make. From Piqua you can either head directly to Greenville or make a quick stop farther south to visit a few sites in Troy. If you choose the latter, take South Main Street south. The road becomes North County Road 25A just outside of town and continues for 7 miles to Main Street in Troy.

For food, there's **K's Hamburger Shop** on Main Street. Since the 1930s, this has been the place to get a burger in Troy. One of the things that set this place apart is that they grind their own beef. You don't have to watch too much foodie television to realize that's an important qualification for any great burger joint.

The staff here still wears white caps and bow ties, and out front, a neon chef hails passers-by with a sign that says *Eat*. Since you're on a road trip, be sure to order a malt and maybe swap out the fries for onion rings. When K's first opened, you could eat well for a quarter. The prices have gone up, but maybe only enough to account for inflation. K's Hamburger Shop is still easy on the pocketbook.

Two blocks toward the Great Miami River is the **Overfield Tavern Museum**.

The Northwest Indian War

From 1785 to 1795, the newly established United States fought a war in the Northwest Territory against the reluctant-to-admit-defeat British and their Native-American allies. The war was fought here, in the Ohio Territory.

The early years of the war were marked by incompetence on the side of the American forces, which were composed mainly of untrained militia. In 1793, General "Mad" Anthony Wayne took command of the newly founded Legion of the United States. By the end of 1794, the Native American forces had been defeated—the final battle being the Battle of Fallen Timbers.

In 1795, the Americans and the defeated Indian chiefs met in Greenville and signed the treaty that would secure the conditions that would open the territory to even more settlement. These conditions would change in the years to come, but the treaty-signing marks a pivotal point in the territory's history.

THE BASEMENT OF THE KITCHENAID STORE IN GREENVILLE IS A MUSEUM DISPLAYING A TIMELINE OF MIXER MODELS

The tavern is the oldest surviving building in Troy. The log structure was built in 1808 by Benjamin Overfield, and no one has ever moved it. The tavern was an important meeting house in the early days of the settlement. The county held court upstairs, and plenty of business was sorted out in the tavern. Overfield gave the community a place to eat, drink, and socialize, and he gave travelers a place to sleep. The Overfield family lived in a log cabin behind the tavern.

The site today includes the tavern and the log cabin. The museum inside includes a collection of furniture and other historical bits from the early 1800s. The museum includes an impressive library of early nineteenth-century medical books. Across the street from the tavern is the Annex, which has a small library of period documents and a gallery space for the occasional show.

From Troy, take OH 41 northwest to the town of Covington, then head west on US 36. Ten miles west of Covington, turn south onto Arcanum–Bears Mill Road. The historic **Bear's Mill** is on the right, just after the road crosses the creek. This mill, built in the mid-1800s, is one of the last water-powered operating gristmills in Ohio. The mill still grinds flour and meal. The four-story structure is impressive—even more so if you get the opportunity to see the mill in action.

The mill is powered by water that flows in by way of the millrace. When

AN EXHIBIT FROM THE GARST MUSEUM, WHICH ALSO INCLUDES EXHIBITS ABOUT ANNIE OAKLEY

the mill was built, the millrace was dug by schoolchildren. Water moves the gears that in turn transport grain through the entire facility.

The shop on the main floor sells flours and meals ground on the site. It also offers a fine assortment of arts and crafts produced by local arts- and craftspeople. There are also locally produced gourmet foods, kitchen goods, coffees and teas, and even clothing. After touring the mill, be sure to head outside and take the short, scenic walk between the creek and millrace.

To read the headlines, it would seem like everything these days is made overseas. The brands have stayed the same, but the hands assembling the goods we buy have changed. There are, of course, a number of notable exceptions, companies who have resisted the temptation to capitalize on cheap labor and move operations elsewhere. One of these is KitchenAid, the makers of the famous stand mixer. Greenville is the home of KitchenAid, and those with a passion for kitchen appliances will want to take the **KitchenAid Factory Tour** and visit the **KitchenAid Experience**.

The KitchenAid Factory is located north of Greenville, and tours are offered several days a week at 12:30. Manufacturing isn't the most glamorous of industries, but the tour is very interesting, especially for bakers to whom the KitchenAid mixer is an essential tool. The tour starts with a look back at early models of the famous mixer and then moves on to the production floor.

A few miles away in downtown Greenville, the company operates the KitchenAid Experience. This is a retail outlet. In the basement, they carry refurbished mixers, and there's an impressive display of early mixers here as well. The Experience also has a test kitchen. From time to time, bakers come in to demonstrate a few recipes for visitors. This can be a fascinating (and tasty) diversion. Of course, KitchenAid also sells blenders and a host of other accessories. In fact, the entire retail catalog is on display at the Experience, and those who love kitchen gadgets will leave with a silly grin they just can't seem to shake.

While in Greenville, it would be a shame not to stop at the **Garst Museum**. This 35,000-square-foot facility is a historic home onto which has been attached a lot of additional space. Inside, you will find the National Annie Oakley Center and the Crossroads of Destiny, an exhibition that commemorates the signing of the Treaty of Greenville in 1795. The Treaty of Greenville marked a significant moment in the country's history. After General "Mad" Anthony Wayne defeated the British and Native American forces at the Battle of Fallen Timbers, the Treaty of Greenville set the stage for the settlement of the Upper Ohio River Valley.

IN THE AREA

Accommodations

THE INN AT VERSAILLES, 21 West Main Street, Versailles. Call 937-526-3020. Website: innatversailles.com. $$.

Attractions and Recreation

ALLEN COUNTY MUSEUM, 620 West Market Street, Lima. Call 419-222-9426. Website: allencountymuseum.org.

ANNIE OAKLEY GRAVE, Brock Cemetery, Greenville-St. Mary's Road, Brock.

ARMSTRONG AIR & SPACE MUSEUM, 500 South Apollo Drive, Wapakoneta. Call 419-738-8811 or 1-800-860-0142. Website: armstrongmuseum.org.

BEAR'S MILL, 6450 Arcanum-Bear's Mill Road, Greenville. Call 937-548-5112. Website: bearsmill.org.

THE BICYCLE MUSEUM OF AMERICA, 7 West Monroe Street, New Bremen. Call 419-629-9249. Website: www.bicyclemuseum.com.

BRUMBACK LIBRARY, 215 West Main Street, Van Wert. Call 419-238-2168. Website: brumbacklib.com.

DELPHOS CANAL COMMISSION MUSEUM, 241 North Main Street, Delphos. Call 419-695-7737. Website: delphoscanalcommission.com.

DELPHOS MUSEUM OF POSTAL HISTORY, 339 North Main Street, Delphos. Call 419-303-5482. Website: postalhistorymuseum.org. The museum is open on Thursdays and Saturdays, but the schedule changes a lot, so check before you visit.

FORT AMANDA CANOE LIVERY, 22638 Dughill Road, Lima. Call 419-657-6782. Website: fortamandacanoelivery.com.

FORT AMANDA STATE PARK, 22901 OH 198, Lima. Call 1-800-283-8713. Website: jampd.com/parks-facilities/fort-amanda-park/.

GARST MUSEUM, 205 North Broadway, Greenville. Call 937-548-5250. Website: garstmuseum.org.

JOHNSTON FARM AND INDIAN AGENCY, 9845 North Hardin Road, Piqua. Call 1-800-752-2619. Website: www.johnstonfarmohio.com.

KITCHENAID EXPERIENCE, 423 South Broadway Street, Greenville. Call 937-316-4777. Website: kitchenaid.com/experience-retail-center.

KITCHENAID FACTORY TOUR, 1701 KitchenAid Way, Greenville. Call 937-316-4777. Website: kitchenaid.com/experience-retail-center.

OVERFIELD TAVERN MUSEUM, 201 East Water Street, Troy. Call 937-335-4019. Website: overfieldtavernmuseum.com.

ST. MICHAEL'S CATHOLIC CHURCH, 33 Elm Street, Fort Loramie. Call 937-295-2891. Website: nflregion.org.

THE WINERY AT VERSAILLES, 6572 OH 47, Versailles. Call 937-526-3232. Website: wineryatversailles.com.

Dining

K'S HAMBURGER SHOP, 117 East Main Street, Troy. Call 937-339-3902. Website: kshamburgershoptroy.com. $.

KEWPEE HAMBURGERS, 111 North Elizabeth Street, Lima. Call 419-228-1778. Website: kewpeehamburgers.com. $.

MICHAEL ANTHONY'S AT THE INN, 21 West Main Street, Versailles. Call 937-526-3020. Website: michaelanthonysattheinn.com. $$.

Other Contacts

VAN WERT AREA CONVENTION AND VISITOR BUREAU, 136 East Main Street, Van Wert. Call 419-238-9378. Website: visitvanwert.org.

LIMA/ALLEN COUNTY CONVENTION AND VISITOR BUREAU, 144 South Main Street, Lima. Call 419-222-6075. Website: lima-allencvb.com.

15

THE INTERIOR OF
NORTHWEST OHIO

FINDLAY, ADA, KENTON, MOUNT VICTORY, INDIAN LAKE,
BELLEFONTAINE, WEST LIBERTY, MARYSVILLE, MARION

ESTIMATED LENGTH: 175 miles

ESTIMATED TIME: 4 hours

HIGHLIGHTS: This itinerary begins in Findlay at a museum that features the art of children's illustrators, the Mazza Museum on the campus of University of Findlay. There are a few places to stop in Findlay, including a couple nice places to grab a bite to eat. Instead of heading straight to Kenton next, the route makes a detour to Ada and the Wilson Football Factory. In Kenton, there is the Sullivan-Johnson Museum. A few miles southeast of Kenton lies the town of Mount Victory, which boasts nearly a dozen antique and craft shops. From there, we take the road west to Indian Lake and Indian Lake State Park. Plenty of places for hiking, swimming, biking, and camping. In Bellefontaine, you can visit Mount Campbell, the highest spot in the state. Visitors also enjoy stops at Zane Caverns, Ohio Caverns, and the Piatt Castles. There are a few B&Bs in the area. Escape Route 508 is one of these. Nearby in Marysville, there's an excellent bluegrass festival held every year in late September. It's a great event if the timing works out for your travel plans. Another great inn is The Barn at Walnut Glen in Waldo. Where's Waldo, you ask? It's located between Marysville and Marion, the final stop on the tour. In Marion, there is the Stengel True Museum and the Buckeye Telephone Museum, as well as the home and tomb of President Warren G. Harding. And while you're in town, be sure to stop at The Warehouse for excellent Italian food in a unique location.

GETTING THERE: This trip begins in Findlay, which is found east of I-75. From there, take Lima Avenue southwest (it becomes C.R. 313 en route) to OH 235 south. The road becomes Main Street in Ada. Continue south on OH 235 to OH 309, which continues east and then southeast into Kenton. US 68 is the direct route to Bellefontaine, but we will take OH 31 south to Mount Victory, and then OH 373 west in order to stop by Indian Lake. From the lake, US 33 East heads toward Bellefontaine. From here to Marysville, you follow back roads

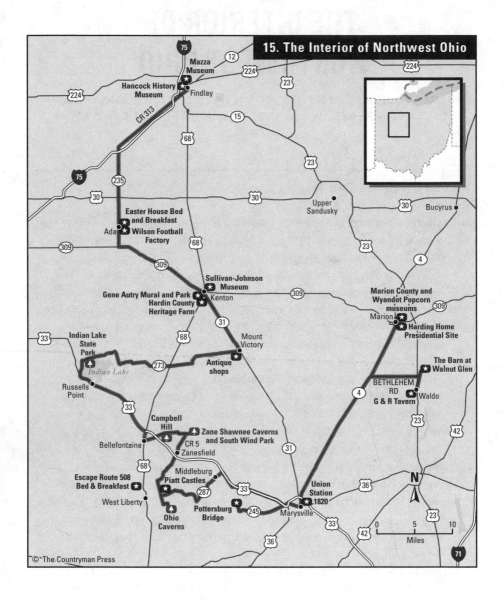

15. The Interior of Northwest Ohio

Mazza Museum

Hancock History Museum

Findlay

CR 313

Easter House Bed and Breakfast

Ada

Wilson Football Factory

Upper Sandusky

Bucyrus

Sullivan-Johnson Museum

Gene Autry Mural and Park
Hardin County Heritage Farm

Kenton

Marion County and Wyandot Popcorn museums

Marion

Harding Home Presidential Site

Indian Lake State Park

Indian Lake

Mount Victory

Antique shops

The Barn at Walnut Glen

BETHLEHEM RD

G & R Tavern

Waldo

Russells Point

Campbell Hill

Bellefontaine

CR 5

Zanesfield

Zane Shawnee Caverns and South Wind Park

Escape Route 508 Bed & Breakfast

Middleburg

Piatt Castles

West Liberty

Pottersburg Bridge

Ohio Caverns

Union Station 1820

Marysville

N

0   5   10

Miles

© The Countryman Press

Like a lot of Ohio, Findlay began as a military outpost. During the War of 1812, Colonel James Findlay built a stockade here on the edge of the Great Black Swamp to keep U.S. troops in supplies. In 1880, gas was discovered under Findlay, and in 1886 drillers discovered the Great Karg Well, which became the largest gas well in the world. A half-acre park on the north end of town commemorates the site. (The historical marker is located in Apple Alley, a short stretch of road where northbound Liberty Street turns into westbound River Street, overlooking the Blanchard River.) As the marker records: "This single well produced 12,000,000 cubic feet (340,000 cubic meters) of gas per day, and when lit it burned with a flame 100ft high and was visible more than 30 miles away."

The most immediate benefit of this resource was that there was no good way to store and transport gas in the nineteenth century (it was simply a by-product of oil drilling), so it was piped throughout town to heat homes and drive industry ... at no cost. Glass manufacturers, unable to pass up free fuel for their furnaces, flocked to Findlay.

The University of Findlay, which takes up 75 acres west of North Main Street, was established in 1882. The school is affiliated with the Churches of God, General Conference, and the Winebrenner Seminary is located next door to the university. Visitors to Findlay should stop by the campus to visit the **Mazza Museum of International Art from Picture Books**. The name of the place pretty much says it all. It's a museum that celebrates the work of children's book illustrators—including the work from the likes of Tomie dePaola, Maurice Sendak, and Mary Engelbreit. There are various galleries, each showcasing different aspects of the art.

The next stop, the Hancock History Museum, is easy enough to get to. Just follow Main Street south to West Sandusky Street. The museum is a third of a mile west of Main on the north side of the street. The first acquisition for the museum was the building you see upon arrival—the Hull-Flater House. Built in 1881, it has been restored to reflect its original Victorian décor. Additions to the house added exhibition space for the museum. More buildings were acquired and moved to the property—including the Crawford Log House, the De-Wald Funk House, and the Davis Homestead. The Marathon Petroleum Corporation Energy & Transportation Annex is added space to explore the role of the energy and transportation industries in Findlay, and a barn on the site offers a look at the county's agricultural heritage.

The fruits of that agricultural heritage—at least the dairy aspect of it—are on full display, a couple blocks north on West Cross Street. Dietsch Broth-

THE HANCOCK HISTORY MUSEUM MAINTAINS SEVERAL HISTORIC BUILDINGS ON THE SITE

ers has been producing fine chocolates and ice cream in Findlay since 1937. This is the best place in town for ice cream. The business has stayed in the same family since it began, and they still use their own recipes for dozens of flavors—I counted 62, not counting seasonal flavors. They also make excellent buckeyes, chocolate nut clusters, and chocolate covered cherries.

Findlay's iconic burger joint is **Wilson's Sandwich Shop**. Wilson's opened a year before **Dietsch Brothers**, in 1936. From all appearances, the restaurant is a somewhat dated and gently worn fast food joint with a drop tile ceiling and Formica tables and benches. Over the years, folks at Wilson's have developed their own lingo. They call them "hamburgs" here, and when ordering, they don't even use that truncated noun. Instead, when customers step up to order, they announce the number of hamburgers desired with cheese and the number without. So, two cheeseburgers and a hamburger comes out: "I'd like two with and one without." Add a frosted malt and some warm fries, and you're golden.

Another fine stop for lunch is just across the street and north a block, **Main Street Deli**. With painted ceiling tiles and chairs, exposed brick, and funky décor, the deli has an eclectic appeal. The menu features stacked sandwiches, stuffed croissants, and eggs for breakfast. They also have a lot of options for those who require a gluten-free diet, including gluten-free cinnamon rolls.

From Main Street in Findlay, take Lima Avenue southwest (it becomes C.R. 313 en route) to OH 235 south. In Ada, the road becomes Main Street. There's a fine B&B in town. **Easter House Bed and Breakfast** has two rooms, one with a queen bed and the other with two twins. The house was built in the Queen Anne style, which means it features gracious wrap-around porches. The inn is located on Main Street and is popular with parents visiting students at nearby Ohio Northern University.

The **Wilson Football Factory** is east of Main Street at the southern end of Liberty Street in Ada. Wilson has been making NFL game footballs for over 75 years. That is to say, every football used in an NFL game since 1941 has been made by Wilson, and since 1955 every one of those balls was made here in Ada. Today, the factory produces about 4,000 footballs a day. To get an employee-led tour of the factory and to see how the old pigskin comes together, call for a reservation (419-634-9901).

Continuing south on Main Street, which becomes OH 235, turn east on OH 309 and drive about 13 miles into the center of Kenton.

Kenton is the county seat of Hardin County. The town is named for Simon Kenton, a legendary frontiersman equal to Daniel Boone. He was captured by the Shawnee and suffered numerous ordeals, trials that usually resulted in a captive's death. He was eventually rescued by an interpreter working for the British. Kenton settled in Urbana, 50 miles to the south, but he was a central figure in the European settlement of the Ohio River Valley and surrounding region.

MAIN STREET DELI HAS GREAT FOOD AND A SUPER CASUAL ATMOSPHERE

Kenton is perhaps best known as the home of the Kenton Hardware Company. The company, specializing in the production of cast-iron toys, had a hard time during the Great Depression. However, a vice president at Kenton Hardware had an idea that one really successful toy could save the business ... and the town. He talked to the famous cowboy of screen and radio, Gene Autry, and created a cap pistol modeled on the guns Autry used in movies. It was an overnight success. The Gene Autry Mural and Park at the northeast corner of Market and Franklin Streets commemorates that success.

There's plenty of Kenton–Hardin County history on hand. Hardin County

Historical Museums, Inc. maintains two historical sites: the nearby **Sulli-van-Johnson Museum** on Main Street, and **Hardin County Heritage Farm** south of town, adjacent to the Hardin County Fairgrounds. The museum contains artifacts passed down from the era of pioneer settlement.

The farm site features several historic structures: Burison Barn, Dunkirk Jail, Staadt Log Home, the Beech Grove School, and the Ada Railroad Building. There are vintage farm implements and a working wood shop in the jail. Guests need to make reservations to visit the farm site, which is only open in the summer. The barn is rented out for special occasions.

Every community deserves a great local pizza place. In Kenton, that place is **Michael Angelo's Pizza**. Michael Angelo's, and the sister shop 15 miles south in Rushsylvania was started by Michael Shepherd, who has won his fair share of pizza championships. The pizza here has an exceptional crust. The restaurant also has a full bar. All around, a great atmosphere for lunch or dinner.

Michael Angelo's is on Detroit Street. Main Street is one block to the east. Head south on Main Street, and it turns into OH 31, turning south by southeast after crossing the Scioto River. It's a 9-mile drive from Kenton to the next set of stops in Mount Victory.

Mount Victory is an antique town, through and through. The 2016 census counts the number of people in Mount Victory at a little over 600, but there are nearly a dozen antiques shops. That's a lot for a town that doesn't even have a McDonald's. Just make your way down Main Street—from Day's Gone Buy Vintage and Antiques, past New Generation Antiques and the adjacent antique malls, all the way south to Eastman Antiques. Even casual browsers will find something to like—and there are plenty of great deals.

From downtown Mount Victory, take OH 373 west about 20 miles west to Indian Lake.

What is now called Indian Lake, began as an area of wetlands, dotted with small lakes. In the middle of the 1800s, the numerous rivers and creeks that fed this area were dammed up to create a large reservoir. Irish immigrants did most of the grunt work. The purpose was to provide water for the Sidney Feeder to the Miami and Erie Canal. The manmade lake was a bit larger than its current 5,104 acres, and it was named the Lewiston Reservoir. The lake became an attractive place for Ohioans to get away in the summer. In the 1920s there was an amusement park and dance halls on the lake's south end in Russells Point.

The lake itself has a large number of islands. Many are connected by bridges. Today the summer crowd keeps the lake humming with motorboats and supports a variety of lakeside bars and restaurants.

Indian Lake State Park maintains a campground and beach area on the northwest side of the lake. Recreation includes camping, hiking, boating, and hunting. There's even a canoe trail that begins at the campground.

Thanks to several canals that cut into the park, there are plenty of water-front campsites to be had.

The park isn't limited to the campground. It also includes the wetlands along the northeast shore and a good portion of Lake Ridge Island and the wetlands to the east of there. There is also great hiking loop on Pew Island, which is just across the water from the campground. (Getting there from the park requires a boat or a roundabout drive over Lake Ridge, Shawnee, Seminole, and, finally, Crane Town Islands.)

From Russells Point, US 33 continues southeast toward Bellefontaine. To get downtown, exit at US 68 and head south less than a mile.

The first stop in the Bellefontaine area is **Campbell Hill** (or Mount Campbell, as it is sometimes called). Located on the campus of the Hi-Point Career Center, this is the highest point in Ohio. At 1,549 feet, it wouldn't be that much of a hike, but even that much of an effort is unnecessary: The official marker is only a short 80-foot walk from the parking lot.

From these dizzying heights, you continue east 5 miles on OH 540 to the **Zane Shawnee Caverns** and South Wind Park. There are many faces to this property, depending on the time of year and your reason for visiting. The park is a campground with cabin rentals that hosts various events throughout the year—from music festivals to pow-wows. Most tourists passing by will stop for a tour of the caverns (though some events may mean cave tours are unavailable). They might also stay to visit the Shawnee Woodland Native American Museum or tour a pioneer and native village. The site is maintained by the Shawnee National United Remnant Band.

The next two stops are the Mac-A-Cheek and Mac-O-Chee Castles. Backtrack a mile west on OH 540 to County Road 5 south. The route soon crosses the Mad River and then follows the river south through Zanesfield to County Road 1. Here you turn left and cross the Mad River again. Mac-O-Chee Castle overlooks the intersection of CR 1 and OH 245. Mac-O-Cheek Castle is less than a mile west toward West Liberty. Collectively, these are the **Piatt Castles**.

These two estates were built by Donn and Abram Piatt in the late 1800s. Each of the castles is three stories. The architecture is gothic, and guests come to tour the inside to see the woodwork and the painted ceilings. The Piatt family still owns the homes, though now instead of living in them, the castles are operated as privately owned museums. They are also rented out for weddings and other occasions.

Continuing south on OH 245 the road makes a little jog (turn left to avoid continuing on OH 223) and just shy of the 2.5-mile mark, the **Ohio Caverns** appear on your left. These caves were discovered back in 1897. According to the historical marker, a farm boy watched water flow into a sinkhole and was curious about where it was going. He dug a little and found this place.

These are some of the best cavern tours in Ohio. The property is open

THERE ARE TWO PIATT CASTLES. THIS IS MAC-A-CHEEK.

and well maintained. Cavern entrances have all been improved and offer guests better access to the tours. There's a relatively new visitor center, and guides offer a variety of tours, so the site can be visited several times and still be fresh. The Historic Tour is a personal favorite. This is the same route followed by the caverns' first tourists, who often decorated the walls with graffiti.

Escape Route 508 is a bed and breakfast in West Liberty. It's located, as the name suggests, on OH 508 (west of US 68, north of downtown West Liberty). The inn features four rooms, each with its own private bath. Rooms have hardwood floors and trim, and there's a pool out back. A unique amenity you don't see at every B&B is the onsite full-service bar. The inn also has a pub room that can be rented for small gatherings.

It's a crooked route from West Liberty to Marysville, the next town on the itinerary. Heading east on OH 245 (back past the Piatt Castles), you continue east on OH 287 11 miles, through Middleburg, to US 33. Exit at West Fifth Street, and take that road east into the heart of Marysville.

The Union County Visitor Bureau runs a visitor center and gift shop in downtown Marysville. It's a great place to stop and get your bearings. The shop is called **Union Station 1820**, and it would be worth a visit even without the tourist info. Located on Fifth Street just east of Main, it's in the heart of the Uptown Marysville Historic District, which is a great place for a little walking and shopping.

An exciting festival is held each September in Marysville. It is the **Covered Bridge Bluegrass Festival**. There are craft demonstrations, artists and artisans selling their wares, and tons of great food. The event is held at the

THE OTHER PIATT CASTLE IS MAC-O-CHEE

OHIO CAVERNS IS ONE OF OHIO'S MOST POPULAR TOURIST ATTRACTIONS

Pottersburg Bridge, which can be found 7 miles west of town just north of OH 245. One of the highlights of the two days is Dinner on the Bridge. The chandelier is hung, and a splendid table is spread, running the length of the bridge, with room for one hundred guests. Diners not only enjoy a sumptuous four-course meal, but also live music and interesting presentations. This part of the festival sells out fast, but there's also the Picnic on the Bridge and Breakfast on the Bridge.

From Marysville, head north on OH 4 to Marion. East of this route, in Waldo, there's an excellent B&B called **The Barn at Walnut Glen**. The barn itself was built in the late 1800s. The suite for lodgers is located inside the old barn, and when guests arrive, they are surprised to push back the old sliding door and find the interior of a barn, complete with exposed beams and a tractor. The suite, however, is completely modern. Three levels in all, there is a queen size bed and bathroom in the loft, as well as a sleeper sofa and daybed for extra guests on the main level. That main level is where breakfast is served. It features a small kitchen and dining area. The lower level is a recreation room with a pool table.

This close to Waldo, it would be a shame to not make the short trip into town for a bite at the **G & R Tavern**. Essentially a hometown sports bar, the menu includes the usual stuff—burgers, pizza, French fries (straight or curly). What sets the place apart, however, is the fried bologna sandwich. Like nothing you've ever had, folks who try this slab of lunch meat on a white-bread bun with cheese and pickles come away with a whole new perspective on bologna.

The easiest way to get there is to take OH 4 north to Bethlehem Road east. The road ends at OH 98, turn north. At Newmans Cardington Road East, turn right and cross the Olentangy River. At St. James Road, turn left. The inn is just about 1,500 feet north on the west side of the road.

Marion is a blue-collar town. Once world renowned for Marion Power Shovel, which produced earth movers that dug the Panama Canal and crawler-transporters that moved rockets for NASA, the city is now known as the home to the largest factory producing clothes dryers in the world.

The city's other claim to fame is as the hometown of Warren G. Harding, the twenty-ninth President of the United States. Harding was born in Blooming Grove, about 20 miles away, but his family settled here in Marion when he was a young adult. He bought a newspaper business, The Marion Star, and then he moved into politics. He died of a stroke in 1923 while in office and is buried here in Marion. As presidents go, Harding doesn't rank very high reputation-wise. He is known these days for the Teapot Dome Scandal,

AMISH FARMS DOT THE COUNTRYSIDE

and his affair with Nan Britton was confirmed by DNA testing just a couple years ago.

The **Harding Home** site offers a look at the life and times of this controversial president. The home itself has been a museum since 1926. In the 1960s, it was restored to the way it would have been in 1900.

When Harding ran for office in 1920, he decided against a whistle-stop campaign. Instead of traveling the country, giving speeches off the caboose in every village and burg along the way, he opted for a "front porch campaign." America had to come to Marion. The small house behind the Harding Home is a remnant from that campaign. It's the Press House, hastily built for journalists who needed a place to write and communicate with their papers.

Currently, big things are afoot at the Harding Home. The Harding 2020 project is restoring the house to the year of the big election, 1923, when the Hardings were living there and busily running a presidential campaign. In addition, a presidential library and museum will be added to the property.

The next stop on the Harding tour is a visit to the **Harding Memorial**. (Head east on Mount Vernon Avenue about a half mile to Vernon Heights Boulevard. The memorial is about a mile down on the left.) The memorial is the tomb of Warren Harding and his wife, Florence. It's a circular structure with Doric pillars. The design honors the couple's wish to be buried outdoors.

THE HARDING HOME IS BEING RESTORED TO LOOK AS IT DID IN 1923

THE WYANDOT POPCORN MUSEUM HAS EXHIBITS ABOUT POPCORN AND A HUGE COLLECTION OF VINTAGE POPCORN MACHINES AND WAGONS

Harding isn't the only attraction in town. On Church Street, just east of Main Street, two museums occupy the old Post Office building, which has been rechristened "Heritage Hall." The first is the **Marion County Historical Society and Museum**.

Also in the same building is the very fun **Wyandot Popcorn Museum**. What would a fair, carnival, or circus be without popcorn and peanuts? There was a time when it was difficult to provide the public with consistently good popcorn and evenly roasted peanuts. When the mechanics of a solution were worked out, manufacturers went to work creating amazingly creative and attractive wagons, carts, and trucks intended to attract customers. This museum preserves the history of this industry, which relied as much on artistry and showmanship as it did on producing a great product.

Marion is the final stop on the tour, but travelers wanting more can easily drive from here to Mansfield, the start of Chapter 7's tour of Amish Country. Or you could head east to Gambier and run the Chapter 8 route in reverse.

IN THE AREA

Accommodations

THE BARN AT WALNUT GLEN, 4505 St. James Road, Waldo. Call 740-360-7476. Website: barnatwalnutglen.com. $$.

EASTER HOUSE BED AND BREAKFAST, 508 North Main Street, Ada. Call 419-558-1071. Website: easterhouse.net. $$.

ESCAPE ROUTE 508 BED & BREAKFAST, 980 OH 508 West Liberty. Call 937-465-1508. Website: escaperoute508.com. $$.

Attractions and Recreation

CAMPBELL HILL, ON THE CAMPUS OF HI-POINT CAREER CENTER, 2280 OH-540, Bellefontaine.

COVERED BRIDGE BLUEGRASS FESTIVAL, The Pottersburg Bridge, 17141 Inskeep-Cratty Road, North Lewisburg. Call 937-642-6279 Website: coveredbridgefestival.com.

DIETSCH BROTHERS, 400 West Main Cross Street, Findlay. Call 419-422-4474. Website: dietschs.com.

HARDIN COUNTY HERITAGE FARM, 14380 Fairground Road, Kenton. Call 419-673-7147. Website: hardinmuseums.org.

HARDING HOME PRESIDENTIAL SITE, 380 Mount Vernon Avenue, Marion. Call 1-800-600-6894. Website: hardinghome.org.

HARDING MEMORIAL, Harding Memorial Park, Vernon Heights Boulevard, Marion. Website: hardinghome.org/harding-memorial.

INDIAN LAKE STATE PARK, 12774 State Route 235 North, Lakeview. Call 937-843-2717. Website: parks.ohiodnr.gov/indianlake.

MARION COUNTY HISTORICAL SOCIETY AND MUSEUM, 169 East Church Street, Marion. Call 740-387-4255. Website: marionhistory.com.

MAZZA MUSEUM, 201 College Street, Findlay. Call 419-434-4560. Website: mazzamuseum.org.

OHIO CAVERNS, 2210 East OH 245, West Liberty. Call 937-465-4017. Website: ohiocaverns.com.

PIATT CASTLES, West Liberty. Call 937-465-2821. Website: piattcastles .org.

SULLIVAN-JOHNSON MUSEUM, 223 North Main Street, Kenton. Call 419-673-7147. Website: hardinmuseums.org.

UNION STATION 1820, 109 East Fifth Street, Marysville. Call 937-642-6279. Website: unionstation1820.business.site.

WILSON FOOTBALL FACTORY, 217 North Liberty Street, Ada. Call 419-634-9901.

WYANDOT POPCORN MUSEUM, 169 East Church Street # B, Marion. Call 740-387-4255. Website: wyandotpopcornmus.com.

ZANE SHAWNEE CAVERNS, 7092 OH 540, Bellefontaine. Call 937-592-9592. Website: zaneshawneecaverns.com.

Dining

G & R TAVERN, 103 North Marion Street, Waldo. Call 740-726-9685. Website: gandrtavern.com. $.

MAIN STREET DELI, 513 South Main Street, Findlay. Call 419-425-3354. Website: mainstreetdelifindlay.com. $.

MICHAEL ANGELO'S PIZZA, 215 South Detroit Street, Kenton. Call 419-673-7101. Website: michaelangelos.com. $$.

WILSON'S SANDWICH SHOP, 600 South Main Street, Findlay. Call 419-422-5051. $.

Other Contacts

HANCOCK COUNTY CONVENTION & VISITOR BUREAU, 123 East Main Cross Street, Findlay. Call 419-422-3315. Website: visitfindlay.com.

UNION COUNTY CONVENTION & VISITOR BUREAU, 227 East Fifth Street, Marysville. Call 937-642-6279. Website: visitunioncountyohio.org.

Index